Manoomin

Manoomin

THE STORY OF WILD RICE IN MICHIGAN

Barbara J. Barton

Michigan State University Press • East Lansing

⊛ The paper used in this publication meets the minimum requirements of ANSI/NISO
Z39.48-1992 (R 1997) (Permanence of Paper).

 Michigan State University Press
East Lansing, Michigan 48823-5245

Printed and bound in the United States of America.

27 26 25 24 23 22 21 20 19 18   1 2 3 4 5 6 7 8 9 10

LIBRARY OF CONGRESS CATALOGING-IN-PUBLICATION DATA
Names: Barton, Barbara J., author.
Title: Manoomin : the story of wild rice in Michigan / Barbara J. Barton.
Description: East Lansing : Michigan State University Press, [2018] | Includes bibliographical
references and index.
Identifiers: LCCN 2017026390| ISBN 9781611862805 (pbk. : alk. paper) | ISBN
9781609175603 (pdf) | ISBN 9781628953282 (epub) | ISBN 9781628963281 (kindle)
Subjects: LCSH: Wild rice—History—Michigan. | Indians of North America—Michigan—
Food.
Classification: LCC SB191.W55 B37 2018 | DDC 633.1/7809774—dc23 LC record available
at https://lccn.loc.gov/2017026390

Book design by Charlie Sharp, Sharp Des!gns, East Lansing, MI
Cover design by Shaun Allshouse, www.shaunallshouse.com
Cover image is of Daniel Greene, member of the Lac Vieux Desert Band of Lake Superior
Chippewa, holding a grain of Manoomin at rice camp. Photo by Barb Barton.

g green press INITIATIVE Michigan State University Press is a member of the Green Press Initiative
and is committed to developing and encouraging ecologically responsible
publishing practices. For more information about the Green Press Initiative and the use of
recycled paper in book publishing, please visit www.greenpressinitiative.org.

Visit Michigan State University Press at www.msupress.org

Contents

Maps, Figures, and Tables

Foreword

B arbara Barton is a gift-giver.

Over the many years our paths have crossed, I am not sure I have ever attended a conference or meeting where I saw Barb arrive empty-handed. Whether it be honey, maple syrup, wild berry jam, or some other product of the land and her hands, she comes laden, and invariably someone leaves those events not only with a new story or insight, but a reminder of her generosity as well.

Perhaps it is not surprising then that once introduced to Manoomin, or wild rice, Barb would develop a deep and lasting affinity for this remarkable and rare "more-than-human spirit," as it is viewed by many Upper Great Lakes Natives. For Manoomin is also a gift-giver.

My own introduction to wild rice could be seen as a fortuitous fluke. Nearing the completion of my graduate studies at the University of Wisconsin-Madison, I interviewed for a wildlife biologist position with an organization I knew little about, and which had only been in existence for a couple of years: the Great Lakes Indian Fish and Wildlife Commission (GLIFWC).

GLIFWC emerged in the 1980s, born out of the reaffirmation of the tribal treaty rights, when federal courts ruled that the tribes that ceded lands to the United States in the Treaties of 1837 and 1842 had indeed retained the right to traditional lifeways of hunting, fishing, and gathering from the ceded lands, all under their own regulation.

The primary job duties were to be related to waterfowl and wild rice. I knew a little about the former, having studied wood ducks for my master's, but next to nothing about the latter. And though I had never imagined working for a tribal agency, something in the position spoke to me. At the time, public protests in Wisconsin against treaty rights—many of them blatantly racist—were sullying a state I loved. I hoped I might be able to contribute something positive to the controversy.

Mostly through good luck, I got the job and the great blessing of being introduced to Manoomin. Now, after more than three decades of trying to apply both Traditional Ecological Knowledge and Western science to protect and restore this remarkable being, it becomes more obvious each year that whatever I might have done on behalf of Manoomin is trivial compared to what it has done for me. Manoomin—understood by the Ojibwe as a gift from the Creator, is a remarkable gift-giver itself.

As you will soon learn, Barb's own introduction to Manoomin had as much to do with her dedication as with luck, but in many ways, the outcome was the same. Wild rice seed is structurally designed to embed itself within a willing substrate. Similarly, there is something about the spirit of Manoomin that seems designed to embed itself within a willing soul. You will see that the late Naganash (Archie McGeshick from Getegitigaaning) had this soul, and was seeded by his ancestors and likely Manoomin itself. He in turn seeded his nephew Roger LaBine, and Roger—in a ridiculously tardy meeting at an Upper Peninsula tribal casino—first planted it in Barb.

This seeding has been highly successful, flourishing in ways Barb herself could not have imagined. Her love for Manoomin and her love for Michigan naturally and quickly melded together. Driven to understand and document the historic storyline that existed where these two passions intersected, she began seeking out every detail she could find about a relationship that was nearly lost. Within these pages, she has captured and preserved a story that could easily have slipped away unnoticed by most of us.

Her work came at a critical time. Like the wetlands that support it, Manoomin has declined throughout its range. In Minnesota—the core of U.S. rice abundance—Manoomin retains a significant presence in both the physical and cultural landscape despite appreciable local losses. Wisconsin started with less and has lost more, but rice has retained a level of abundance in the northern part of the state adequate to provide ecological benefits and maintain a rice-harvesting culture. Michigan has not been so lucky.

Manoomin: The Story of Wild Rice in Michigan is the living tale of a plant whose once significant role in the state's history was rapidly being forgotten. With dedicated sleuthing and detailed record keeping, Barb has brought this hidden antiquity to light. It is a story with deep ties to the region's Native American communities, and is told in part through their own words. These reflections highlight the struggle to rekindle connections that have been weakened by generations of separation, not only from Manoomin itself but also from the traditions, practices, and ceremonies that once sustained both people and rice. And it is a story remarkably interwoven with the last two centuries of history on the land that came to be called Michigan, with connections to the unfolding of European settlement, the lumbering era, navigation improvements, the birth of muck farming, industrialization, and even early efforts at disease control.

It is a story of loss, to be sure. A once significant feature of the state's landscape has dwindled to near relic status, without most of us ever being aware of what was once here. Barb's work ensures we do not forget that loss, and teaches us that we need to cherish and respect the few remaining strongholds for Michigan Manoomin as we would a remnant patch of wild prairie or stand of old-growth forest.

And at the same time, she plants the seeds of recovery. Before the last of this gift is gone, Barb brings it back and holds it in front of us, reminding us why it is important and why we should care—regardless of our origins.

Barbara Barton is a gift-giver.

Preface

My friend Colleen Deatsman and I had just left Isle Royale National Park after backpacking for several days and were sitting in the restaurant discussing wild rice at the Keweenaw Bay Indian Community's casino with Todd Warner, a biologist for the tribe. I was anxiously watching the clock, as we were to be joined by Roger LaBine from Getegitigaaning (also known as the Lac Vieux Desert Tribe), but he had not yet arrived. After finishing our dinner, I received a call from Roger. He was out on an island with a youth group and would be at the restaurant in an hour and a half. So we waited some more.

Another hour went by before Todd said he had to go. We bid him adieu and continued waiting. And waiting. Finally, five hours after the meeting was to start, Roger showed up. Most folks would have left after half an hour, but something told me I needed to stay, no matter how long it took. Thank goodness I am blessed with patience because the relationships that developed from that meeting with Roger changed my life.

In 2008, I was working as an endangered species biologist for the Michigan Natural Features Inventory (MNFI), a program within Michigan State

University Extension. I was interested in working with the tribes on endangered species conservation and was looking for potential partnership opportunities. I had heard from MSU Extension's tribal liaison Nick Reo that a fellow from Getegitigaaning was interested in hosting a wild rice camp. He suggested that perhaps I might apply for an internal grant to help fund it. Before that time, I knew nothing about wild rice. And I had never heard of the Anishinaabemowin word "Manoomin."

I did apply for and receive funding for the camp, which was held in the fall of 2009. Roger and his brother-in-law Charlie Fox (Sokaogon Chippewa Community) instructed the fifteen participants, and other members of their family helped out where needed. They taught about Manoomin's cultural and spiritual importance and how to make the tools used to harvest and process the rice. We were taken out to the wild rice beds and shown how to pole the canoe and properly harvest the seeds. We were taught the importance of reseeding and the protocol for praying and putting down *Asema* (tobacco) during certain times of the year. I developed a deep respect and love for this sacred plant and for my friends and "family" at Getegitigaaning.

We hosted several more camps at Getegitigaaning (the last one had two hundred participants) and also held camps for two years at Tubbs Lake in lower Michigan's Mecosta County. These camps were making a difference, exposing many people who came through to the beauty and importance of wild rice.

But in October 2009, things changed for me in a significant way. I lost my job at MNFI due to budget cuts and was unemployed for the next three years. One month later I was "posthumously" given the 2009 Michigan State University Extension Cultural Diversity Award for my work on the wild rice camps. This of course softened the blow of entering the world of unemployment a little and inspired me to keep working on behalf of Manoomin.

After that first camp, I began to wonder where Manoomin lived in the rest of Michigan. Roger and Charlie call the western Upper Peninsula home, and I knew there were beds scattered about where they went ricing. But what about the rest of the UP and the Lower Peninsula? I had to know, so I began my quest to learn as much as I could about the story of Manoomin in Michigan. I spent time meeting and talking with tribal folks and tribal natural-resources staff. I started to research the European historical literature. When I began to read about Manoomin in modern-day books, I found very little information about wild rice in Michigan. There was plenty written about the vast beds in Wisconsin and Minnesota, but hardly any mention at all about rice occurring here. Perhaps Michigan was on the edge of its range? Or the Europeans didn't pay much attention to it or think it had enough value to include in their writings? I began to dig.

The journey first took me back to the 1800s when the U.S. government began mapping Michigan as part of the General Land Office (GLO) surveys. Starting with those maps and notes from the surveyors, a picture began to develop in my mind. I could see this land as it was, wild and free. Unspoiled. I could feel it. The trail took me deeper into written history. I went back even further to the writings of French explorers in the 1600s. An even more vivid story began to unfold with the beautifully detailed descriptions of this land. The forests, marshes, prairies, rivers, and lakes were pristine and abundant, unpolluted. As I began to work my way through time toward the present day, my heart became heavy. Roads began to appear on each subsequent map and multiplied in places that had once been empty spaces. Towns emerged from wilderness. Wetlands were drained. Rivers were dredged. Forests were leveled. Manoomin beds shrank, then disappeared. The waters became polluted. It took the colonizers less than half a century to completely alter land that had remained unspoiled for thousands of years.

So what happened to all the wild rice? Historical literature suggests that the decline of wild rice in lakes, rivers, and tributaries may be attributed to habitat destruction/alteration due to several factors associated with logging, including straightening and dredging of streams and rivers for ease of running logs, mill debris deposition, increased sedimentation from log runs, and the alteration of hydrology due to the installation of dams. Additionally, Manoomin was often thought of as a nuisance plant by the Europeans, and efforts were made to remove it to allow clear passage for boats and ships. Sometimes removal was inadvertent as channels were dredged to allow ships to navigate from the harbors along the Great Lakes inland to cities and towns.

Public health concerns and the desire for agricultural lands also drove efforts to drain the marshlands of Michigan. The Swamplands Act of 1850 provided a mechanism for the transfer of federally owned swamps to selected state governments, as long as they were drained and turned to productive use. Michigan received 5,680,054 acres of those federal lands and they were put on the market in 1857, sold on condition that they would be drained by the purchaser. The pressure to drain Michigan was coming from many sides. Then in the late 1800s came the advent of Michigan muck farming. The wetlands and Manoomin were in trouble.

From what we know today, there are scattered small stands of Manoomin around the state, but we have lost the grand marshes that existed prior to the logging era. Our wild rice beds are still under threat today from hydraulic changes due to water-control structures and dams. Additional impacts come from chemical or mechanical treatments used to remove it when it is deemed a "weed"; wave action and/or direct impacts from boat traffic; disturbance and ingestion of seeds by carp; heavy browsing by swans, geese, and muskrats; and multiple impacts due to climate change. Unfortunately, there is limited protection for Manoomin in Michigan. The tall river rice, *Zizania aquatica*, is listed as a state threatened species. The northern lake rice, *Zizania palustris*, has no protection at all. But efforts are underway to change this as people have become more aware and appreciative of the importance of this sacred plant.

My hope is that this book reflects all aspects of Manoomin—its cultural and spiritual significance to the Anishinaabek, the important ecological role it holds in our landscape, its historical significance, the human impacts that have harmed it, and the vital work that is being done on behalf of Manoomin to restore and protect it. I invited several of my tribal friends to contribute introductions for each chapter so that the tribal story is told in their own words. I contacted every tribe and organization in Michigan that was doing restoration work and invited them to contribute stories about their projects to include in the restoration chapter. Several contributed and shared their great work. I also asked for favorite recipes so that these wonderful dishes can be shared and enjoyed by all. For the generosity and kindness of all the Anishinaabek friends who helped create this book, I say *Miigwetch*, thank you.

I have collected and presented as much information as I could find about wild rice in Michigan, both historical and present-day, so that the future generations will know of what we once had and the good work going on today to return the traditions and wild rice beds to our lakes and rivers. Manoomin is and has been an extremely important part of the story of this land and its people. It is my hope that one day the vast wild rice beds will return to Saginaw Bay, the Monroe Marsh, and other lakes and waterways across Michigan, so that we can once again see the huge flocks of migrating waterfowl, hear the delightful whinny of the sora rails, and listen to the rhythmic knocking of cedar sticks as ricers pole through the grassy marshes. So to the children of tomorrow, this book is for you.

A note on the Anishinaabemowin words. There is no consensus on the spelling of words in Anishinaabemowin (the language of the Ojibwe, Odawa, and Potawatomi) as it was not a written language. There are also regional dialects, and some believe that there are three separate languages and regional dialects within those. So you will see words with the same meaning spelled differently, depending on who the writer is. For example, the Anishinaabek word for wild rice may be spelled *Manoomin, mannomin, mnomiin, mnomen,* or *mah-no-min,* depending on the author. Additionally, Potawatomi is spelled differently as well. The Match-E-Be-Nash-She-Wish Band of Pottawatomi Indians (Gun Lake Tribe) spells it Pottawatomi (Bodewadmi). The Nottawaseppi Huron Band and the Pokégnek Bodéwadmik (Pokagon Band of Potawatomi) spell it Potawatomi. Chief Simon Pokagon spelled it Pottawatomie. In general reference I use Potawatomi, but if the sentence is in reference to a specific band or Chief Pokagon I use their spelling.

Acknowledgments

This book would not have been possible without the knowledge, love, and friendship given to me by Roger LaBine, Charlie and Terry Fox, and Giiwegiizhigookway Martin of the Getegitigaaning Ojibwe Nation. Special thanks to Elder Rose Polar Martin for sharing her memories and stories of wild ricing. *Mchi Miigwetch* and much love to all of you.

Special thanks to Julie Loehr and all the staff at MSU Press for their help, kindness, and exceptional work in making this book come to life. *Mchi Miigwetch* to Peter David of the Great Lakes Fish and Wildlife Commission for writing the foreword to this book and providing helpful suggestions. Frank Ettawageshik shared stories with me and provided valuable wisdom, comments, and feedback. *Mchi Miigwetch*, Frank!

I want to thank Jason Tallant for his hard work at creating maps and partnering with me on maintaining the statewide map of Manoomin

Mchi Miigwetch to Stu Lindsay for his brilliant idea, and to the wonderful folks who contributed chapter introductions: Roger LaBine, Panoka Walker (Anishinaabe/French), Kelly Willis (Saginaw Chippewa Tribe), Dr. Kyle Whyte (Potawatomi), Rose Polar Martin (Getegitigaaning Ojibwe Nation),

Renee "Wasson" Dillard (Little Traverse Bay Bands of Odawa Indians), Gi-iwegiizhigookway Martin (Getegitigaaning Ojibwe Nation), and Dr. Martin Reinhart (Sault Ste. Marie Tribe of Chippewa Indians). Additional thanks to Kyle for all his support and for providing a student worker and a computer when I needed it!

Thanks also to everyone who provided written summaries of their restoration efforts: Little Traverse Bay Bands of Odawa Indians, Dr. Pat Rusz (Michigan Wildlife Conservancy), Alisson Smart (Little River Band of Ottawa Indians), John Rodwan (Nottawaseppi Huron Band of the Potawatomi), Keith Stiles (past president of the Houghton Lake Lake Association), Dr. Jennifer Kanine (Pokagon Band of Potawatomi), and Lauren Romstad (Ottawa National Forest).

Miigwetch also to those who provided delicious recipes for the readers to enjoy: Giiwegiizhigookway Martin, Terry Fox, Renee "Wasson" Dillard, Shiloh Maples (Odawa and Ojibwe), Marty Reinhardt, Karen Schaumann-Beltran (Passamaquoddy Nation, European American), Aaron A. Payment (Biiwaagajiig, Bahweting Anishinabe), Cathy Abramson, Wabanang Kwe (Ojibwe Sault Ste. Marie Tribe of Chippewa Indians), and Adel Easterday, (Seneca descendant, Sault Ste. Marie, Michigan).

James McClurken graciously provided valuable information on the history of Getegitigaaning (Lac Vieux Desert). James Robertson provided assistance on the archaeological history of Manoomin. Thanks also to the staff at the Library of Michigan, especially Diane Donham, Janice Murphy, and Jessica Harden, for their tremendous help in researching and finding old things. Janet Geronime, Barbara Nehring, and the folks at Land O' Lakes Historical Society worked hard to provide me with information and photographs of the old dam at Getegitigaaning, as did Cindy Pekral from Land O' Lakes, Wisconsin. Wisconsin Historical Society provided the letters from Chief Pokagon and documents from the Albert Jenks collection. Dick Micka shared his wealth of historical information about Monroe and provided valuable documents and stories. Peter David of the Great Lakes Fish and Wildlife Commission provided information, knowledge, moral support, and inspiration. Sean Dunham provided historical information on Manoomin in the Upper Peninsula. Cathy Wendt of the Wisconsin Valley Improvement

Company shared historic photos and information about the Getegitigaaning dam. Rebecca Rogers of Michigan Natural Features Inventory and Bev Walters of the University of Michigan Herbarium provided data and taxonomic information for the master map.

There are so many people that have been part of this journey. Thank you, *Mchi Miigwetch*, for your teachings, inspiration, encouragement, research, and contributions to the book: Adrianne Daggett, Gale Nobes, Jesse Soelberg, Evelyn Ravindran (Keweenaw Bay Indian Community), Lauren Romstad (Ottawa National Forest), Steve Allen, Linda Robinson, Mike Belligan, and to the many others whose paths have crossed mine at rice camps. Thank you to Michael Loukinen from Up North Films at Northern Michigan University for his inspiring documentary "Manoomin: Spirit Food," and his continued support of my work.

But most importantly, *Miigwetch* to Manoomin for the teachings you impart and for calling the People home.

CHAPTER 1

Manoomin

Many seasons have passed since our Ancestors inhabited the area around the entrance of St. Lawrence Seaway. There the Confederacy of Three Fires members lived in balance and harmony with Mother Earth. It is said the campfires could be seen in all four directions and as far as one could see. It is at this time the Great Spirit delivered Prophecies with instructions to our Spiritual Leaders that we were to migrate in the direction of where our Grandfather sets at the end of the day. If we stayed we would be confronted with death and destruction. The Anishinaabe people were further instructed to follow the Megis until we found the land where the food grows on the water. The Megis guided them to the rich land and pristine waters of the Great Lakes and to the settling point on Madeline Island.

Throughout the region on the watersheds which feed the Great Lakes and along its vast shorelines the Sacred Manoomin could be found and harvested. This Gift from the Creator once found fulfilled the prophecies and became one of the staple foods of the Anishinabek.

The Manoomin beds are considered to be the Great Spirit's Gardens and are a source of medicine and food. Manoomin is respected, honored, and feasted and has become part of the identity of the native communities in the Great Lakes region.

—Roger LaBine, Elder from the Getegitigaaning Ojibwe Nation

Many centuries ago, the Indigenous people who now call the Great Lakes home lived on the northeast coast of North America. Their stories tell of a time when they were given Seven Prophecies, the first and third directing them to travel westward to the place "where food grows on water." So began a great migration that lasted hundreds of years. That food was Manoomin (wild rice) and it brought the Odawa, Ojibwe, and Potawatomi to the Great Lakes region.

The land that welcomed the Anishinaabek was a much different place than what we know today. Lakeplain prairies and miles of Great Lakes shoreline greeted the people when they arrived at the western edge of Lake Erie. Those who traveled westward traversed vast beech/maple forests with nutrient-rich soils that brought forth blankets of wildflowers in the spring. Mature woodlands of oaks and hickory dominated the drier moraine ridges left behind by the glaciers. Prairie chickens and lark sparrows made their homes in the oak savannas and tall grass prairies of the southwestern Lower Peninsula. Great herds of plains bison roamed the prairies in the extreme southern part of this land, grazing on the sweet grasses and tilling the soil with their hooves. Nearly one million acres of tamarack swamps, golden yellow in the fall, hugged the bottom of moraine ridges.

Some bands of Anishinaabek moved northward and found extensive forests of enormous white and red pines emerging from the dry, sandy soils, and soft hemlock trees joining the sugar maples to create a beautiful autumn palette of yellow, orange, red, and green. Mixed oak and pine forests were home to passenger pigeons, whose nesting areas covered many square miles. The skies would darken as millions of the now extinct birds took flight. Arctic graylings flashed their colorful dorsal fins as they courted females in the cold northern rivers. Traveling across the Upper Peninsula, the people encountered vast leatherleaf and sphagnum bogs and muskegs in the central part, and maple/hemlock forests in the east and west. Indeed this land we now call Michigan was a much different place than exists today.

Manoomin was not to be found in the vast forests, dry prairies, airy savannas, or dark forested swamps, but rather in the open shallows of lakes and rivers. The largest beds of Manoomin were part of the vast coastal marshes that lined Lake St. Clair, Lake Erie, and the St. Clair River Delta. Extensive marshes were also found in the many river mouths and bayous along Lake Michigan, as described in 1820 in *Geographical, Historical, Commercial, and Agricultural View of the United States of America*:

> The rivers are numerous, and mostly navigable for boats and canoes, nearly to their heads. Grand river, the largest tributary of lake Michigan, rises in lakes and ponds in the south-east corner of the territory, interweaves its branches with those of Raisin, Black river, Mastigan, and Saganum, and falls into the lake about twenty miles north of Raisin. This river is described as running through a country consisting alternately of woodlands and prairies, abounding with most kinds of wild game. It is navigable for small craft to its source; in high water boats of a considerable size pass from lake Michigan into lake Erie through this and Huron river. A canal connecting Grand river with the Saganum, running into lake Huron, could be opened at a small expense. This canal is among the number recommended by Judge Woodward, of Detroit, in his able report on the subject of internal navigation.
>
> The other streams which run into lake Michigan are, the St. Joseph's, which heads in the state of Indiana, and interlocks by its several branches with Black river, St. Joseph's-of-Miami, Eel river, and Tippecanoe: it enters the south-east end of the lake, is rapid and full of shoals, but navigable 150 miles, and is 200 yards wide at its mouth. The Pottowatomy Indians, who reside on the shore, catch prodigious quantities of fish in its waters: it runs about forty miles in the Michigan territory. On the north bank of this river stands the old fort St. Josephs, from which there is a bridle road to Detroit.

Black river, Marame, Barbue, Raisin, Mastigan, White, Rocky, and Beauvuis; the last three are short rivers, running a westerly course, and emptying themselves into the lake in the order named, at the distance of from ten to fifteen miles apart. St. Nicholas, Marguerite, Monistic, Aux Sables, Lassiette, and Grand Traverse; the four last are small streams, which enter the lake between Marguerite and the straits of Michilimackinac.

The greater part of the rivers just mentioned, expand and form circular bays or small lakes behind the sand-hills near the lake. This effect is produced by the frequent conflicts between the currents of the rivers and the surf of the lake; for the latter not only repels, as it were, the tributary streams, but at the same time washes the sand of the shore into their mouths, causing the smaller ones to contract at their entrance into mere brooks. These basins are from two to three miles across, and are, at certain seasons, literally covered with wild ducks, geese, and other water fowl, which resort here to feed on the wild rice, profusely sown by the hand of nature.—The pious and benevolent St. Pierre could have found in these bays materials for an eloquent chapter on the beneficence of the Deity. (688–89)

Open embayments in Saginaw Bay, with their curving shorelines and shallow, gently sloping bottoms, protected Manoomin from high waves and strong lake energy. The fine-textured soils were resistant to shifting and provided a stable substrate on which the Manoomin beds could grow. Thousands of acres of wild rice blanketed Saginaw Bay and its tributaries and drew in millions of waterfowl during their migration season, providing food and a resting area for their long journey south (Bradford 1917; Stout 2007).

Sand spits developed in other areas of Saginaw Bay, creating protective embayments behind them. Organic and fine sediments settled and provided a nutrient-rich bottom from which the marshes could thrive. Some embayments became sheltered over time due to near-shore currents depositing a barrier across their mouth. The barrier beach lagoons, as they are now called, were shallow and full of organic soils, and created the perfect habitat for rice.

There are two species of Manoomin found in Michigan, the state threatened *Zizania aquatica* (river rice), and *Z. palustris* (northern lake rice), which has two varieties according to the University of Michigan Herbarium, *Z. palustris var. palustris* and *Z. palustris var. interior*. As its name implies, the elegant *Z. aquatica* is found along the shorelines of shallow, slow-moving rivers in the southern part of the state (plate 1). *Zizania palustris* prefers the shallow inland lakes, rivers, and coastal marshes and is the species most frequently planted for restoration projects due to the large size of the seeds (plate 2).

The life story of Manoomin is a fascinating one and somewhat unique in the world of plants. During autumn, when the leaves begin changing color and the morning dew glistens at sunrise, ripe seeds drop from the tall plants and shoot straight down, embedding in the bottom sediment. The seeds rest during winter and need to be surrounded by water temperatures at or near freezing for three to four months. When the ice finally breaks in the spring and the sun gains strength, it melts the ice and provides the warmth and light needed for sprouting. The wild rice seeds will start to germinate when water temperatures reach around 45° F. The thin little plants grow up toward the light and develop long, slender leaves that float on top of the water—called "the floating leaf stage" (plate 3). As the roots reach further into the sediment to anchor Manoomin into Mother Earth, the plant "stands up" and grows taller, turning into an elegant emergent plant.

By early summer, Manoomin starts producing small white flowers, which are pollinated by the wind. These flowers are placed at the top of the main stem, and the pollen-producing male parts develop a few inches below (plate 4). To encourage cross-pollination, the male and female parts mature at different times. Later in the summer and early fall, nutritious grains form where the female flowers once were. Each seed has an awn or "tail" that serves as a rudder, and when the ripe seed drops into the water, the awn guides it straight down into the muck. Seeds on the same plant ripen at different times so that in the event of a strong wind or rainstorm, there will still be more ripe seeds to carry on the plant's lineage (figures 1 and 2).

Manoomin favors clear water 2 to 3 feet deep. Sometimes plants grow farther out from the shore in slightly deeper water, but they have to put so

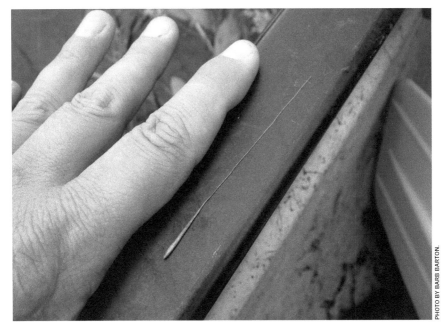

FIGURE 1. Seed of *Zizania aquatica*.

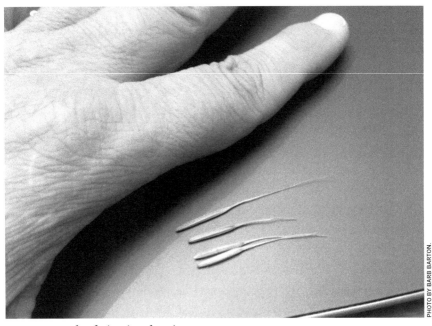

FIGURE 2. Seeds of *Zizania palustris*.

much energy into growing tall to get above the surface of the water that there is little left to produce seeds. So the densest beds are found in the shallower zones. Manoomin requires some flow and stable water levels in any given year, but also needs periodic disturbance. Multiple stable years generally favor perennials, and disturbance will set them back, providing a foothold for the wild rice (an annual plant), according to Peter David, wild rice biologist with the Great Lakes Indian Fish and Wildlife Commission. This is best illustrated in the Great Lakes rice beds, where Manoomin appears and disappears over time, always in tandem with the lakes' cyclic, fluctuating water levels. Low water levels produce miles of shallow coastline and support the growth of large beds; high water levels reduce the size of the shallow zones, which results in small, few, or no beds. Sometimes there are decades between the high and low water cycles. During times of high water, the resilient seeds of Manoomin remain buried in the sediment, waiting for shallower water to return so that the rays of the sun can once again reach them at the bottom and invite them to sprout.

On inland lakes and streams, stable water levels are particularly important during spring and early summer when the plants are in the floating leaf stage. Their roots are not yet well-established, so wave action from passing boats or flash floods can easily uproot and kill the plants. But when conditions are right, beautiful lush beds of Manoomin can grow and thrive, providing food and cover for many species of animals and opportunities for harvesting.

Manoomin has a fairly large range that covers most of the eastern half of North America, yet the archaeological record is scant given the broad geographic area in which it is found (NatureServe 2016). To date, we know of twelve locations where remains of Manoomin have been found (table 1). In 2003, Crawford and Smith published a list of thirty-seven sites containing archaeological evidence of Manoomin, only two of which were in Michigan. The Dunn Farm site in Leelanau County was our first to produce preserved wild rice fragments. Discovered in 1973, the rice fragments were radiocarbon dated in 1992 to between A.D. 460–520 and A.D. 540–620 (Brose 2017). In 1991, archaeologists found Manoomin grains in five separate soil layers in excavations at the Schultz site near Saginaw, Michigan. Radiocarbon dates

Table 1. Archaeological Evidence of Wild Rice in Michigan

SITE NAME	SITE #	COUNTY	TYPE OF FIND; ABSOLUTE DATE OF FIND/RELATIVE AGE	YEAR FOUND	YEAR PUBLISHED
Dunn Farm	20LU22	Leelanau	Seed Fragments; C14 A.D. 460–520; A.D. 540–620/ Late Middle Woodland—Early Late Woodland	1973	1999 (2016)
Casassa	20SA1021	Saginaw	1 Seed; No Absolute Date/Late Woodland; 1 Seed; No Absolute Date/Late Woodland	1991	1995
Cloudman	20CH6	Cheboygan	1 Seed; No Absolute Date/Late Woodland	1992	1995 (2017)
Schultz	20SA2	Saginaw	4 Seeds Stratum 6; C14 A.D. 160 and A.D. 380/Middle Woodland; 3 Seeds Stratum 7; No Absolute Date/Middle Woodland; 2 Seeds Stratum 8a; C14 A.D. 300/Middle Woodland; 24 Seeds Stratum 8b; No Absolute Date/Middle Woodland; 3 Seeds Stratum 8c; C14 A.D. 310/Middle Woodland	1991	2001
Converse	20KT2	Kent	2 seeds; No Absolute Date/Contact Period; 1 seed; No Absolute Date/Contact Period	1999/2000	2003
N/A	20SA367	Saginaw	2 Seed Fragments; C14 A.D. 950/Late Woodland	2006	2009
Kantzler	20BY30	Bay	Phytoliths, No Absolute Date/Middle Woodland	N/A	2010
Surath's Junk Yard	20BY77	Bay	Phytoliths, No Absolute Date/Late Woodland	N/A	2010

Site	Number	Group	Description		
Schultz	20SA2	Saginaw	Phytoliths; C14 70 B.C./Middle Woodland	N/A	2010
			Phytoliths; C14 90 B.C./Middle Woodland	N/A	2010
Shiawassee #13	20SA1276	Saginaw	Phytoliths, C14 A.D. 20/Middle Woodland	N/A	2010
Solms	20SA57	Saginaw	Phytoliths, C14 A.D. 950/Late Woodland	N/A	2010
			Phytoliths, No Absolute Date/Late Woodland		
Fritz	20OT3	Ottawa	Phytoliths, C14 A.D. 1450/Late Woodland	2012	2016
			Phytoliths, C14 A.D. 1470/Late Woodland		
			Phytoliths, No Absolute Date/Late Woodland		
			Phytoliths, C14 A.D. 1640/Contact Period		
Fisher	20OT283	Ottawa	Phytoliths, No Absolute Date/Late Woodland	2011	2016
			Phytoliths, A.D. 1470/Late Woodland		
			Phytoliths, No Absolute Date/Late Woodland		
			Phytoliths, No Absolute Date/Late Woodland		

CHRONOLOGY: Middle Woodland Period ca. 200 B.C. to A.D. 500, Late Woodland Period ca. A.D. 500 to A.D. 1600, Contact Period ca. post-A.D. 1600 indicate that those soil layers were aged between about A.D. 90 and A.D. 636 (Lovis et al. 2001a).

Unpublished reports on file at the Michigan State Historic Preservation Office document five other sites where evidence of wild rice has been found in Michigan. These include the Casassa site, located about eleven miles southwest of Saginaw (Branstner and Hambacher 1995); the Cloudman site, which is found on Drummond Island at the eastern edge of the Upper Peninsula (Branstner 1995; Christine Branstner, personal communication to James Robertson, March 31, 2017); the Converse site in Grand Rapids (Hambacher et al. 2003); site 20SA367 along the Flint River in Saginaw County (Hambacher et al. 2009); and the Fisher and Fritz sites in Ottawa County, which are along the Grand River about twenty miles west of Grand Rapids (Hambacher et al. 2016). Based on radiocarbon dates and artifacts, these five sites date between about A.D. 500 and the seventeenth century.

Research published by Maria Raviele (2010) in her PhD dissertation adds to our list of archaeological sites that produced evidence of Manoomin. As part of her research project, Raviele microscopically examined cooking residues that were adhering to prehistoric potsherds (pieces of broken pot) from the Kantzler and Surath's Junk Yard sites in Bay County, and the Schultz, Shiawassee #13, and Solms sites in Saginaw County and successfully identified wild rice phytoliths in the residues. Phytoliths are microscopic fossilized particles of plant tissue made of silica, the primary mineral used to make glass. Phytoliths were also found in soil samples from underground storage pits at the Fisher and Fritz sites in Ottawa County.

It is noteworthy that phytoliths are much more likely to be preserved than the seeds of Manoomin, and the analysis of phytoliths provides a valuable method to track the use of Manoomin at archaeological sites. Certainly, these finds support the argument that Manoomin has been collected and eaten by people from this land for at least two thousand years.

Documenting places where Manoomin once grew is a daunting and difficult task. Some of the information passed down orally within the Anishinaabek tribes of the Upper and Lower Peninsulas has likely been lost due to historical disruptions of the culture, or, if stories survived, may be kept private within a given tribe. In the early writings of the French explorers and land surveyors, Manoomin was often referred to as "folle avoine" (French for wild oats), or it might have been called rice, wild rice, or wild oats. Many early references in travel guides, encyclopedias, and historical atlases were highly generalized, simply stating that Manoomin grew in a nameless lake or stream, or was abundant in Michigan. Later in the 1800s, more accurate locations began to appear in print in newspapers of the day.

Chief Simon Pokagon, a renowned Pottawatomie leader and author, described Manoomin in southwest Michigan in two letters to Albert Jenks dated November 10 and November 16, 1898. In the first letter, Chief Pokagon presented the first documentation of Manoomin in that part of the state, reporting that "our people used to gather much wild rice through the St. Joe valley" (meaning the St. Joseph River valley). He said that two Pottawatomie words were used to describe wild rice, "Me-no-maw" and "Man-o-min," and that *minominkike* meant "I gather wild rice" (Pokagon 1898).

Albert Jenks was one of the first scholars to write about Manoomin in the Great Lakes region in his 1901 paper *Wild Rice Gatherers of the Upper Lakes*. He presented the concept of a wild rice district, which he said encompassed the northeastern and northern parts of Wisconsin and the part of Minnesota lying east of the Mississippi River. He believed that Manoomin was so abundant in the district that it was able to sustain an indigenous population equal in number to the Native population in the rest of the Northwest Territory (southwestern Wisconsin, Illinois, Indiana, Ohio, and Michigan). He dubbed the Indigenous people who lived in the district "wild rice gatherers." Jenks had a difficult time finding sources of information on wild rice distribution within its range, as botanical textbooks of the day were of little to no assistance. Instead, he corresponded with postsecondary teachers of botany and also directors of experimental stations to solicit what he could. It was truly the first attempt at defining the distribution of wild rice nationwide and provided a base for others to build upon. In describing where Manoomin grew in Michigan, Jenks wrote:

> Michigan. Found throughout the state in mud-bottomed lakes and sluggish streams; also found commonly in Grand river valley (letter of C. F. Wheeler, Michigan Agricultural College post-office, Michigan).

It is found also in Huron river, Washtenaw county (letter of F. C. New-combe, Ann Arbor, Michigan, December 9, 1898). The plant is also very abundant in St Joseph river in southwestern Michigan, and is found also in various streams and small alluvial lakes in Kalamazoo and Barry counties.

Jenks also mentioned that the Ojibwe people of Saginaw and Lake Superior were two of several tribal groups outside the wild rice district that produced Manoomin for sale from 1852 to at least the late 1870s. But as wild rice began to disappear from Michigan's landscape in the late 1800s and early 1900s and most of the Saginaw Ojibwe moved inland to Isabella County, the harvesting and selling of Manoomin from the Saginaw River Basin most certainly ended.

The next major publication on wild rice came out nearly nine decades later when Thomas Vennum published *Wild Rice and the Ojibway People* in 1988. It was the first comprehensive book on Manoomin in the United States (*Wild Rice in Canada* by S. G. Aiken was published the same year). The text is filled with valuable historical information on ricing traditions, ecology, spirituality, and wonderful historical figures, but he focused even less on Michigan than Jenks did. While Jenks primarily presented information on Manoomin and harvesting by Chief Pokagon and the Pottawatomie in the southwestern part of the state, Vennum focused on interviews and photographs of western Upper Peninsula tribal members from the Keweenaw Bay Indian Community and the Lac Vieux Desert Band of Lake Superior. The reader is left with the impression that Manoomin was not a significant part of Michigan's landscape or local Anishinaabek traditions, yet oral history and the written word contradict this perception.

In a 1943 Michigan Department of Conservation report titled "Wild Rice in Michigan," biologist Herbert Miller wrote, "Unlike Minnesota, Michigan is on the edge of the range in which wild rice grows, and accordingly has dense natural stands in only a few localities. Lac Vieux Desert in the western end of the upper peninsula is the only Michigan lake on which the rice stands are harvested annually" (1). It is understandable that Miller would have had that belief, as most of the Manoomin beds had disappeared or

BAIRD AND JONES 1919.

FIGURE 3. A 1919 effort to seed Manoomin by broadcasting it across the water.

significantly declined by then. If he had delved deep into Michigan history or perhaps consulted with the tribes, he would have learned that Michigan did have some significant beds of Manoomin, only most were gone by the time he entered his profession.

In addition to documenting the historical distribution of Manoomin, it is important to learn about whether beds were naturally occurring or planted. Early on, the Anishinaabek seeded Manoomin to ensure a continuing source of food. Later, nontribal sportsmen planted it, seeking to increase habitat for waterfowl (figure 3). The difference between the two cultural groups was that the Anishinaabek most likely used local seed sources for planting, whereas the sportsmen's groups initially obtained seed from local sources if they could, but more often imported it from Wisconsin, Minnesota, or Canada.

Historically, Manoomin was widespread in both peninsulas and also could be found in the vast coastal marshes along the Great Lakes, with large beds (some thousands of acres in size) occurring at the mouths of major rivers. While there were many human causes of the decline and disappearance of these beds, natural forces also impacted them. In the early spring of 1946, large expanses of marshlands in Lake Erie from Cleveland to the Detroit River, Lake St. Clair, and Saginaw Bay died off (McDonald 1955). Once lush and green, they stood bare and silent as the weather warmed and new growth returned to the rest of the land. Extremely high water levels were thought to be the cause, essentially drowning out the emergent plants, particularly the cattails and Manoomin. This completely changed the composition of the plant communities in these marshes, with some species that were less abundant becoming more dominant and vice versa.

To the nontribal biologists, these changes seemed catastrophic, and indeed they were in that moment of time. But lake levels have changed for hundreds of years and the marshes always adapt. The Anishinaabek know this; this land has long been their home and they have seen these cycles for many generations. This difference in experience and relationship with place is no more evident than in the way Western science-trained biologists manage the land and waters, striving to keep things in a static state. Even in our natural areas, the temporal perspective is lost. Yet that is not how the cycles of Earth flow. Change is part of the natural order of things. It is necessary for the health of the land and waters and for diversity. Manoomin has also ebbed and flowed over time, responding to an ever-changing environment. The newcomers have not yet learned to see from a wider temporal perspective.

In the written record, which includes old newspaper stories, books, letters, magazines, and government reports, there exists information about some of these historical rice beds—where they once were and how and when they disappeared. Manoomin was traded between the trappers and the Anishinaabek during the fur trade era of the 1700s and valued by them as an essential food item. However, during the logging era of the 1800s, the newcomers were no longer living as explorers but rather colonizers, viewing Manoomin as a hindrance to movement, settlement, and development rather than as a food source. The Anishinaabek were still harvesting where they could, maintaining their relationship with the sacred plant. These stories illustrate the shifting and diverse relationship between Manoomin and the Europeans.

Benton Harbor, Paw Paw River Marsh—Berrien County

The St. Joseph River begins its journey at Baw Beese Lake in Hillsdale and snakes 206 miles across southern Michigan and northern Indiana before outletting into Lake Michigan between St. Joseph and Benton Harbor. In the mid-1800s, the river flowed through a vast marsh that stretched from Lake Michigan to the bluffs along both the Paw Paw and St. Joseph Rivers. Much of this large wetland was covered in wild river rice, *Zizania aquatica*, which grew 10 feet tall.

In the mid-1830s, the St. Joseph River was the primary transportation artery for the entire region. Everything that was imported, exported, or shipped went through the busy harbor of St. Joseph. It was in 1839 that orchards became a boom in the area and the port became more important than ever, and it was then the "fruit belt" was born. Farmers were dependent on the river to transport their fruits.

The village of St. Joseph is located directly on the western shore of the river. Benton Township is east of the river, and at that time east of the large wild rice marsh. Township residents had a difficult time getting to St. Joseph to sell their crops and purchase supplies. Up through the 1850s, Benton Township residents had to travel over an often muddy, sandy road around the marsh to get to the Spinks Bridge, which was some distance upstream from St. Joseph.

The idea to build a canal through the marsh first came to life in 1834 but never went anywhere. But in 1859, the idea resurfaced and started to gain momentum as the vision of a new village in Benton Township grew. Township farmers Charles Hull, Henry Morton, and their friend Sterne Brunson were appointed to pursue the canal, and so off to Chicago the new committee went. It took them three tries before finally locating a contractor to dredge the canal. Michael Green and his crew of local men dredged a new canal 50 feet wide and 10 feet deep with a turning basin at the end—right through the wild rice marsh. The Bung Town Canal was completed in 1862, and development on the newly drained lands followed rapidly. The Manoomin bed that has existed for hundreds of years at the mouth of the St.

Joseph River was quickly forgotten, swallowed up by the brand new village of Benton Harbor.

New Buffalo, Pottawatomie Lake—Berrien County

South of St. Joseph and north of Michigan City lies the coastal town of New Buffalo, through which flows the Galien River. Before the river outlets into Lake Michigan, it once flowed through Pottawatomie Lake, reported to be nearly three and a half miles long and 800 to 2,400 feet wide. The lake was partially covered with Manoomin, and the water levels fluctuated with those of Lake Michigan. The lake was dredged by the U.S. Army Corps of Engineers in the mid-1800s to create a shipping canal.

St. Joseph River—St. Joseph County

The St. Joseph River flows through the villages of Colon and Mendon on its way to Lake Michigan. Late in the 1800s, some enthusiastic hunters from Colon planted Manoomin in the river, which made its way downstream to Mendon, much to the chagrin of the local health officer. From the Twentieth Annual Report of the Michigan Board of Health (1894):

> Edwin Stewart, M.D., health officer of Mendon village, St. Joseph county, wrote to this office, August 20, 1891, as follows:
>
> "I enclose a clipping from our local paper of last week. It is like others made directly to me. I can see no remedy, can you? These are the facts, and conditions. Several years ago a quantity of wild rice was procured by parties in Colon, a village nine miles above us on the St. Joseph river and the rice sown in the river to bait ducks. It is said the practice is still continued. The result is, the seed floats down, seeds the shallow waters and produces the obstruction and the evil complained of. I have been requested to lay the matter before you and inquire if anything can be done to abate the nuisance."

Following is the clipping mentioned by Dr. Stewart:

"The rice in the St. Joe river is getting so thick that it threatens a pestilence. The heat has been almost overpowering the past few weeks and sweltering humanity has been turning in every direction for fresh air. Some of our neighbors residing near the river, on Main street, complain that when out on their back porches they would be cool and comfortable were it not for the stench that comes from the river. The rice is so thick it clogs up the river, dead fish, dead frogs and turtles, rats, cats, etc., are caught and detained and they impregnate the air with a sickening smell that threatens disease and death. Let the health officer look into this matter and apply the remedy. This case should be agitated until something is done to save our people from an epidemic, or at least from numerous cases of sickness." (309)

Muskegon Lake/Muskegon River—Muskegon County

The Muskegon River originates in Houghton Lake and flows for 216 miles before entering Lake Michigan. Historic rising of Lake Michigan water levels pushed the river water back upstream and created Muskegon Lake by filling in the low-lying area and creating a beautiful marsh full of Manoomin and other aquatic plants. A mile-long swamp covered the flats at the mouth of the river on the east end of Muskegon Lake.

Manoomin was abundant in the marshes where the river forked before entering the lake at its western end. The rice was said to never grow in water more than 8 feet deep, and boats navigated by this vegetated boundary.

There were many marshes along the Muskegon River, and of course Manoomin could be found in abundance. But when the fur trade ended in the late 1830s, eyes turned to the trees as a source of income, and the first mill in the area was constructed in 1837. At the peak of the logging era, there were forty-seven lumber mills around Muskegon Lake, with the greatest concentration along the southern shore. Men were sent to the head of the marsh where the river entered Muskegon Lake to pole logs

(Detroit) *Evening News*   October 11, 1900

Mendon's Erstwhile Beautiful Streams

MENDON—Several years ago Mendon had a beautiful river flowing through the village. Some fool hunter sowed wild rice in the stream, thinking to attract ducks to the vicinity and make good shooting, and now, as a result, there is nothing but a marsh where the river was for several miles above and below the village. One man has benefited by the change, however, and that is a dairyman whose farm borders on what was the river. His pasture was very poor this summer, so he turned his cows into the St. Joe, which is so shallow that they waded in and devoured acres of the wild rice and at the same time defeated the flies in their attempt to pester them. The flow of milk increased at once, and the quality was sweet, though no one has accused him of watering his milk.

through channels along the shoreline. The logs were guided to the mills, then shipped to Chicago and other cities and towns in the Midwest. The impact of logging on Manoomin was profound, and whatever rice remained was further decimated by the industrial era that followed. In the 1930s, up to 1,000 acres of marsh was contaminated by excessive oil pollution and all the vegetation died off. Manoomin disappeared from Muskegon Lake, but small patches still survive upstream in the river today.

Pointe Mouillee—Monroe County

This historic coastal marsh is in the northeastern corner of Monroe County. In 1910, Manoomin nearly covered the entire marsh. But between 1910 and 1944, cattail slowly moved in and displaced the Manoomin, an event studied by University of Michigan graduate student Malcolm McDonald in 1951. Coastal marshes are affected by changing water levels in the Great Lakes, and in 1945, Lake Erie saw its highest levels in seventeen years. The large reed marsh, 1,205 acres in size, was devastated, with seven species of emergent plants killed off. The marsh filled in with submerged aquatic plants, and within just two years, Manoomin started to appear again, spreading into the newly vacated areas; but its spread was slowed as the cattail recovered. By 1949, the emergent plants had taken back about one-fifth of the marsh, but heavy browsing by muskrats and uprooting of plants by carp were suspected of knocking the Manoomin back that summer. Within two years wild rice disappeared from Point Mouillee.

Detroit River Area—Wayne County

Huron and Potawatomi villages and burial mounds were once found near a stream that flowed into the Detroit River in what is now called the township of Springwells. Manoomin grew in the area and provided a good source of food for the people. In the very early 1700s, the original French settlement was established, and the land was divided up into long, linear lots unique to that area of Detroit. The Knagg Farm was built later in the century on the west side of the creek, about 20 feet back from the road on what is now the corner of River St. and Swain. Around 1795, a red windmill was erected at the mouth of Knaggs Creek, and in 1812, the creek was 300 feet wide and came to within a few yards of the farmhouse. Twenty-five years later, the outlet of Knaggs Creek was filled with ducks and red-winged blackbirds enjoying a 3-acre wild rice marsh. Several years later, the stream and surrounding land would be purchased by a man named Bela.

Bela Hubbard was a renowned geologist and naturalist who left a wonderful gift to us in his 1887 book *Memorials of a Half-Century*, which chronicles his life and the incredible beauty of the Detroit River since he moved to Detroit as a boy in 1837. The chapter "Birds of My Neighborhood" tells the tale of the unwelcome flocks of blackbirds that would descend upon the marsh in fall:

> Of all the birds that visit us in flocks we love least to see the blackbirds,— those arrant thieves, that steal our corn and oats so pertinaciously. The

Muskegon Chronicle   December 26, 1896

The following question was read to the [Farmer's Institute] society:

"Hunters and sportsmen are now sowing wild rice in all lakes and rivers for wild game but this is detrimental to our grain crops; how are we to protect ourselves?"

The objection was that the wild rice attracted black birds which destroyed the farmer's grains. No blight or anything similar, it was said, is half as destructive as a flock of blackbirds.

river marshes afford such congenial habitats for these birds that their numbers scarcely diminish, notwithstanding the havoc made among them by the guns of boys and outraged farmers. They congregate by thousands in these river borders and coves, where they find a favorite food in the wild rice (*Zizania aquatica*). The cove or pond near my farm house, covering an area of some two or three acres, is nearly every season filled with this plant, and is often black with the birds. On firing, or throwing a stone into their ranks, they rise in dense flocks, with a loud rushing sound, fly a short distance, wheel about, and again settle to their repast; or they collect in dense, black masses in a neighboring tree. Here they hold council over their misdeeds, or rather, it is probable, over the unauthorized insult to which, in their opinion, they have been subjected. The chatter is loud and incessant. (286)

Bela Hubbard's farm encompassed 240 acres of land that included Knaggs Creek. The mouth of the creek was a cove covered with wild rice, and the Manoomin was said to be an excellent source of food for cattle and considered profitable for pasture in the mid-1800s. But the land was eventually sold to brothers Lew, John, and Hiram Ives, and in 1851 they obliterated Knaggs Creek by building a dry dock for shipping. Over time, the little creek

Detroit Free Press   October 17, 1906

MORBID MOB AT FUNERAL
Gaping Throngs Attend Services over Victims of Ill-Starred Fishing Trip.
UNFORTUNATES ARE BURIED SIDE BY SIDE

Horrible as the death which overtook Mrs. Mary A. Cadwell and Stephen A. Stuart in the imprisoned duck boat in the marsh near Fighting Island, was the funeral which was the mark of the last respect this world could show them.

The unfortunate man and woman, out for a day of pleasure at fishing and blown into the desolate labyrinth of wild rice, died a miserable death of cold, exhaustion and mental torture. But for the bereaved widow and husband, the grey-haired mothers and a score of near and dear relatives who are left to mourn, the torture of yesterday afternoon, scarcely could have been less.

Together the black caskets were carried from the little cottage home of the Stuart family at 341 Twenty-fourth street. Behind them came the veiled and sobbing mourners, men and women wracked by sorrow. The procession of grief was forced to run the gauntlet of a thousand people, the aged about the doorstep, the lawn, the curb, where the hearses and carriages were drawn up. Across the street gaped another thousand.

that had provided habitat for blackbirds and Manoomin for the Anishinaabek simply disappeared.

Numerous islands, including Belle Isle and Grosse Ile, are found in the Detroit River, and all had Manoomin growing in the marshlands surrounding them. Wild rice beds can be very dense and thick with tall plants and deep muck, and it is not unreasonable to assume one could get lost or even stuck in them. Even standing in a boat, you cannot see very far over the vegetation, and it can be quite disorienting.

Wildfowl and Sebewaing Bays, Saginaw Bay—Huron County

These bays lie between Sand Point and Fish Point on the east side of Saginaw Bay, and are unique in that they contain several islands. Hunting pressure increased in this area in the early twentieth century due to the advent of automobiles and outboard motors, and hunters were much less likely to get a good shot due to the number of sportsmen on the bay. But the hunters did not see the gas-powered machines and overcrowding as the problem behind poor hunting conditions; rather they believed the lack of Manoomin and other duck foods were to blame. They repeatedly asked the Department of Conservation to furnish wild rice seed and to remove the carp at Wildfowl Bay to solve their hunting problems. In 1935, the bottom sediment in the shallow bays was chiefly hard sand and clay. Manoomin, duck potato, cattail, and bur reed were scarce, except in drainage ditches and boat channels. However, a few localities in the Middle Grounds of Wildfowl Bay had deep muck, and these plants could be found growing there. In fact, many places had a good depth of muck according to samples taken back then, but it had been covered by hard sand and clay due to sedimentation and wave action. Fifty years earlier, wild rice beds blanketed the Middle Grounds, but they were replaced by sedges and phragmites. Given that Lake Huron water levels were at the bottom of a low cycle in 1935, one would expect Manoomin to be most abundant at that time. But it was not. M. D. Pirnie, Department of Conservation ornithologist, recommended that due to the change in sediment it was futile to try and plant Manoomin seeds (Pirnie 1935).

St. Clair Flats—St. Clair County

The flats of Lake St. Clair are well known for their extensive beds of Manoomin, and based on historical descriptions of the rice plants, the state threatened species *Zizania aquatica* may have been growing in parts of the marsh. It was often described in early accounts as "Indian rice," the name commonly applied to *Z. aquatica* in those days, and the tall plants were said to be over 8 feet tall and as high as the common reed. Manoomin was reported to grow all around the shallow lake margins of Lake St. Clair and, as with the other hunting hot spots, attracted duck hunters from across the country. The ducks were so numerous that Cadillac, the founder of Detroit, said in 1701 that ducks covered the water so that they "drew up in lines to let boats pass through." It wasn't long before Lake St. Clair had its own hunting club, with an interesting story attached. According to Leonadis Hubbard Jr., in the magazine *Outing* in 1901,

Twenty-eight years ago three men landed from a little steamer at the building where lived the superintendent of the ship canal which the government had been obliged to cut through the shallow water at the lake's head. They hired the superintendent's son to row them to a point a few rods north of the opening of the canal, and there, on the bank of the channel, in water some six feet deep, they drove four stakes. Then followed a barge with a pile-driver that drove great timbers into the bottom of the lake, and carpenters who built on the tops of these timbers a small frame house.

This was the beginning of the Lake St. Clair Fishing and Shooting Club. At that time it was nine miles from the nearest land. There the members came to hunt and fish. There, with cool, clear water on every side, with game-filled marshes in their rear and abundant supplies of bass, pickerel, mascalonge and perch in the channels, they found rest and sport after the hot summer months of the city.

The marshes had islands in them, and on these lived the old French settlers, famed far and wide for their musk-rat dinners. These were employed as "punters," and with one of them to paddle his boat the sportsman would push through the marsh, shooting such ducks as he frightened from the rushes, or would lie hidden to catch the morning and evening flight. (450–51)

An old duck hunter named Yusef, in a story published in the November 3, 1889, edition of the *Detroit Free Press*, describes what we will never see again, the vast marshes of the St. Clair Flats:

The wild ducks are the denizens of this region of tall rushes, damp marsh grass and wild rice that grows thriftily on the submerged soil of the Flats. There are thousands of acres thus submerged, cut through by deep channels and wrongly called swamps. The eye cannot perceive the limit of the river, disappearing in the horizon into which it blends at this time of the year in a distinct brown. The region is extensive, perhaps as much as forty miles across and from three to ten miles broad. Many and intricate channels divide it; so many and so intricate that the hunter in a small boat and without a guide is pat to lose his head. The grass, the rushes, and the wild rice grow higher than a man's head. To the hunter in his boat the place looks like a boundless field of grass without a distinguishable landmark. (6)

What happened to the vast rice beds along the northern shore of Lake St. Clair? Residential development is blamed for the loss of much of the coastal emergent marshes and wetlands along the coastline, with the St. Clair River Delta the last refuge for Manoomin (Albert 2003).

Houghton Lake—Roscommon County

Houghton Lake is the largest inland lake in Michigan, covering just over 20,000 acres and was described in the 1921 publication *Inland Lakes of Michigan*:

This lake, although more than eight miles long and over four wide, does not anywhere exceed twenty-five feet in depth and is filled with an almost continuous weed bed, except in a zone about the shore. This is the lair of countless fish of many kinds and accounts in part for the attraction of this lake to sportsmen. Interesting and instructive though a study of the plants and animals of these waters might be to one capable of undertaking it, the writer must dismiss it with the mere mention of wild rice. This furnishes food supply to migrating birds which flock here in great numbers to feed and rest in the fall of the year, thus the attraction to the hunters. (16)

In the mid-1930s, Pirnie described a very large wild rice bed one mile long near Houghton Lake village on the lake's southern shore. Other lush beds grew in Muddy and North Bays and continued to provide high-quality habitat for waterfowl and fish.

As was common in those days, a timber logging dam with flash boards was constructed in 1926 on the Muskegon River about three-quarters of a mile downstream from the lake, and the legal lake level was set at 1,138.1 feet above sea level. Over time, the dam fell into disrepair, and so in 1938 the Roscommon County Board of Supervisors decided to replace it. Engineers at Michigan's Department of Conservation were concerned about the new dam being sized appropriately and recommended to the board that they make sure the spillway was of sufficient design. During construction, however, the contractor on the job told the board that the dam didn't need to be so large and suggested they make it smaller. Again the state warned against reducing the length, saying that while low water levels were the main concern of the day, high water levels might be a concern in the future. But the board went ahead with the contractor's recommendation and built a dam shorter than the one in the plans. The new concrete dam was completed in 1938 about 35 feet southwest of the old timber structure, which was finally torn down in 1940.

As predicted, water levels in Houghton Lake exceeded the legal limits by as much as 1.7 feet from 1943 to 1954 (except 1946 and 1949, when they were at legal levels). These high lake levels would surely have impacted wild rice growing in shallower waters by preventing their growth or limiting seed production.

It wasn't until 1989 that Manoomin faced its most serious challenges on Houghton Lake. During the spring of that year, huge mats of dead rice plants washed up on the eastern shore of the lake in such high volume that dump trucks had to be brought in to haul it away. Donald Bonnette speculated in his 1998 master's thesis that lake water froze from the surface into the sediments in the shallow rice beds during the previous winter, and when the ice broke up, wave action lifted out the rice plants and the sediment including the seed bed. It was after this event that the Manoomin beds began to decline. First Muddy Bay disappeared in 1989, followed by North Bay in 1990. Middle Grounds lost its rice in 1992. Sporadic sightings of individual plants occurred up through 1994.

While no one has been able to point to a single cause for the decline of Manoomin on Houghton Lake, there were likely multiple contributing factors. Bonnette (1998) and Ustipak (1995) suggested several causes, including sediment contaminated with lead (due to outboard motor use), high lake levels, and wave action due to boat traffic and hardened shorelines. Additionally, Bonnette (1998) suggested that the loss of wild rice straw from the bottom sediments may have increased turbidity in the lake and also created nutritional deficiencies through the loss of nitrogen in the straw, as well as the continued cutting of Manoomin from the 1930s into the 1950s.

One additional factor came into play and that was the highly invasive Eurasian milfoil (*Myriophyllum spicatum*), which was believed to have entered the lake in the 1990s and quickly spread. By 2001, some 11,000 acres of the lake were infested with Eurasian milfoil, and 5,300 of those 11,000 were considered to have common to dense colonies. This was of great concern from the perspective of recreational usage and the ecological health of the lake. After several years of study, the entire surface of Houghton Lake was treated with low concentrations (6 ppb) of the herbicide fluridone on May 15, 2002. A few weeks later a second application was administered, and the Eurasian milfoil was severely knocked back. In 2003, the U.S. Army Corps of Engineers conducted a study of the response of Manoomin to select herbicides (including fluridone). What they discovered was that wild rice is most resistant to these chemicals during the later growth stages, but when they are in the floating leaf stage or are young plants with aerial leaves and early tillers, plant vigor is reduced and their biomass inhibited. From mid-May to early June, Manoomin on Houghton Lake would have been in the early stages of growth and negatively impacted by the application. But a few years after, wild rice plants started to appear again. The vast beds are long gone, but the dream that wild rice can be returned to Houghton Lake still persists in its believers as plants still can be found in the Middle Grounds.

Tawas Lake—Iosco County

Historically, Tawas Lake was a well-known wild rice bed and is now the largest remaining bed in Michigan. On its southwest shore existed an Anishinaabek village, whose residents must have enjoyed the bountiful Manoomin, fish, and waterfowl found living there. In 1874, medical professionals were examining the Tawas area for potential sources of malaria and reported in the *Transactions of the American Medicine Association* that "Tawas produces an annual growth of 'wild rice,' so abundant that it bids fair to convert it into a great marsh in course of time" (423). Indeed, by 1935, the majority of the 1,820-acre lake was completely covered by wild rice, and today it covers nearly three-quarters of the water body. Local folks at that time wanted to have access for fishing and hunting, so plants were hand-pulled to make boat channels. Tawas Lake has been a favorite of duck hunters and anglers, who in the 1930s wished that the muskrats would do a better job of clearing out some of the Manoomin for better fishing.

Munuscong Bay—Chippewa County

Munuscong Bay was considered a hunter's paradise back at the turn of the twentieth century, when five men from Detroit and one Canadian decided to create a new hunting club about forty miles by wagon road from Sault Ste. Marie. The club had 8,000 acres of shooting ground and 3,000 acres of emergent marshland in Munuscong Bay, and Manoomin thrived in these marshes in 1906. The reason Manoomin disappeared from the bay is unknown, but in 1936 efforts were made to reseed the area, with no success.

MAP 1. Historical distribution of Manoomin in Michigan.

CARTOGRAPHY BY JASON TALLANT.

Manoomin's Historical Distribution in Michigan

To date, 212 historical sites have been identified in Michigan, and that number will likely grow as research continues (map 1; appendix 1). Of those 212 historical sites, 14 are still known to exist. However it must be remembered that there has been no comprehensive survey of wild rice and so additional sites may have persisted. Today, we know of at least 139 extant (existing) Manoomin locations in the Upper and Lower Peninsulas (map 2).

The ecological devastation that was caused by logging and industrialization, along with the draining and filling of over 200 million acres of wetlands in the past two hundred years, drastically reduced the number of our wild rice beds. It is clear that Manoomin was once widespread across Michigan, with several very large beds occurring along the Great Lakes, which were an important part of Anishinaabek culture and our ecological landscape. With the exception of one remaining bed in the St. Clair Flats, the large marshes of Manoomin in the Great Lakes are now gone.

MAP 2. Present distribution of Manoomin in Michigan.

CARTOGRAPHY BY JASON TALLANT.

CHAPTER 2

The Industrialization of Western Lake Erie

MANOOMINIKE GIIZI AUGUST, THE WILD RICE MAKING MOON

Our Stories tell that the people of the Dawn were visited by eight Prophets that came out of the water and gave seven Prophecies to follow. The third Prophet directed them to travel westward until they found the place where "food grows on water." When they arrived in the Great Lakes region they discovered massive beds of wild rice. They called it Manoomin "The Good Seed" Food that grows on the Water, a gift from Gitchi Manitou through the Spirit of the water and the land. This land they would call home and the Manoomin would help teach them Bimaadiziwin, how to live a good life.

The sunlight glistens on the water as a dragonfly darts among the reeds and the cattails where a Red-wing black bird sings its song. The Willows bow low as their long finger-like branches touch the water's edge that is dotted with rich colors of purple, gold and oranges, the colors of the flowers and shrubs that make their home along these banks. A pair of Mallards bob their heads as they dance together there under the protection of the Willows. The Lotus are in full bloom with their bright yellow faces gracing the sky as they sway together on top of their strong stems, in clusters like a village camp. You can smell their sweet aroma in the air, which draws us near to them. We see the water droplets on their leaves as it beads up like tiny crystal jewels. The sound of an Egret and the Great Blue Heron can be heard in the distance as we paddle our kayaks gently along the Otter Creek. It is quiet here except for the occasional sound of the paddle as it goes through the water. There is a gentle breeze that blows through our hair and you can smell late summer all around us. A family of small box turtles sun themselves on an old log that has moss and grass growing out of it. A fish jumps high in jubilation bringing water droplets with it and lands with quite a splash that gets our attention. It was the full Moon called Manoomin Giizi August Wild Rice Moon. We as a family floated our kayaks down Otter Creek, imagining them as bark canoes floating down the creek like the ones the people of this land used so many years ago. We look around again and try to understand that our relationship to everything in nature is a part of the story, part of the missing link to the Manoomin. Everything we see—the trees, the marsh, the winged ones, the swimmers, and yes, even Water has a spirit. It is their spirits that call softly to us on the wind trying to stir us to waken an ancient memory that is deep inside us. It brings us back to the thoughts of the wild rice, Manoomin and how at one time everything we needed came from the land and the water, and how everything we did had a spiritual component to it. But now there is a loss of relationship to that spirit of the Water and to the sacred vibration of land and those who make their home here. You can see the evidence of this everywhere. Plastic bags, plastic bottles, and trash are a true sign of this loss of connection to Nibi and Aki, the Water and our Earth Mother.

In 2008 through the River Raisin Institute and the Biology teachers of Monroe High School at Bolles Harbor Math & Science Center, Bill Paulson came from White Earth Reservation in Minnesota as part of a National Fish and Wildlife Foundation Grant to bring the Wild Rice Manoomin back to waters of Monroe. We remember that event and reminisce about it.

It was a cool day in early December. The dew was still heavy on the grass; there was crispness in the air. The Canadian Geese flew in V formation overhead. I could smell smoke from a camp fire in the air and could hear voices of excitement and laughter as I came into view. Bill Paulson was instructing the students on how to build a fire in the earth that was slightly banked up behind a large cast iron kettle, placed just so on an angle so that the wild rice could be placed in it and stirred to be parched without falling out on the Earth. Mr. Russ Columbus, their biology teacher, guided them through the task. I met up with my daughter Felicity who, in turn, introduced me to Bill. I offered him our assayma for his sharing and teaching of the Manoomin, Wild Rice. He accepted it and we exchanged stories for a minute or two. The students listened attentively as Bill continued to share stories of the Spirit of the rice and its connection to the people, and weaves them among the instruction and the steps that would be taken after the parching of the Manoomin. As the Manoomin was parched it was taken in batches to be "Danced on." The parched rice was placed in a shallow pit that first had a clean white cloth placed into it. Bill demonstrated to the students how the "Dance" was done with clean Moccasins that had been made with the ricing harvest in mind. Stepping with the balls of his feet first one then the other, he twisted and turned on the rice. Then, lowering his heel he began again. This breaks loose the rice hulls from the grains. Over and over, holding on to a pole to help keep his balance, he danced on the rice. The students happily took turns dancing on the rice as Bill and I kept rhythm for them through drumming and singing to the spirit of the Manoomin. Next came the stories of the birch baskets. I remember the story of how the spirit of the birch protected Nanaboozhoo. Bill shows the students a beautiful hand woven birch basket. He shows them how the basket has a slight curve to it to fit into the belly space of the grandmas. The students laugh, I imagine all the older women's hands on it and the love that must be in the basket. He continues to share with them it was Grandma that hand winnowed the first rice offered to the spirits because of the sacredness of it. He demonstrated how the rice was placed into the baskets and with a kind of shifting and quick flicking-like motion, the chaff is blown into the air leaving behind the clean rice. All day the students continued to parch, dance, and winnow the rice. Even at the end of the day the excitement stayed as they talked about the process of planting the Manoomin seed that would follow in the upcoming weeks. Before leaving, Bill offered assayma back to me and gifted me with the basket to help keep the spirit of the Manoomin alive.

The waiting and watching was the hardest part. Manoomin is very sensitive to its environment, and the seed didn't seem to take to the water as we had hoped it to. We heard that a Muskrat was found dead floating in the water with its belly full of rice. Our stories tell us it was the Muskrat that had saved the people of Monroe from starving so many years ago. It's with heavy hearts we re-lived this part of the memory, the whys and why nots of it all. Perhaps the water had not been offered assayma and sang to and the ceremony had not been done to let the animals and birds know something sacred was coming. Perhaps it's because the spirit of the rice connects to the spirit of the people. After all it was through the Prophet that we had been guided to find the food that grows on the water. My daughters and I talk about all these things, noting that there is still much work to be done to help clean the water and remove the invasive plants. We believe that the people are wakening to the spirit of the land and of the water and beginning to understand that we are part of the land not separate from her. We can see good work being done all round us. As they waken and call to the Spirit of the land, to the spirit of the Water and the spirit of all creation and yes, the spirit of the Manoomin, they will deepen their understanding and it will grow like a fire of hope and from that more good work will be done. My daughter turns to me and says, "Mama you know we planted the seeds in a good way and it's down there waiting for when the time is right and then it will grow and call to the people just like it did to Nanaboozhoo and the spirit of the rice will help the people." Now that is what we call faith to understand truth. It make me feel proud to be her mother, to live by faith, and to remember Bimaadiziwin—how to live a good life. Gakina gegoon bimaadan. Everything is alive. Gakina awiya-bimaadisiwag. Everyone is alive. And as the elders say, "Remember to move our feet when we pray."

—Panoka Walker, Deer Clan, French/Anishinaabe

When the Europeans arrived in Michigan, broad coastal marshes lined the many river mouths and bays of the Great Lakes. These marshes, often transition zones that could extend for miles, could be found in tributaries that were affected by the changing Great Lakes water levels. The amount of protection from high winds and wave action determined whether Manoomin could grow there. Open embayments had curving shorelines with shallow, gently sloping bottoms that reduced wave height and energy. This was particularly important for Manoomin in the springtime when it was in the floating leaf stage, its roots still shallow and vulnerable. If the embayment had too much sand, waves would cause the particles to shift and thus marshes could not form. Protected embayments had deeper shorelines, and often tributaries emptying into them brought organic and mineral sediments from the uplands, creating ideal conditions for wild rice to grow.

Early French explorers Pierre François Xavier de Charlevoix and René Robert Cavelier de La Salle provide us with a glimpse of what the western shore of Lake Erie looked like in the late 1600s and early 1700s, from Bulkley's 1913 book *The History of Monroe County*:

Listen to the words of the enthusiastic Charlevoix and of La Salle in their journals of voyages and adventures amid the lakes and streams, in their batteaux and canoes propelled by the hardy voyagers: "Great and luxuriant fields of wild rice and the sweet flags, of grapes and berries extend ahead of us and around us for miles; the streams and the trees along their borders are festooned with magnificent vines bearing the great clusters of purple grapes, and the morasses swarming with waterfowl." (301)

They, of course, were not the only explorers to notice Manoomin. Massachusetts-born explorer Jonathan Carver left Boston in 1766 on a sailing trip to Fort Michilimackinac by way of Albany and Niagara. His travels carried him into Lake Erie, up the Detroit River into Lake St. Clair, and through Lake Huron to the Straits of Mackinac. Carver's journal entry upon reaching the Detroit River area states that there were "great quantities of [wild rice] in the watered lands near Detroit, between Lake Huron and Lake Erie, but on enquiry I learned that it never arrived nearer to maturity than just to blossom; after which it appeared blighted, and died away" (Carver 1778, 524). Carver blamed this blight on high winds coming down the river channel.

In addition to the vast wild rice beds in the Detroit River, there were three large marshes along the western coast of Lake Erie. The southernmost Erie Marsh extended intermittently from near Otter Creek to the Ohio line, broadening in places and including some small areas of open water. The Monroe Marsh encompassed an area one mile south of Brest to the mouth of Plum Creek and included the mouth of the River Raisin, and the third marsh, Pointe Mouillee, extended from the mouth of the Huron River to Stony Point. Manoomin was abundant in these places and extended up the coastal tributaries, providing important habitat for many different species.

In those days, towns were springing up all around the Great Lakes at the outlets of their rivers, and commerce was growing. Within these river mouths, sand and clay had been deposited at the point where river currents meet the still water over many years. These bars were a hindrance to navigation, which was required to move goods inland from the big lakes. This problem was discussed by Colonel Graham in his 1855 report, referred to in *The General History of the Great Lakes*:

These bars at the natural river-mouths had frequently not more than two or three feet of water; and some of them have entirely closed up the entrance, although, at a short distance inside there might be a depth from twelve to fifteen feet, or even twenty feet of water.

The channels of these rivers have also a tendency to be deflected from their courses, on entering the lake, by the shore-currents, which, driven before the prevailing winds, bend the channel off at right angles, and carrying it parallel with the lake-shore, form a long spit of sand between the river and the lake.

Thus in constructing an artificial harbor at one of these river-mouths, the first object aimed at by the early engineers was to prevent the further formation of a bar; and the second, to deepen and improve the river-channel. The former is attained by running out piers into the lake from the mouth of the river; and the latter, by the use of the dredge-boat to cut through the obstructions. (265)

Of particular interest were the rivers leading into Lakes Michigan and Erie, as the populations of these soon-to-be harbor towns were large enough to warrant the improvement of navigational channels and harbors. In 1824, the U.S. Army Corps of Engineers was contracted to remove snags and sandbars from waterways outletting to the Great Lakes in the interest of common navigation. Of course, many of these outlets contained marsh-lands that were full of wild rice. Such was the fate of the River Raisin and the Monroe Marsh, where piers were built and the river straightened. And it is the case study of how dredging and water pollution likely destroyed one of the largest wild rice beds in Michigan.

Our story begins in the early 1800s at a time when the marsh was a famous waterfowl hunting ground for the Europeans. Four to five thousand acres in size (reports vary), the marsh was dominated by Manoomin and wild celery, favorite foods of the hundreds of thousands of ducks that visited the wetland each year. The Monroe Marsh extended three to four miles along the Lake Erie coastline, and wild rice could be found growing up the creeks and rivers that emptied into the big lake. Within the heart of the marsh snaked the natural channel of the River Raisin, which joined with Riviere Au Sable and the Mason Run and wound around several islands and shoals, creating excellent growing conditions for Manoomin and other coastal marsh plants. Mill Creek (now called Plum Creek) and LaGrande Coulee (now called LaPlaisance Creek) emptied into the southern end of the marsh. And in the middle of the vast wild rice bed at the mouth of the River Raisin rose House Island, an important place for the Native people in the area, described in the *History of Monroe*:

In June, 1871, Mr. Joseph Guyor, one of these veterans [of the War of 1812], at that time eighty-eight years old, and vigorous, hale and hearty as a man twenty five years his junior, concluded that it would be an excellent plan to assemble together as many as possible of his old compatriots. Following up this admirable impulse, he at once extended an invitation to every one of them living in this county, to meet him at his home on Guyor's Island, now the home of the Monroe Marsh Club; and which was once known as "House Island." This had been the scene of large gatherings of the Pottawattomie and Shawnee tribes of Indians, and the ancient site of a small village of the former; many relics of their occupancy had been found in the earlier years; while, during the construction of the railroad from Monroe to the Piers, an extension of the line of the Michigan Southern Railroad Company to connect with its steamers on Lake Erie; in building its tracks across this island, there were exhumed, in the course of excavation, quantities of bones, skulls, stone axes, arrow heads, copper utensils and other implements used by the aborigines, unmistakable evidences of Indian occupation at some remote period.

It seemed a fitting place therefore, that on this historic island, this gathering should take place. Besides this, it was a most attractive spot, located on the north bank of the stream, shaded by huge forest trees, and surrounded by the immense beds of Egyptian Lotus, wild rice and luxuriantly blooming members of the lily family, and the home of all manner of wild fowl. (Bulkley 1913, 126)

La Plaisance Bay was the first to receive attention in this effort to improve navigation for the Monroe area. A survey of the bay was ordered by an act of Congress and carried out by Captain T. W. Maurice of the U.S. Army Corps of Engineers (USACE). Captain Maurice reported that the bay was broad and shallow, 9 to 10 feet at its deepest. A great marsh one mile broad surrounded it on all but the lake side, with extensive shoals separating the bay from the river. He recommended construction of a harbor of refuge by building a breakwater of stone-filled cribs, and work began in the spring of 1828. By September of that year, the 1,050-foot breakwall was completed.

Detroit Daily Free Press   August 8, 1858

Incidents of the War of 1812

A few days before the surrender of Detroit, Capt. CICOTTE was ordered to march his company to Monguagon and Brownstown, and see if the enemy's Indians were there. He mounted thirty (about half) of his men on ponies, and the remainder marched on foot. When they arrived at what is now known as Wyandotte, he saw the great chief WALK-IN-THE-WATER. He had not then joined the enemy.

The chief told him that the Indians knew of his coming, and were in force, lying in ambush in a marrais of wild rice, some miles down the river, and he advised CICOTTE to return with his men, as they would be greatly outnumbered and destroyed. The Captain replied that he was ordered to *see*, not to *hear*, if the enemy were there, and on they marched some distance below, where they met WILLIAM WALKER, a white man and Indian interpreter to our government.—He confirmed the statement of the chief.—He said the Indians were in ambush in the rice on each side of the road, in large numbers—that they would let the men pass the bridge over the creek, but that none who passed would ever return, and advised the men to go back. "But I am ordered to *see*," said the Captain, "and I *must see*," and on they went. When within about a half mile of the bridge, he halted the footmen, and with the mounted men advanced to within a rifle shot of it. All was silent as death, no living thing was to be seen, not even the black birds, which, at that season, collect in large flocks to feed on the wild grain.

Captain Maurice then recommended connecting the navigable waters of the bay with the River Raisin and proposed parallel piers and dredging. The work was approved in 1829 and completed in 1830, with the breakwall extended 210 feet. He continued to push for opening up the River Raisin to vessels that could navigate Lake Erie.

But in 1831, a violent storm hit and destroyed much of the new breakwall. Repairs were made and by 1835 the structure had been extended to 1,320 feet. It remained in good shape for three more years, but began to sustain minor damage in 1838, and no more repairs were made to the structure as funding and improvements were switched to Monroe Harbor. In just seven years, La Plaisance Harbor was built and abandoned. The breakwall was gradually destroyed over time and totally disappeared by the late 1800s.

Captain Smith had several times recommended that the navigable waters of the River Raisin be connected to Lake Erie, and had even submitted a plan for making a direct connection between the river and La Plaisance Bay. But his successor, Captain Henry Smith, had another idea in mind—to straighten the River Raisin and make a direct connection to the lake. He proposed cutting a canal 4,000 feet long and 100 feet wide through the peninsula known at the time as River Raisin Point, from the river just north of House Island to Lake Erie. The entrance would be protected by two parallel piers 726 feet long and 20 feet wide, which would run out to a depth of 10 feet right where the proposed canal would cross Sandy Creek. The creek would be turned toward the canal.

Captain Henry's plan was approved and work commenced in early May of 1835. Permanent dams were constructed on both sides of the canal to harden the shoreline and protect it from the wash of steamboats and the current. By 1837, a little over 3,000 feet of the canal was completed and the piers had been built out to a depth of 10 feet. But it was deemed necessary to take them out further to a depth of 12 feet. The following year, the piers and canal were lengthened and six new cribs of stone had to be added to the north side of the canal, which was rapidly wearing away. With the exception of limited dredging and repairs, no further funds were made available by the U.S. government until 1866, due to a change in federal policy. After that time, dredging continued unabated until the late 1800s. And what

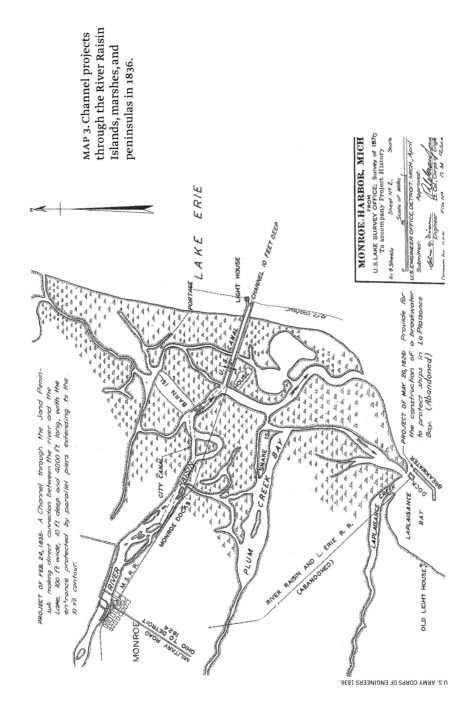

MAP 3. Channel projects through the River Raisin Islands, marshes, and peninsulas in 1836.

PROJECT OF FEB. 24, 1835: A Channel through the Sand Peninsula making direct connection between the river and the Lake, 100 ft. wide, 10 ft. deep and 4000 ft. long, with the entrance protected by parallel piers extending to the 10 ft. contour.

PROJECT OF MAY 20, 1826: Provide for the construction of a breakwater to protect ships in La Plaisance Bay. (Abandoned)

LAKE ERIE

PORTAGE

LIGHT HOUSE

CHANNEL 10 FEET DEEP

U.S. CANAL

BARN ISL.

STATION

CITY CANAL

SNAKE ISL.

PLUM CREEK BAY

BREAKWATER

DOCK

LAPLAISANCE CREEK

LAPLAISANCE BAY

MONROE DOCKS

RIVER

MONROE

M.S.R.R.

MILITARY ROAD
OHIO TO DETROIT
1824

RIVER RAISIN AND L. ERIE R. R.
(ABANDONED)

OLD LIGHT HOUSE

MONROE HARBOR, MICH
U.S. LAKE SURVEY OFFICE; Survey of 1870
To accompany Project History
In 4 Sheets   Sheet No. 2,   Scale
Scale of Miles
U.S. ENGINEER OFFICE, DETROIT, MICH., April
Submitted: Approved:
Engineer   Lt. Col. Corps of Engrs.
Drawn by   File No.   O. M. No.

became of House Island, former home of the Potawatomi and Shawnees? It was cut in two by the new canal, filled and shaped, and eventually lost any resemblance to its former self (map 3).

All of this work was done right through the heart of the Monroe Marsh, and the impacts of channelization were significant. Dredging is done in two ways, mechanically and hydraulically. For large projects such as Monroe Harbor, hydraulic dredging is the preferred method and involves mixing a large volume of water with sediment to form a slurry, which is then sucked from the bottom and pumped through a pipeline or into a hopper bin, or side-cast away from the channel being dredged. Dredged materials that aren't side-cast may be taken offsite and deposited.

In addition to direct physical harm, dredging can affect plant life by altering the physical environment and quality of the water. The mechanical process suspends the sediment, which increases turbidity and lowers light penetration. The heavier particles settle out quickly, but the fines stay suspended for longer periods and may be transported away from the site with the current. There are changes in the bottom topography as well that alter water circulation and cause changes in the mechanical properties of the sediment. Physical destruction of Manoomin from dredging surely occurred, and if the seeds were not covered by the disposal of spoils or the shifting of bottom sediments, lower light penetration would have prohibited them from sprouting. Additionally, wave action from boat traffic would also have uprooted any new plants in the spring.

By the late 1800s, the first great disturbance to the marsh was completed. Yet through all those years of being dredged and built upon, a portion of the marsh still held on, though smaller than it originally was. Manoomin continued to provide habitat for migrating waterfowl, which attracted shooters from far and wide.

Wealthy businessmen from Buffalo and Detroit frequently hunted together in the rice beds of the Monroe Marsh and decided to organize by creating the Golo Club around 1854. The club was named after an unusual bird nicknamed "golo" by a French punter (the duck was infrequently seen in the marsh and, based on the description of their whistling wings, was most likely a golden eye). The members used Joe Stearn's hotel as their

MAP 4. Hand-drawn map by Landon Cooke of the Monroe Marsh in 1900 showing the vegetation. Wild rice is indicated by three upward lines.

clubhouse and lavishly refurnished the building to supply great comfort. The staff included a chef, servants, and punters—the name given to men who poled the flat-bottomed boats with square-cut bows (punts) used in the marsh. The club was open in the fall and Golo hunters only targeted the largest ducks, keeping detailed records of the number and type of waterfowl shot by each shooter. But the Golo Club was short-lived as their numbers began to decline late in the decade due to some of their members passing away or moving out of the country. The final blow was delivered by a violent storm that hit the Monroe Piers and destroyed their clubhouse. The Golo Club, one of the first of its kind in the nation, was dissolved.

Great waterfowl hunting was not the only benefit derived from wild rice beds in those days. The tall, soft plants also provided a very comfy bed for a young boy's pig and made fine paper for the *New York Tribune*. The story "Something New: Wild Rice for Paper Stock—How It Is to Be Gathered" appeared in the *Detroit Free Press* on August 10, 1871.

> Last spring a gentleman connected with the Niagara Falls Paper Company was on a visit to Monroe, in this State, and one evening observed a lad carrying through the streets a bundle of wild rice which he had cut in one of the marshes so numerous on the lake coast of that locality. The lad stated that he had gathered the stuff to make a nest for his pig, but was glad to exchange the bundle for a few coppers. The gentleman was aware of the fact that experiments had been made with the wild rice plant of Minnesota, and that the article had been found unfit for newspaper material. The stalks taken from the boy were so soft and tender as to induce the paper man to decide upon an experiment. He next day secured the services of a man to cut him a good sized bale, and this was sent to Niagara Falls. The result was all that could be asked for. The rice not only made a soft paper, but paper firm and white. A further supply was obtained, and a share of the edition of the New York Tribune was worked off on the paper manufactured. The publishers being satisfied, and anxious to contract for a supply, the company determined on securing the stalks at its own expense and to make it a business of importance. Two or three weeks since, a New York machinist and engineer

named Thomas W. Griffith was sent out here to perfect some sort of a machine for gathering the rice, and his labor thus far is to be seen tied to the wharf near the D&M Railroad elevator, foot of Hasting street. He has first constructed a flat boat or scow sixty feet long and eighteen feet beam, drawing one foot of water the whole length. The boat is not provided with bulwarks, but merely sits upon the water like a shallow box, having no "hold" to speak of. Abaft the center is a boiler sitting flat upon the deck. The scow is provided with a regular stern wheel, the same as the steamers plying on the Ohio and Mississippi Rivers, and to the right of the boiler is an engine of eight or ten horse power, which will furnish the propelling power. The craft is to be steered by two rudders, each situated inside the wheel, and it is expected that they will work as easily as the patent wheel of a sailing vessel.

Going forward, a twin engine has been fastened down near the bow of the boat, on the port side, and this one is to be used for cutting the rice and hauling it inboard. At the bow, a solid frame, seven or eight feet high, has been erected, and a framework extends from the bow over to the water for several feet. From two of these timbers, seven feet apart, a huge knife, working on the same principle as the knife of a mowing machine, is to be hung, with means at hand to lower or raise it at will. When at work, the knife will be under water two or three feet, cutting a swath seven feet wide. Directly over the knife, or perhaps a little ahead of it, will be rigged a large fan worked by the engine. As the boat runs into the marsh, this fan will blow the grain over toward the knife, and will also serve a more important service. Resting upon the surface of the water is a large wooden roller, revolved by steam, and over this will travel an "apron" which will take up the rice and carry it [illegible] between two other rollers for the purpose of squeezing out the water. From thence the stalks can be stacked up in the center of the boat, or loaded into a barge alongside.

The boat, when finished, will have cost about three thousand dollars. It is an odd thing to look at, but there is no reason to believe that it will disappoint the anticipations of the designer. When using both engines to cut and run too it is not expected that the craft will make more than two miles an hour, but when using all steam to move about, she will get along at fair speed. A steam pipe runs under the deck to the forward engine, so that only one engine need be used at once. The article to be gathered abounds not only at Monroe, but at the mouth of the Detroit River, in the vicinity of Belle Isle, along the coast of Lake St. Clair, on the Flats, and in various other places. The stalks grow about seven or eight feet long, three feet or more of this being under water. Heading the scow for a marsh, with the knife in good order, and it is expected that she will not stop until cutting all that there is to cut. If she works as hoped for, at least one more craft will be built, and the business of gathering and shipping the stalks will give labor to a respectable number of men and boys, and the manufacture of the paper itself may cause something of a revolution in present prices. By Tuesday or Wednesday next the boat will be ready for a voyage to Lake St. Clair, and a trial of her cutting capacities will then be made.

The gentleman who happened to meet that young boy on a fine spring day in Monroe was Mr. George M. Worden, a contractor hired by the Niagara Falls Paper Company to furnish stock for the manufacturing of its product. Mr. Worden came up with the idea that the abundant beds of wild rice found at the mouth of the River Raisin would supply a limitless amount of fiber for papermaking, so he obtained a sufficient quantity and took it back to New York for testing. The Manoomin was worked into paper and found to produce a quality much superior to straw. The wild rice paper was free from silicates, as strong and flexible as that made from rags, easily bleached, and economical in respect to chemicals. In addition, it was pure in color, free from blemishes and specks, had perfect evenness, and received clear impressions from printer's type. (Wild rice paper was later found to be the strongest fiber known for making bank note parchment.)

Paper companies were always looking for cheap fibrous material, and the limitless supply of Manoomin was enticing to Mr. Worden, so he came up with a design for a rice-harvesting machine. The boat was built, and on August 17, 1871, went out on a trial run but unfortunately broke a belt and became disabled in the middle of the river. The harvester was towed back to the dock by a tug boat and repaired, and on the 18th made a successful test run. It took a few more trips on the river to test its effectiveness at harvesting wild rice before it was finally deemed a success. The machine was scheduled to cut a large amount of Manoomin in September of that year, at which time the rice would have been dropping its seed.

There were plans to build a second machine in the coming year, one that was larger and had a sheet-iron metal bottom and wider cutting blades. They were even planning to make Monroe the headquarters for gathering Manoomin and preparing it for shipment. Mr. Worden believed he would have no difficulty securing 100,000 tons of Manoomin annually for paper, it was considered so abundant. But they quickly learned that the harvested plant material was so heavy that its weight prohibited shipment. It was at that point in history that the story of Mr. Worden and his wild rice harvesting machine went cold. There was no further mention of this venture in the press. It simply vanished into the mist of history. This, of course, was lucky for the Manoomin because if he had been successful, the wild rice beds of Monroe Marsh might have disappeared before the twentieth century.

While the wild rice paper business faded into memory, hunting continued on the marsh. While several years had passed since the dissolution of the Golo Club, Manoomin continued to provide food and shelter for thousands of migrating ducks, geese, and swans. Market hunters continued to shoot in the marsh, providing canvasbacks, redheads, mallard, and teal to the local people of Monroe at a cost of twenty-five to fifty cents each. Hunting pressure on the marsh's waterfowl was so great that it was described as an "indiscriminate slaughter" by J. M. Bulkley in his 1913 book *The History of Monroe County*. The ducks were clearly in trouble.

Enter into our story the Monroe Marsh's second hunt club. The marsh had long been a favorite hunting spot and was known around the country, with shooters from the East, South, and even Canada traveling to the sportsmen's paradise (figure 4). Joseph Guyer, a former Monroe resident, saw a golden opportunity with all the national interest and purchased a house owned by Joe Sears on the southern bank of the lower channel of the River Raisin. It was converted to "Uncle Joe's Marsh Hotel" and every spring and fall it was filled to capacity with shooters.

At that time hunting was an unregulated activity with no limits on how many ducks one could shoot in a day. These gentlemen noticed the decline in the number of ducks they bagged and came up with ideas on how to restrict hunting in order to preserve the magnificent opportunities afforded by the marsh. It was proposed that an organization be formed to accommodate rules for hunting and that it include both local and visiting sportsmen. So, in 1880, several visiting shooters paid money to Mr. George Dawson to purchase the marshlands and form a club, and the books were left open for one year for local residents to sign up. But the cost seemed insurmountable for the folks who lived in the area, and thus not one joined the club. The Monroe Marsh Club then incorporated under the laws of New York with a membership of twenty-four wealthy gentlemen from different parts of the United States and Canada, with none of them from the Monroe area. The company soon tore down the old hotel and replaced it with a handsome clubhouse and a number of other buildings. It possessed leases and ownership over 5,000 acres of the Monroe Marsh, and strict rules were put in place and rigidly enforced in order to ensure continued good hunting.

Shooting rights were reserved for club members, which rankled the local sportsmen who had hunted there for years. So upset were the locals that they formed their own organization, the Liberal Hunt Club, specifically to test the claims of the Monroe Marsh Company. One day, Liberal Club member Mr. H. C. Jackson put on his hunting gear, grabbed his gun, and placed himself at a point opposite where the visible boundary between the Marsh Company's property and Lake Erie had washed away. He was told to leave but stubbornly refused and was subsequently arrested for trespassing. The case went all the way to the Michigan Supreme Court not once but twice, and a final ruling in 1886 ended the battle with the right to hunt in the marsh given exclusively to the Monroe Marsh Company.

A new threat to the marsh appeared in the early 1900s in the form of a fish. Carp, introduced into the country around 1865, was most abundant in the United States in the western end of Lake Erie and in the Illinois River and its tributaries at that time. Sportsmen were quick to blame the fish for most everything, from fewer ducks in their bags to vegetation damage in the marshes. Carp are known to feed on roots and tender plants, uproot

FIGURE 4. Monroe Marsh, date unknown. Taken by the mother of Mrs. Carl Kiburtz in the marshes while picking lotus. Circa 1907.

plants by rolling and burrowing into the sediment, and a new study suggests they eat rice seeds as well (Johnson and Havranek 2013).

The Monroe Marsh Company thought of the poor carp as a curse, as the bottom feeders uprooted Manoomin and destroyed the wild celery in their marsh. One club member, W. C. Sterling, took advantage of the problem and created the Monroe Carp Pond Company in 1916. Carp were removed from Lake Erie and reared in six open-water "ponds" created within the marsh. The fish were fattened up with cracked corn all summer, transported up the River Raisin to Monroe, then shipped alive in cars to East Coast markets and sold as gefilte fish to the Jewish communities.

While the sportsmen were enjoying great duck hunting and Mr. Sterling was selling his carp, other entities began taking advantage of the River Raisin. Industries sprang up on its shores, including paper mills, manufacturing plants, and even municipal dumps. Waste was freely released into the waters of the River Raisin, causing major pollution issues. It wasn't long before Mr. Sterling noticed the changes in the marsh, and he blamed

Mirror of Michigan

While Lewis Shettler, aged 34 years, was in bathing at the iron bridge over the Huron river, four miles south of Pinckney, he became tangled in the weeds and wild rice growing in the river, and before help could reach him was drowned.

the effluent from the Monroe Paper Company for killing off his carp and the wild rice and celery once so abundant in the area. He filed suit against the paper company with the goal of having an injunction placed against the mill to stop the discharge of effluent into the River Raisin and to receive compensation for the loss of his carp. Mr. Sterling lost his case in the circuit court and appealed to the Michigan Supreme Court.

The state's highest court heard the case and found that while the effluent did indeed lower the dissolved oxygen content of the water, sewage from the City of Monroe and other sources of waste from industry and other paper companies also contributed to the problem (figure 5). Mr. Sterling was awarded $23,141 for the loss of his carp, and the polluters were allowed to continue to discharge effluent and other pollutants into the River Raisin.

Water pollution was not restricted to the River Raisin and Mr. Sterling's carp ponds; unregulated discharges of numerous chemicals, organic materials, and garbage occurred throughout the region. In the 1951 "Report of the International Joint Commission of the United States and Canada on the Pollution of Boundary Waters," they identified and quantified the problem of pollutants being discharged into the major rivers of the Great Lakes along the U.S.-Canadian border:

Industrial wastes, which were of little concern in 1912, are now a major problem. The daily discharge into these boundary waters now averages more than 2 billion U.S. gallons (approximately 1¾ billion Imperial

COURTESY OF THE LIBRARY OF MICHIGAN ARCHIVES.

FIGURE 5. Pollution from a paper company in Monroe 900 feet from the footbridge, circa 1920.

gallons). While much of this is condenser and cooling water which has not been adversely affected by its use for industrial purposes, an appreciable volume of harmful pollutants is discharged daily. These include some 13,000 pounds of phenols, 8,000 pounds of cyanides, 25,000 pounds of ammonium compounds and large quantities of oils and suspended solids of all types. In addition to the toxic effects of some of the pollutants . . . the industrial waste discharge has a biochemical oxygen demand (B.O.D.) equivalent to the oxygen demand of the untreated sanitary wastes from a population of more than 4,000,000. Thus the industrial wastes produce a greater oxygen requirement on the receiving streams than the combined total of the domestic wastes of the area. (International Joint Commission 1951, 17)

The wild rice of the Monroe Marsh, touted as one of the best waterfowl-hunting spots in the nation, was not mentioned again in any available

Detroit Free Press   August 9, 1896

CAPITOL SQUARE FOUNTAIN
People Had Their First View of It Yesterday.
WHEN COMPLETED IT WILL BE THE FINEST OF ITS KIND IN THE WEST

The handsomest bit of work in Detroit, in the landscape gardening line, was thrown open to public inspection yesterday when the board fence around the Capitol Square fountain was removed. The basin is of stone and cement and is surrounded with flowers and vines. It is in the shape of a clover leaf. In the center is a great basin ten feet high, supported on a massive pillar. Projecting into the three arms of the basin are three graceful arches joining at the top with the basin. All of this interior work is made of a peculiar sort of rock called tuffa. It is a petrefaction [*sic*] of incrustation of vegetable matter, found in marshes near Sandusky, O. It seems that ages ago, the washing of the water on the vegetation coated it with lime and by a gradual process the whole mass was turned to stone. The rock shows the traces of vegetation very plainly and bits of cane and wild rice can be easily distinguished. Several shells, perfect in outline, are also to be seen. A peculiar thing about this rock is that the longer it is exposed to air or water, the harder it becomes. It is very porous and soaks up the water much as a sponge does. At the top of each arch is a large basin filled with water plants. At each angle of the cloverleaf basin is a like vessel filled with palms and vines. All of these are of tuffa rock.

newspaper, book, or published paper after the 1920s. To find out when the Manoomin disappeared and what caused it, we turn our attention to the waterfowl. There was a significant die-off of ducks in the 1940s, and because hunting was important to the Michigan Department of Conservation, they initiated a study.

The Detroit River connects Lake St. Clair and Lake Erie and carries the outflow of Lakes Superior, Michigan, and Huron. Prior to the 1930s, there were no wintering ducks because the food-rich lower half of the river froze every year due to its shallow depth (Hunt and Ewing 1953). The upper part of the river, which remained ice-free because it was deeper, did not have much food for the ducks; thus it did not encourage them to stay. But when the industrial plants began to appear on the lower west banks of the river, they began to discharge effluent, which warmed the water and prevented ice from forming. This allowed the waterfowl, which numbered up to fifty thousand ducks, to stay the winter in the lower half of the river.

In the Detroit River and near its mouth in Lake Erie, it was estimated that ten thousand wintering canvasbacks, scaups, redheads, and black ducks perished in 1948 (Miller and Whitlock 1948). There was speculation that this massive loss was caused by a combination of cold weather, lack of food, and pollution. J. S. Hunt and H. E. Ewing of the Michigan Department of Conservation wanted to find out why and conducted a study to investigate the question (Hunt and Ewing 1953).

The first step they took was to look at the diet of the ducks to determine if something in their food might have contributed to the die-offs. Bottom samples taken from food beds during that time showed the bottom coated with oil or impregnated with sludge in some places. The 1951 International Joint Commission's report *The Pollution of Boundary Waters* stated that seventeen industrial facilities were releasing oil directly into the River Rouge in the mid-1940s. The lower three miles of the River Rouge were dredged annually, and 17,000 gallons of oil and grease were scooped up from the bottom daily for fifty days, then taken to the Detroit River where it was dumped to be carried away by the current. The researchers predicted that 2,000 gallons of oil per day were settling on the bottom of the River Rouge and likely more in the Detroit River.

The dumping of industrial chemicals, oil, and grease would certainly impact Manoomin, and in some cases this would depend on the time of year it was done. In late fall through early spring, oil-laden sediment would smother the seed bank and inhibit sprouting. Oil-saturated particles would suspend in the water column and increase turbidity, prohibiting sunlight penetration and sprouting. If Manoomin was in the floating leaf stage, the vegetation would be covered by floating oil. It is unknown what effects those particular industrial chemicals would have had on Manoomin because it hasn't been studied. However, Miles Pirnie, a respected wetland biologist who worked for the Michigan Department of Conservation in the mid-twentieth century, believed that chemical pollution often eradicated thriving stands of young rice plants (Pirnie 1935).

Pollution continued to flow into this area for the next twenty years, with additional die-offs of waterfowl reported. These losses were attributed directly or indirectly to pollution and thermal changes due to the release of effluent from industrial plants as they rose up along the western bank of the Detroit River. Wild rice, a source of trade in the area for the Huron Indians in the 1600s, disappeared from the Detroit River by 1960 (Michigan Department of Natural Resources 1991). Its disappearance was likely due not only to pollution, but to the filling of the extensive marshes that once existed along the western side of the Trenton Channel.

There was another culprit in the decline of waterfowl, and the conditions causing the disease that killed them also likely killed or damaged the Manoomin. In 1962, H. J. Miller from the Michigan Department of Conservation presented a statement to the Detroit River–Lake Erie Conference on Pollution Problems regarding heavy losses of waterfowl since the early 1940s (Miller 1962b). He described the first serious botulism outbreak east of the Mississippi, which occurred in the Monroe Marsh beginning September 10, 1941, and spread by late fall of that year to the marshes of Maumee Bay near the Ohio line. The devastating losses were estimated at ten thousand ducks. The dumping of decomposing organic matter into the River Raisin by the local paper mills was named as the principal factor in creating the anaerobic conditions (low oxygen) that encouraged the growth of the organism that causes botulism. Anaerobic conditions were likely very detrimental to wild rice as they are known to limit growth of the plant's roots and the protective covering of the emerging shoot.

The combination of pollution, dredging, and filling contributed to the disappearance of the great wild rice beds along the western coast of Lake Erie and the Detroit River. As with other ecological events in history, it is often difficult to identify the sole cause of Manoomin's decline, and there may be even more reasons yet to be uncovered. But this one is certain. There are historical accounts of extensive wild rice beds prior to the early 1900s, evidence of their decline during the early and mid-twentieth century, and none left today. Prior to industrialization of the area, Manoomin flourished. During and after, it was gone. The loss of these great coastal marshes was a high price to pay for "progress."

CHAPTER 3

Logging in the Saginaw River Basin

In the fall of 2013, my daughters Olivia and Alexandria Sprague, Alexandria's son Noah, and I joined a great group of enthusiastic Hunters of Wild Rice (Manoomin). It was our first time ever doing anything like this, and we were all very excited to be part of this group and to be the first Ojibway to gather wild rice in this area in almost a century. We started out our journey in Caseville, looking for the long grain rice. Daisy Kostus and Barb Barton did the water ceremony and prayed. The Winds were not too bad out there on Lake Huron, but enough to make it a bit more challenging to paddle into the wind. It was a challenge to get to the Manoomin due to the cattails and phragmites and as we pushed our way through all of that, we found there wasn't too much Wild Rice out there. We tried multiple spots and had found the same situation at each spot we put the canoes in. So, after a little bit of discussion amongst the group, we decided to head on over to Tawas Lake. An hour and a half later we arrived at what seemed to be the perfect setting for Manoomin. The depth was just right, the winds weren't too strong, and the current didn't seem to be overly powerful. We put the canoes in and headed out to the middle of the lake. And there it was, a big beautiful patch of Manoomin! We got the push poles out, our knockers ready, and in we went with great excitement, and expectation. I took lessons for push poling from Roger LaBine, he made it look so easy, as opposed to my style of swinging it over my head to switch sides. Poor Daisy was getting wet in front.

As we were going along I started to sing songs that I knew, which were random top 40 radio songs. Thankfully Daisy jumped in during my intermission and started to sing a beautiful water song in the language. Everybody within 300 yards appreciated her gift of song, including myself. We spent a good amount of time out there, it was wonderful. As we made our way back to shore, we ended up in a bit of a race, which didn't end well for Daisy and I. We tipped the canoe over in 4' deep water and lost half of our Manoomin. As we were standing in the shallow water, I had a visitor (water snake) swim up my pant leg. I hit the high C note for about a minute or two, until he finally exited and went on his way. The other canoers started to make their way back to us to give us a hand (and take pics of our mishap). What are friends for, right? After all the laughter subsided, I emptied the water out of the canoe, flipped it back up and jumped back in. Daisy was doing her best to save the Manoomin, bless her heart. So that was our first adventure out on the lakes to find Manoomin. We retell these stories when we see each other, and have a great laugh about all of our idiosyncrasies and mishaps. To follow up with the gathering of the Manoomin, we did all come together at Barb's home in Lansing to prepare the rice for consumption. Which is quite the process and a great story to tell in itself.

Miigwetch,
Kelly R. Willis, Saginaw Chippewa Indian Tribe

Saginaw Bay lies along the southwestern coast of Lake Huron on Michigan's eastern shore and contains the largest contiguous freshwater coastal system in the United States. Its gently sloping, shallow margins provide excellent habitat for emergent marshes, which grow from sand-covered clay sediments in most areas. In the lower part of the bay is an area named the Inner Bay, whose currents are driven by the wind due to the shallowness of the water. In the upper Outer Bay, Lake Huron's circulation determines which way the water flows.

Prior to European colonization, the Saginaw Bay watershed was estimated to be covered with approximately 700,000 acres of wetlands, and 37,000 of those were emergent marshes around the bay proper (Public Sector Consultants 2012). These "swamplands" were bisected by many creeks and rivers carrying water to the bay. Six rivers converge to form the Saginaw River: the Tittabawassee, Chippewa, and Pine to the north, and the Shiawassee, Flint, and Cass to the south. This important waterway passes through the cities of Saginaw and Bay City before emptying into Lake Huron. The Saginaw River was the hub of multiple trade routes used first by Indigenous people, then by European trappers, traders, and travelers. It is that intersection of time and place where we awaken history to tell the story of how logging, dredging, and draining impacted Manoomin.

We begin just prior to European colonization, when the vast majority of the population were Indigenous people. Many Ojibwe villages could be found along the streams and rivers of Saginaw Bay, often near the shores of the Pinconning and Kawkawlin Rivers and also adjacent to a trail that ran along the western edge of the bay (Hinsdale 1931). The Ojibwe had easy access to excellent hunting, trapping, and fishing opportunities in the vast marshes of Saginaw Bay. They also had thousands of acres of wild rice beds to harvest in, as Manoomin grew inland in the marshes and along the coastline.

In 1819, the Ojibwe, Potawatomi, and Odawa in this region ceded more than 6 million acres to the U.S. government (Powell 1899). Numerous reserves were created in the Saginaw Bay area, including several that encompassed large wild rice beds: the Kawkawlin Reserve (6,000 acres), located on the north side of the Kawkawlin River at the Indian village; Crow Island and vicinity (1,000 acres) in the Saginaw River; Big Rock on the Shiawassee River (10,000 acres); Little Fork on the Tetabawasink (Tittabawassee River) (6,000 acres); Red Bird Reserve at Black Bird's town on the Tetabawasink

(Tittabawassee River); and a large tract (40,000 acres) on the west side of the Saginaw River.

As time went on, the reserves were replaced by European settlements and the Anishinaabek were moved once again. The Treaties of 1855 and 1864 established the Isabella Indian Reservation, and the Saginaw, Black River, and Swan Creek Bands, who together were known as the Saginaw Chippewa Indian Tribe of Michigan, relocated to Isabelle County. Today, additional reservation land exists on the Saganing Reservation near the coast of Saginaw Bay. The land they were moved to was a far cry from the extensive marshlands they had known. And the Manoomin, an important food source for the people, was nearly nonexistent on their new reservation.

The rice beds of the Saginaw River and Bay are perhaps the best documented of any in Michigan. Early explorers, colonists, lumbermen, and hunters were clearly moved by the vastness of these marshes and their resident birds. General B. F. Partridge elegantly wrote in 1881 that "the smooth waters of this broad river were streaked and spotted with islands of high grass and wild rice . . . innumerable bayous and creeks covered with the waterfowl listening and peering shyly through the high grass" (338). Leeson and Clark wrote that same year that the "bayous and extensions of the Saginaw River were bordered with a plentiful supply of wild rice" (289). L. S. Foote (1917) penned a story in *American Angler* a quarter-century later, describing the Saginaw section of the bay as "one of the finest duck hunting areas of the United States. Along the bay and river shores and on the main tributaries are thousands of acres of wild rice marshes, to which, in the season, the wildfowl resort by the thousands" (342).

Perhaps the most detailed descriptions of the wild rice beds came from W. B. Mershon in *Recollections of My Fifty Years Hunting and Fishing* (1923). Mershon was born in Saginaw in 1856 and began hunting at the age of ten. An accomplished naturalist, he went on to become the State of Michigan forester for two years, mayor of Saginaw, a lifelong member of the American Ornithologists Union, and a third-generation lumber businessman. Mershon painted his picture of the marshes and wild rice beds in a beautiful way:

Back from the river edge, both below and above Saginaw, stretched great areas of marsh land. I don't know why I call it "marsh land," other than that it is the common expression, for this was marsh pure and simple with no land to be seen in it, tremendous beds of wild rice miles in extent, pond holes with cattails, muskrat houses, pond weed, water lilies—both yellow and white, and all the surroundings and inhabitants that an ideal old fashioned duck marsh ever contained, even to the sonorous old bullfrog that on moonlight summer nights concerted and bellowed, making a music that many a night has lulled me to sleep even in the heart of my home town, East Saginaw. Of course these tremendous stretches of marsh land meant quantities of wild fowl.

Around the mouth of the Flint River was the Mishtegay. I have spelled it phonetically; I don't know what the meaning of the word is, probably derived from the Chippewa language. Then the Ferguson Bayou put off from the Shiawassee and extended up towards the Flint, its earlier reaches being tremendous rice marshes. Then the shores of this bayou became fringed with trees of black walnut, elm, basswood, oak and hickory, to which clung enormous wild grape vines. This was home of the woodduck, and black and gray squirrels innumerable. These up river marshes were miles in extent. The combined length of the two marshes I have mentioned was upwards of twenty miles, and in breadth from a mile to three or four miles. All along the margin of the river were rice fields from a few hundred feet to hundreds of yards in width. Below Saginaw the rice beds of Crow Island, Cheboyganning and Squaconning were of great area.

Years back the duck season began September 1st, and many blue winged teal and mallards, that we called gray ducks, raised their broods on our home marshes. The rice was high, still in the milk; water lilies, both white and yellow, filled the open places; the pickerel weed with its blue spikes had not yet lost its beauty. The redwinged blackbirds had flocked in clouds, taking wing were uncountable and for brief moments appeared from nowhere, they were out of sight again, but listen!

What a concert you can hear from the dense rice cover, for when the rice is in the milk these cheery birds love it best.

While hunters dearly loved the Saginaw marshes, others did not look so favorably upon the tall, dense grass. In 1848, the Reverend Ferdinand Sievers led his flock of German Lutheran emigrants from Franken, Germany, into the wilds of Bay County to establish a new colony and church. In a letter dated August 11, 1848, to Reverend Loche in Germany, Rev. Sievers described lush wild rice beds on the south arm of Squaquanning Creek—a tributary of the Saginaw River:

> This time we stayed at the first bridge of the south arm. This was as far as our boat could go. The raft loaded with 8,500 board feet of lumber, which as tied on the back of our boat, we had to leave further upstream because in spots the river was too overgrown with wild rice, which made it very difficult to get through with our big load … it was required that all surveying would start in the middle of the stream. On both sides of the river there is quite a large swamp area with marsh grass growing up to six feet tall.

The Lutherans weren't the only ones looking to move into this region; the Presbyterians were right behind. An "intelligence" report by the Presbyterian missionary Reverend J. Ambrose Wight in the 1867 issue of *Presbyterian Monthly* described the Saginaw Bay area as a land full of potential—as long as the marshes were drained.

> Its soil is everywhere rich. It produces abundantly grain, small grains, vegetables, dairy products, fine wool, horses; and all the most valued fruits, say apples, pears, plums, peaches, and grapes; and Indian corn ripens well in all parts of it so far as known. But the swamps! The swamps are such as are mostly made by a close subsoil, a want of hills, and the forests. Cut off the timber, cut a few ditches, and your swamp is hard, dry, productive land. And when the swamps are gone the fever and ague disappears. There are thousands of acres about the Saginaw

River, which only two years ago were dismal-looking marshes, which are now firm, dry land, under cultivation; and at but a trifling expense. Towns are now covering just such grounds.

Then as to the forests; they are very rapidly disappearing. The year 1866 shipped from the Saginaw Valley alone, three hundred and fifty millions of pine lumber, to say nothing of timber, staves, lath, and other like products. The year 1867 is cutting a larger quantity yet.

Then in salt manufacture, clearing for settlement, etc., the forests are very rapidly giving way. (280)

The Saginaw Valley was in the heart of Michigan's great pine forests. The best pine in the state was along an eighty-mile stretch of the Tittabawassee River, with trees up to 175 feet tall and 7 feet in diameter. Along the Cass River, W. B. Mershon (1923) described the trees of his youth as "big soft glorious pine cork pine of old," and observed logs from the Cass River that would produce "perfectly clear white pine planks four inches in thickness and four feet in width" (57).

The Saginaw Valley was part of the eastern district of the lumber industry and the first to be exploited for its timber, with much of the wood going to the Northeast, where it was used to build cities and homes. With a convergence of six rivers forming the Saginaw River, the network of waterways provided easy access to the interior supply of pines, and ample places to store logs.

After timber cruisers found the best stands of pine, logging crews would come in and begin their work. Logs were cut during the winter months, the time when Manoomin seeds were resting in the bottom sediments of the marshes and streams. The 16-foot logs were too heavy to drag, so instead they were loaded onto sleds and skidded over ice-covered roads to the river banks, where they were piled 20 to 30 feet high to await the spring thaw. Once the rivers melted, the logs were pushed into the rivers and floated downstream to the booming grounds and mills at the mouths of the Tittabawassee, Shiawassee, and Cass Rivers, where they were marked and sorted (figure 6). The logs were at last cut into boards, dried, and put on ships and transported to various places. Mershon (1923) described a continuous string

FIGURE 6. Many lumber mills lined the Saginaw River.

of lumber mills for nearly twenty miles on either side of the Saginaw River above Saginaw City, past East Saginaw, Carrollton, Crow Island, Zilwaukee, Melbourne, and Bay City. When the sawing season was over in the summer, there was a nearly solid lumber pile on both sides of the Saginaw River from Saginaw to Bay City and logs covered the surface of the water so thickly "it was hard for a steamer to find a channel."

As time went on, improved technology allowed for quicker harvest of the timber. When the logging railroad was built in the 1850s, the small engines and portable narrow-gauge track allowed for logging farther away from the rivers during all times of year. Plank roads were built through the marshes. The axe was replaced by the crosscut saw, a tool that cut trees much more quickly. The big wheels transported logs much more easily, and circular saws improved cutting in the mills. All these improvements increased the rate at which trees were taken from the forests.

The ecological impacts of the logging era on the rivers, streams, and marshes were many and severe. As the industry developed, towns and lumber mills sprang up along the rivers like mushrooms. The storing of logs on their banks and their transport down the rivers physically altered the shorelines and seriously disturbed the bottom sediments and vegetation. Saw ash settled on the surface of the waters and commonly filled in low marsh areas along the water's edge. Marshy areas were filled to stack logs. Waterways were deepened and cleared. The rivers were clogged with logs and strewn with acidic bark that was churned about by boats and ships of all kinds. Bottom sediments were covered by an accumulation of sawdust and wood debris, smothering plants and seeds (figure 7). Sedimentation increased turbidity, and the castoff bark would create tea-colored acidic water due to the release of tannins; both reduced sunlight penetration to the bottom, which was needed by Manoomin seeds to germinate.

The quality and health of the water was also severely impacted during the logging era and the industrialization that followed. The discharge of

COURTESY OF WEST MICHIGAN SHORELINE DEVELOPMENT COMMISSION.

FIGURE 7. Wood debris in Muskegon Lake left by the lumber mills during the late 1800s.

sewage and other pollutants from the cities, mills, and industries degraded water quality in the rivers and caused a change in the fish communities. Conditions favored bottom-feeding carp, and their populations increased significantly. The fish disturbed the sediment and uprooted young plants in the spring through their "churning" behavior. They may also have impacted the seed bank by feeding on wild rice seeds in the sediment.

Burning refuse, oil slicks, salt spills, sewage, and plant wastes were routinely dumped in the waters. During the years between 1870 and 1890, nearly all the trees had been cut in Michigan, and by 1923, not a single saw-mill was cutting pine anymore (Mershon 1923; Kilar 1990). Dr. R. C. Kedzie of the Michigan Agricultural College presented his observations of the condition of the Saginaw River to the East Saginaw Sanitary Convention in December of 1880.

> You have water-works a few miles up Saginaw River, taking water from the river a little below the confluence of the Titabawassee and the Shiawassee. This water is taken at a point above the outlet of the sewers of both east Saginaw and Saginaw City, and would thus seem to be safe from sewage, for it is supposed to be the first and main business of a river to flow downstream. If the inlet pipe of your water-works was placed below or among the sewer mouths, you would condemn the system by a unanimous verdict without the jury leaving their seat. I know some of you want to tell me what your sister Saginaw City does, but we are not discussing Saginaw City just now, and the only argument adequate for her case is to hold your nose! Wisdom comes from the east, and East Saginaw has wisely rejected sewage as a source of water. You seem to be safe, for the attraction of gravitation is on your side, and gravity never takes a vacation during the heated term or for the holidays. The fact that water runs down hill is in your favor. But does it always? A short way up one of the affluents of the Saginaw I am told that there is a marshy lake covering nearly 100 square miles, and when the wind blows strongly upstream the contents of Saginaw river are carried up stream—the waters overflowing into this lake, and thus the sewage of all the cities on the river is carried to and past your water-works, and

both the upper flow and the refluent tide may give you your sewage water at times, gravity to the contrary notwithstanding.

Once more, these streams which feed the Saginaw are the water-beds of millions of saw-logs, lying in store for the use of the saw-mills. These logs have parted with their bark which lies in the bottom and along the banks undergoing slow decay. This is reinforced by driftwood of every kind, infesting the streams in their whole length. The banks for miles are only marsh, and the lake is a flag and rush swamp rather than a lake. Yet these are your reserve forces from which are drawn the active troops for the daily battle of life. Would you stoop down and drink from these slimy marshes? But how is the water made any better by forcing the water by a steam pump through long lines of pipe, to be finally drawn off through a faucet? It is the same water still, essentially unchanged in properties. I have heard of a housewife who reproved her dog for thrusting his dirty nose into a pan of milk: "You nasty dog! Now I have got to strain that milk over again." How much is your method better than hers?

This for the present; how about the future? What will be the condition of the water in Saginaw river when the Saginaws have reached their possible limit of growth, and the banks of these streams are lined with vast manufactories of every kind to contribute to the defilement of these waters? No civic control is possible to preserve these streams in their present condition without hampering the expansion of the manufacturing interests of both the Saginaws, and when the conflict comes between business and health, you may safely count that business will win the day. (51–52)

Dredging and draining of the marshes in the Saginaw Basin also played a key role in the loss of habitat for Manoomin. The dikes and ditches in the Saginaw River Basin claimed thousands of acres of marshland, turning them into prairie farms. Railroad tracks were being laid throughout the region, running right through wetlands. In 1867, the interurban railroad was built from Saginaw to Bay City and went directly through a large wild rice marsh near the Saginaw River.

All these impacts acted in concert during the logging era of the 1800s and likely caused the destruction of nearly all wild rice beds in Saginaw Bay and the Saginaw River Basin. Several miles of rice beds tried to hold on along Cheboyganing Creek, but they too disappeared within the first half of the twentieth century. Today, Wildfowl Bay is the only known location in Saginaw Bay where Manoomin still survives.

But the threats to Manoomin didn't stop here. Next came the war against malaria and the little mosquito that carries it, and the birth of a new kind of farmer in Michigan—the muck farmer.

CHAPTER 4

Draining the Swamplands

As a Potawatomi person and member of the Citizen Potawatomi Nation, my ancestors originally lived in what is now the Lower Peninsula of Michigan and other nearby regions. As I now live in Michigan, I have worked with Potawatomi and other Anishinaabe/Neshnabe persons and communities to protect the environment for the sake of human and ecosystem health and promote the resurgence of cultural and spiritual practices that renew relationships across human, plant, animal, and physical (e.g. water) relatives. "Renewal" is a complex ecological process. As Anishinaabe/Neshnabe people, we have long traditions of relating to particular relatives, whether water, whitefish, wild rice, sandhill crane, blueberries or sturgeon. We call them relatives, in part, to refer to our seasonal round system of governance in which humans have multiple responsibilities throughout the year to monitor, steward, harvest, process and recycle refuse involving all of these relatives and how they relate to one another.

The seasonal round is at once a cultural, political and ecological system. It is deeply physical, as these relationships among relatives ensured the ecological flows of nutrients through plants, animals and humans and ensured high quality soils, clean waters and woodlands teeming with life. In our seasonal round system, a part of what makes it work is what humans do; but another part involves the ecological conditions that interact reciprocally with what humans do. Ricing is a good example of this. Governing wild rice involved human cultural and spiritual practices which included ceremonies, harvesting camps, monitoring regimes and leadership traditions (i.e. the rice chiefs), and much more, of course. The cultural and spiritual cohesion involved in these practices is something many Anishinaabe/Neshnabe societies very much want to continue today—as, in short, it gets to the heart of what many Indigenous persons understand to be their sovereignty or collective self-determination.

But our efforts to restore these processes always must reckon with the physical depth of settler colonialism. While settler colonialism did not entirely wipe away our memories of these practices, settler colonialism has degraded the physical or ecological aspects of these practices to a degree that makes restoration extraordinarily challenging. Settler colonialism refers to a particular form of domination in which at least one society seeks to exploit what they perceive to be the benefits that lie on the territories of Indigenous peoples. Here, I say territories and not ecosystems because settlers have no experience in the territories they want to settle, seeing them not as ecosystems in which humans, plants and animals relate as relatives within ecosystems based on reciprocal responsibilities, but rather, as bearers of "benefits," or "resources," that are understood in isolation. Examples are "farmland," or "minerals," or "trading routes," and so on. Settler colonialism differs from other types of colonialism because the settler population seeks to stay in the territory permanently. Given most human societies I am aware of cannot handle the cognitive dissonance of seeing themselves both as people aspiring to the moral life and as people who commit genocide, settler societies seek to erase Indigenous peoples, either through direct forgetting, such as in the U.S. educational system, or through romantic portrayals of the destruction of Indigenous peoples that let current, wistful settlers living today off the hook.

One of the significant forms of erasure is destruction of the ecosystems required for Indigenous peoples to engage in the spiritual and cultural practices that express collective self-determination. Again, boarding schools and other forms of genocide did not entirely erase our memories of these practices. But settler land-use essentially upended the physical or ecological aspects. So, even if you have some memory of ricing traditions, that only goes so far when rice no longer grows in lakes or rivers or when the remaining rice beds are on state lands or some settler's private property. As Anishinaabe/Neshnabe persons engage the soils, waters, flora and fauna, and so on, of Michigan, we learn just how much settlers have sedimented colonialism through multiple layers into the ecological aspects of this place. Settlers did this to make way for creating ecological aspects that they believed would lay the groundwork for their agricultural and industrial economies and their cultural and spiritual practices.

The history of logging and malaria in Michigan in the 19th century is deeply disturbing. By the 19th century, the remaining rice, already threatened by previous historical circumstances of settler and other forms of colonialism, was destroyed in order to eradicate malaria, a disease settlers were having a tough time with. Ironically, the prevalence of malaria is quite possibly related to the massive and now infamous logging of Michigan. The logging of Michigan, to woodlands peoples such as the Potawatomi, was devastating, as one can imagine. Yet the changes in hydrology, soil composition, and so on of logging makes for the exact type of stagnant pools that anopheles mosquitoes thrive in. Settler logging destroyed Anishinaabe/Neshnabe reciprocal ecosystems; logging also created a further hazard to settlers that they only knew how to solve through using means that further degraded the environment, drying up the "swamps" and oiling the waters. These latter anti-malarial practices are not good for wild rice. Of course, the drying up of swamps was not based on settlers knowing about the origin of malaria in mosquitoes. They had other hypotheses about where malaria came from. But that did not stop them from doing so.

This history then raises the issue of a pattern of settler colonialism. Settler societies seek to erase Indigenous peoples through multiple tactics, one of which is ecological destruction. But given settlers know so little about ecosystems, the initial acts of degradation create new problems that they only know how to solve through further ecological degradation. As Indigenous persons, when we put our hands and hearts back into the soils, waters—the physical and ecological aspects of this place—we experience this history. And we have to reckon with this history every day, both when we address the immediate problems our societies face but also when we take the time to engage in the resurgence of cultural and spiritual practices that hold one of the keys to our having a future as original peoples of the Great Lakes region.

—Kyle Whyte, Potawatomi

As we have learned, wild rice disappeared from many places in Michigan due to the dredging of river channels to facilitate the running of logs and the passage of boats and ships. Marshes and swamplands were also drained for agriculture, roads, railroads, and the development of towns. This widespread practice was fueled in part by the Swamplands Act of 1850. The act essentially turned over all federally owned swamplands to the state with the caveat that they would be drained for public health and, presumably, agriculture.

While the ecological impacts of logging are not hard to imagine, it wasn't until the last decade or so that researchers have been exploring the effects of deforestation on public health (de Castro et al. 2006; Garg 2014; Hahn et al. 2014; Fornace et al. 2016). And what they are finding is a positive correlation between logging and the incidence of malaria. What was the connection between logging, malaria, and Manoomin? It is a fascinating story of cause and effect, misperception and irony.

Malaria comes from the medieval Italian word *mala-aria*, which means "bad air." It was known as ague in the 1800s, which comes from the Latin *acuta* or *febris acuta*—"sharp fever." If you get malaria, you really don't feel so well. The little *Plasmodium* protozoa enters your blood through the bite of a mosquito and travels to your liver, where it matures and reproduces. The classic symptom of malaria is paroxysm, a cycle of cold, violent shivering followed by fever and sweating. You will also experience fatigue, vomiting, and headaches, or worse yet, seizures, coma, or death.

Malaria is spread by mosquitoes in the genus *Anopheles*, and in Michigan is most commonly associated with *A. quadrimaculatus*. Eggs are deposited in water, where the larvae develop into adults during a life cycle that lasts 14-27 days. They have multiple generations per year and the fertilized females of *A. quadrimaculatus* overwinter, then die after laying their first set of eggs in the spring. Larvae can be found in many freshwater aquatic environments, including swamps, bayous, ditches, slow-moving canals and streams, and ponds. To a lesser extent *Anopheles* may use manmade objects that fill with water, such as cans, barrels, and old tires. In other words, similar habitat to where one might find Manoomin growing—minus the manmade objects, of course.

Malaria was rampant in Michigan during the nineteenth century and believed to be the origin of the most prevalent diseases at that time. The highest rates ever recorded in the state occurred from 1859 to 1860 due to two consecutive years of significant rainfall, and the sickness was believed to originate from the horrible effluvia (odor) coming from the flooded marshes. Malaria had the dubious honor of representing 50–75 percent of all sicknesses prior to 1880, according to *Occurrence of Malaria Mosquitoes in Southern Michigan* (Sabrosky 1946). A popular poem circulated along the East Coast during those days: "Don't go to Michigan, that land of ills; the word means ague, fever and chills."

While today we know that malaria is spread by mosquitoes, it was still a great mystery back then. Medical professionals had many different theories about what malaria actually was and where it originated. The New York engineer E. B. Van Winkle presented some of these in his article "Draining for Health" in the August 13, 1881, edition of *Engineering News*. Mr. Niemeyer proposed that the decomposition of vegetative matter influenced the growth of the poison. Mr. Bolestra, however, believed it was caused by small spores

in putrefied marsh water. Others theorized it was carbonic acid gas ema-
nating from decomposing organic matter. Mr. Liebigs attributed malaria
to some deoxidizing process, and mechanically diffused germs that were
organic in nature took the blame from a Dr. Thompson. Still others thought
malaria was meteorologically influenced. Some believed malaria lived in
water-saturated soils and blamed logging activities for (1) releasing it from
the soil through the churning of the earth, and (2) damming streams and
rivers, which then created overflows filled with decaying vegetation. While
there were many theories floating around, it seemed everyone agreed on
one condition that was always present—stagnant water. And the only way
to eliminate that was by draining it.

In those days, it was estimated that there were about 1.92 million acres
of marshes and boggy, saturated lands in the southern Lower Peninsula,
where most cases of malaria occurred. Doctors and engineers promoted the
draining of those swamplands for health, believing that the source of malaria was within foul swamp odors or wet soil. In his 1880 article "The Reclaiming of Drowned Lands," Dr. Henry F. Lyster (a University of Michigan
surgeon who treated the state's first Civil War battle casualty) promoted the
drainage of these wetlands and even went so far as to suggest that the whole
State of Michigan could be drained.

> There can be no doubt from a study of the of the State but that a very
> large portion of these lands can be drained and made available and
> profitable to agriculture, and in the meantime, diminish very notice-
> ably the amount of sickness and mortality from diseases of a malarial
> type. The clearing out of the smaller creeks and streams, and the con-
> struction of county drains and of private drains, would enable vast
> quantities to be reclaimed and made salubrious. The gradual decline
> of several hundred feet in the surface of the country from the central
> portions of the State toward the littoral margins, shows the possibility
> of accomplishing a complete drainage of the State. (238)

Lyster presented several examples of drainage projects that helped improve both public health and agricultural opportunities. In Macomb County,

between the mouth of the Clinton River and Lake St. Clair and just north of the ghost town of Belvidere, was a wet marsh full of wild rice, marsh grass, and flags. The 175-acre parcel was owned by Mr. William M. Campbell, who in 1875 dug a 6-foot ditch all the way around the marsh, threw the dirt up on the sides of the ditch, and installed a windmill and large pump to make certain all the water was removed. Wrote Dr. Lyster, "He has now fifty acres of wheat growing on land formerly covered by water and growing wild rice and marsh weeds and frequented by muskrats" (Lyster 1880, 237).

In another example, Dr. Lyster wrote of a 5,000-acre lake that existed in Ingham County just twelve miles from the capital that had filled up over time with "vegetable material and the sod of marsh grass over it." The Chandler farm owned 2,000 acres of it, including an open pond known as Park Lake (formerly called Pine Lake). Mr. Chandler and a neighbor created over forty miles of ditches, drained the marshland, and lowered Park Lake by about 3 feet. After the drainage, Dr. Lyster reported that it was "remarkably healthful" on the farm (Lyster 1880, 238).

On a farm near Flint, owned by the late Governor Crapo, 800 acres of wetland was drained in 1862. The wetland had acquired the name Dead Marsh due to the "peculiar virulency and intensity of the malaria generated in the ground." After draining, it was deemed one of the healthiest localities in the area (Lyster 1880, 239).

C. E. Hollister read a paper before the Michigan Association of Surveyors and Engineers in January 1884 describing the drainage methods of several large Michigan marshes. Nearly 4,000 acres were drained along the Maple River in Clinton County by the county's drain commissioner, Mr. J. N. Smith. This was accomplished by deepening and straightening the small streams that ran through the marsh, which were dug 5 feet deep and 12 feet wide:

> The South Maple, or south branch of the Maple, has its source in a pond on sec. 16, T. 6, N. R. 1 W.; finds its way without much channel in a southerly direction through wide marshes for about 2 miles, then makes a sweep east and then northerly to the Maple River on section 4 of T. 7, N. R. 1 W. At the point where it turns cast it is about 1 mile from the Looking-glass River, which at that point flows west in wide marshes.

Marsh land extends continuously from the creek to the river and drains into both. It is a noteworthy fact that if the creek is cut to the depth of 5 feet from the surface of the marsh and a branch extended to the Looking-glass River, it will bring water from the channel of the latter river through the creek into Maple River. The creek drains about one third of the town of Victor, and about half of Ovid Township. In some places it flows through a narrow bottom or swale only a few rods wide, but most of the way through marshes or elm swamps 1/8 to 1/5 mile wide, the main line being about 17 miles long, and having two branches one about 4, the other about 2 miles long, laid out and dug at the same time.

From the mouth of the creek for a distance of 5 miles the bottom as dug is to be 12 feet wide, and is to be deepened gradually as the valley widens until a depth of 5 feet from the surface is attained. At this point the drainage of about a square mile of marsh and the adjacent highlands enters the creek. Above this place the bottom is narrowed to 8 feet. About four miles up the stream is another branch of some miles in length. Here again the width at the bottom is contracted to 4 feet. At a point about 4 miles further upstream another branch comes in and the width beyond is again reduced to 2 feet on the bottom. The whole elevation from Maple River to Cedar Lake is about 95 feet.

It was proposed to make the bottom of drain 4 feet below the surface of the water at the stage when the preliminary survey was made, but the square mile of marsh that drains into it lies so flat that it was necessary to increase the depth to 5 feet. The work was put under contract in August, 1882, and most of the work was done by Jan. 1. 1883. The people along the line were amazed at the idea of going so deep, and thought it unnecessary; now they wish the ditch were deeper. (Hollister 1884, 6843)

Mr. Hollister described another class of marsh, one with a creek leading from or going into it such as on the Chandler farm described above. These types of marshes are perfect wild rice habitat, providing the slow flow of water through the bed that Manoomin is so fond of. To drain them,

Mr. Hollister recommended opening an outlet and cutting deep enough to allow the marsh to settle yet still be able to drain the further edges of the wetland to a depth of 3 feet. The outlet also needed to be able to carry the water off freely. His method proved successful.

Dr. C. V. Tyler of Bay City shared with the Michigan State Medical Society that Swartz Creek was formerly very swampy with a prevalence of malaria, but had been thoroughly drained since 1868. Similar observations were made by Dr. H. McColl of Lapeer County, who attributed the near absence of malaria in his county to the efforts of the drain commissioners. According to Dr. Tyler, the entire Lower Peninsula had been completely drained thanks to the commissioners. Of course, we know that not to be true as there still are wetlands today, but indeed we lost thousands of acres to the malaria eradication effort (quoted in Gibbes 1888, 32, 134-35).

There are many more examples and stories to be told, but suffice it to say their efforts paid off. Dr. Lyster announced in *Michigan and Its Resources* (1883) that the drainage of swamps reduced malaria by 75 percent between 1863 and 1883. This was further supported by Dr. R. C. Kedzie (1874), who surveyed physicians and township clerks to determine how effective drainage was on reducing cases of malaria. He estimated from the clerks' reports that more than 20,000 miles of ditches had been dug between 1864 and 1874, and there was general consensus among the physicians that, indeed, drainage did result in a significant decrease in malaria.

It was ironic, and perhaps lucky, that their hard work paid off, because the cause of malaria was not found in the rotting vegetation but rather in an insect. It wasn't until the turn of the century that scientists finally discovered that malaria was linked to mosquitoes. In 1903, Dr. George Dock informed the Sixth Conference of the Health Officials of Michigan that it was "five years since Ross first demonstrated the true role of the mosquito in the spread of malaria." At that time, very little was known about the insect, such as how the illness was transmitted, which species were involved, how they reproduced, and where they lived. As more information was gathered, it was clear that the *Anopheles* mosquito was the vector for the parasite, and a more targeted effort to eradicate the mosquito and its habitat replaced the generalized dredging and draining of marshes and swamps.

According to recommendations by sanitary engineer J. A. A. Le Prince in the 1915 Public Health Report, *all* water had to be removed to eliminate the mosquitoes, and proper planning, construction, and maintenance of ditches was required to accomplish this. Drain tiles were used for subsoil drainage to lower the water table or ground water, or to intercept seepage from hillsides. Streams were to have steep banks directly above and below the flow line, be of uniform grade and width, and have a straight, unobstructed course. For wider streams, channels were to be reconstructed with boards or stones and backfilled behind the barriers. Fill material was used when it wasn't economically feasible to drain an area, and common materials included soil, clay, cinder, and lumber-mill waste.

A second weapon was added to the arsenal against the mosquito and malaria, and it negatively impacted wild rice as well. Mosquito larvae float on the surface of the water, and it was known that placing a light film of oil on the surface of the water would suffocate them. Oiling with kerosene had been done for nearly a hundred years to get rid of mosquitoes, but had not been used specifically to eradicate malaria because the relationship between the two had not been known. Once the connection was made, oiling was used as a supplement to drainage. Mr. Le Prince also provided recommendations for its application and noted the importance of completely covering the surface of the water with the oil film. This was thought to be especially effective against *Anopheles quadrimaculatus* due to the larvae's horizontal floating position. Kerosene or illuminating oil was useful but more expensive because it evaporated more quickly and, because the film tended to be invisible, caused the sprayer to add more, which then increased costs. But kerosene had advantages over oil. The film it formed was thin, spread rapidly, and was easy to obtain. More oil was required when treating ditches and streams overgrown with vegetation, as the plants impeded the formation of a complete film of the thick substance.

How did oiling for mosquitoes affect Manoomin? The answer may be extrapolated from a study done back in 1918 on a related family member, white rice (*Oryza sp.*). Arkansas began large-scale rice production in 1896, and there was great interest in learning the effects of oiling on the rice paddies, as they were known habitat for malaria mosquitoes. J. C. Geiger and W. C. Purdy of the U.S. Public Health Service set out to answer that very question. The researchers monitored the health and growth of rice over an entire growing season while different types of oil, application methods, and rates were applied to the paddies. Two of the tests showed a negative effect on the rice. The first was the application of fuel oil at a drip rate of 30 gallons per acre to a bed of rice with plants 18 to 20 inches tall. At this stage of growth, the oil would "climb" the stalks and discolor and sometimes kill the plants. The second test involved applying a "2 plus 1 mixture" (two parts kerosene, one part black oil) to a paddy, which puddled around the drip point where the oil was being administered. The rice plants were just getting ready to blossom during this test, and those that were within a few yards of the drip were killed. Dense vegetation restricts the dispersion of oil, and certainly dense wild rice would act in this fashion, causing puddling and "climbing" (Geiger and Purdy 1919).

It is impossible to know exactly how much Manoomin was damaged by this method of mosquito control, but certainly there was some impact. If the oil was applied in late spring during the floating leaf stage, it is likely that all oiled Manoomin plants would have been killed. Later in the season, plants in close proximity to the oil or kerosene would have been damaged before they set seed and thus would not reproduce.

So, let's now return to logging and examine its connection to malaria. In the past ten years or so, there has been an increased focus on the link between deforestation and public health as some of the last large tracts of forests on our planet are experiencing heavy logging pressure. Several researchers have found increased incidences of malaria in areas that are experiencing deforestation. This is partly because cleared lands receive more sunlight and are susceptible to the formation of puddles containing water with increased pH, both conditions that favor *Anopheles*. Deforested areas also have lower biodiversity, which eliminates or reduces the number of natural predators of mosquitoes. It is also due to increased human population in these areas as logging progresses.

The effects of logging in creating conditions favorable to malaria in the form of saturated and flooded land, and the subsequent draining of the same land, were described over one hundred years ago by Dr. J. N. Eldred of Chesaning. He had been practicing medicine in Saginaw County for twenty-five years when he made these comments to the Michigan State Medical Society in 1888 regarding malaria in the county:

> When I first commenced practice, malaria was very prevalent there, as two of the gentlemen who have preceded me have remarked. Consumption, on the other hand, was very rare for the first ten or fifteen years. I call to mind very few cases of consumption—but one, the first four or five years. Saginaw County is extremely level. It is what is commonly called a low country, and at the time of which I speak a large portion of the timbered land, which comprised nine-tenths or more of the whole area, was under water the larger part of the year, on account of the water courses being obstructed with fallen timber; and the dense growth of vegetation and thick, heavy timber prevented evaporation. A marked change has now taken place in the face of the country. The water courses have been opened, the heavily timbered lands have been turned into fertile farms, the stagnant water is nowhere to be found, and the dense, sickening fogs are now a thing of the past, remaining only in the memory of the old pioneers. At the present time, and in the last ten or fifteen years, a change has taken place in the prevailing diseases. Malaria is now very rare, in fact, it is almost unknown. I do not see a case of malaria now where I used to see fifty. (Gibbes 1888, 137)

Our Civil War surgeon Dr. Lyster noticed that when new land opened up here in Michigan, particularly alluvial or bottomlands, malaria would develop in the local populations and increase for a few years before eventually declining and leveling off. This phenomenon, now known as "frontier malaria," has been recently documented in populations in the Amazon, and the ecological impacts and sociological situations are strikingly similar to those of the logging era of the 1800s in Michigan.

While the war against malaria raged on, another threat to the health of Manoomin began to develop. Reports from the first surveyors back in the early to mid-1800s described vast areas of swamplands in Michigan, and these mucky areas dampened enthusiasm and delayed the colonizers' move here for nearly a quarter-century. The land was too wet to farm in a great many places, ague was rampant, and who wanted to get their horses and wagons stuck in the muck? Compared to other options it just wasn't appealing. But over time, come they did, and efforts to drain the swamps for farmland commenced. This was referred to as "reclaiming" the land, a term that implies the land was taken from the colonizers somehow and they were taking it back as theirs. It is a word that illustrates the possessive relationship between the newcomers and the land, one still used today.

The early muck farmers had no experience growing crops in former swamplands, unlike folks over in the Netherlands who had been highly successful. So they had to learn from experience. Mr. Chandler, the former U.S. senator mentioned earlier in this chapter, began buying marshlands near Lansing in the mid-1880s. By 1871, he owned 3,160 acres. Senator Chandler began experimenting with drainage, trying to figure out how to grow crops in the muck soils and which vegetables would grow the best. He invested tens of thousands of dollars draining Park Lake and the surrounding marshlands into the Looking Glass River. His farm created much interest across the state, and he was starting to find some success for his efforts when he died before completing his project.

In the south-central part of Newaygo County lies an area deep in muck and muck farmers. It has been dubbed the onion capital of Michigan, due to the propensity of these globes of goodness to grow so well in the organic soils. The rich history of this area includes farms across the Lower Peninsula; muck farms began to spring up in "reclaimed" land as the swamplands were being drained. And this is another example of an activity carried out by the colonizers that, while creating wealth for some and food for others, caused the loss of Manoomin and an important source of food for the Anishinaabek.

One afternoon in the summer of 2016, Frank Ettawageshik, a soft-spoken Elder from the Little Traverse Bay Bands of Odawa Indians, shared a story with me that he remembered about his people harvesting Manoomin from a lake near the town of Grant that had been drained and converted to an onion farm long ago (figure 8). Frank's story was confirmed within the memory of a white man named Robert Thompson, who was born in 1890 in Newaygo just six miles north of Rice Lake. Mr. Thompson was eighty-eight years old in 1977 and wrote a story about Rice Lake for the Grant Public Library, excerpted here:

> The lake and surrounding land was teeming with wild life. I well remember when a boy, accompanying my father on Rice Lake. He rented a punt, a special flat boat, and had to guide pole it through the numerous channels formed by the luxurious growth of wild rice that reached the height of six to eight feet. Ducks came by the thousands for evening feeding which made hunting excellent. The dog was necessary to retrieve the downed ducks.
>
> Indians always came in the fall of the year to Rice lake, to harvest the wild rice. They flailed the tall stalks bearing rice with their paddles, the kernels falling into the canoe. This was one of their staffs of life.

FIGURE 8. Rice Lake, before it was drained in 1917. Wild rice bed in the distance.

MICHIGAN STATE UNIVERSITY, 1968.

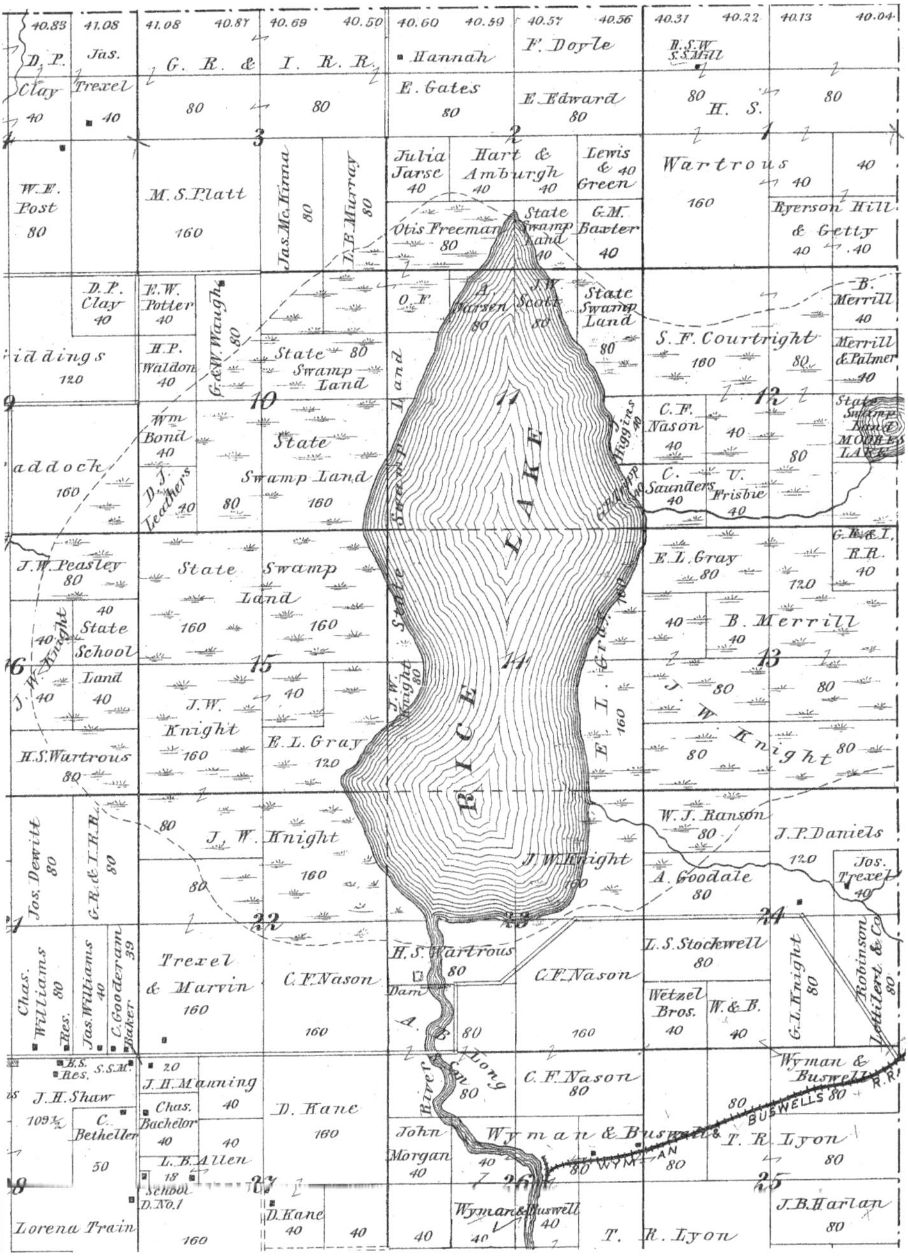

40.83 41.08 41.08 40.87 40.69 40.50 40.60 40.59 40.57 40.56 40.31 40.22 40.13 40.04

D.P. Clay 40 | Jas. Trexel 40 | G. R. & I. R. R. 80 | 80 | Hannah | F. Doyle | B.S.W. S.S.MIL | | |
E. Gates 80 | E. Edward 80 | 80 | H. S. | 80

3 — **2** — **1**

W.E. Post 80 | M. S. Platt 160 | Jas. McKinna 80 | J.B. Murray 80 | Julia Jarse 40 | Hart & Amburgh 40 40 | Lewis & 40 Green | Wartrous 160 | 40 | 40

Otis Freeman 80 | State Swamp Land 40 | G.M. Baxter 40 | Ryerson Hill & Getty 40 .40

D.P. Clay 40 | E.W. Potter 40 | G.&W. Waugh 80 | O.F. | A. Larsen 80 | S.K. Scott 80 | State Swamp Land 80 | S. F. Courtright 160 | B. Merrill 40 | Merrill & Palmer 40

iddings 120 | H.P. Waldon 40 | State 80 Swamp Land |

10 — **11** — **12**

Wm Bond 40 | D.J. Leathers 40 | State Swamp Land 80 160 | C.F. Nason 40 40 | State Swamp Land MOORES LAKE

addock 160 | C. Saunders 40 | U. Frisbie 40

J.W. Peasley 80 | State Swamp Land 160 160 | E. L. Gray 80 | 12.0 | 40

40 | State School Land 40 | J.W. Knight 160 | E.L. Gray 120 | 40 | B. Merrill 40 | 80 | 80

16 — **15** — **14** — **13**

H.S. Wartrous 80 | J.W. 80 | J.W. Knight 80

Jos. Dewitt 80 | G.R.&T.H.R. 80 | J.W. Knight 160 | 80 | W. J. Ranson 80 | J.P. Daniels 12.0 | Jos. Trexel 40

22 — **23** — **24**

Chas. Williams Res. 80 | Jos.Williams 40 | C. Gooderan Baker 39 | Trexel & Marvin 160 | C.F.Nason 160 | H.S. Wartrous Dam 80 | A. 80 | C.F.Nason 160 | A. Goodale 80 | L.S. Stockwell 80 | Wetzel Bros. 40 | W.& B. 40 | G.L.Knight 80 | Robinson VdeTiert & Co 80

J.H. Shaw 109½ | B.S. S.S.M. Chas. Bachelor 40 | 20 J.H.Manning 40 | D. Kane 160 | John Morgan 40 | Long 80 | C.F. Nason 80 | Wyman & Buswell R.R. | BUSWELLS 80

C. Betheller 50 | L.B.Allen 40 | School No.1 D.No.1 | D.Kane 40 40 | Wyman&Buswell 40 | 40 | WYMAN & Buswell AN 80 | T. R. Lyon 80

27 — **26** — **25**

Lorena Train 160 | Wyman&Buswell 40 | T. R. Lyon | J.B.Harlan 80

MAP 5. Rice Lake in 1880, near Grant, Michigan.

Looking into old map files, one can find an 1880 map of Newaygo County showing an arrowhead-shaped lake forming the headwaters of the Rouge River, which was completely surrounded by an enormous marsh (map 5). The lake was called Rice Lake. The shallow lake and its marsh covered nearly one-quarter of Grant Township and was a favorite hunting spot for many. The book *Grant Area: Yesterday and Today* (1979) includes a story that Elmer Nichols wrote for the *Grant Herald-Independent* newspaper in 1938 about how the lake was formed. Elmer believed that a very long time ago, beavers had built a dam that blocked the flow of a stream that ran through the area and created a lake. This was an old lake, he claimed, collecting its black, mucky bottom over many years. As the muck deepened, the water rose, and an island developed in the middle of it with a wonderful stand of white pines rising from its sandy soil. Eventually rising waters drowned the trees, and their skeletons were dug out when the lake was drained many years later.

Before Grant officially became a town in 1893, and was nothing more than a bare patch in the woods, the first European folks to arrive mid-century came for the trees. The logging industry boomed in the area, and logs were hauled to the shores of Rice Lake and floated to the lake's outlet, the Rouge River. Stored there until spring, the logs were then released down the Rouge toward the Grand River.

Richard Kincaid was born in 1873 and moved to Grant in 1899, where he ran a drugstore in town. In his leisure time, Mr. Kincaid was an avid outdoorsman and spent every Sunday during duck season hunting on Rice Lake and exploring his 200 acres of marsh. Since most of the ducks coming in were late-evening "black mallards," he spent his daylight hours rowing around the lake, shooting at other birds. It was on such a day when Mr. Kincaid spotted a man at the eastern edge of the marsh. Mr. Beldt, a very successful onion farmer, motioned him over and told him that he was growing more and more frustrated with losing his crops during periods of heavy rains. He asked Mr. Kincaid if he would consider getting Rice Lake drained, as he had heard that in the Netherlands they successfully drained swamplands to make them suitable for farming. Mr. Kinkaid stored the idea in the back of his mind.

GRANT PUBLIC LIBRARY 1975.

FIGURE 9. The dredged channel that drained Rice Lake and its wild rice bed, 1917.

After losing yet another crop of onions to flooding the following year, Mr. Beldt finally threw in the towel, sold his land to Mr. Kincaid, and moved away. In 1914, Mr. Kincaid began buying more Rice Lake marshlands and eventually acquired over 3,000 acres with hopes of creating a hunting and fishing club. With little interest from the local hunters, he abandoned the concept and began to think about the idea Mr. Beldt had proposed a few years earlier. After hiring a surveyor to see if it was possible, which it was, he soon realized he could not afford to drain the lake by himself. So Mr. Kinkaid convinced several other farmers to join him in petitioning the drain commissioner to drain the land for farming so that they could grow onions, celery, carrots, and mint. Their petition was successful.

In 1912, the farmers were jubilant when they learned that the job to drain the marshlands would be put up for bid. A channel 20 feet wide at the bottom would be dredged from the mouth of the Rouge River at the south end of Rice Lake for five miles, running straight through Rice Lake. It was believed that water would eventually be drained from Ashland, Grant, Ensely, and Croton Townships and emptied into the Grand River, freeing up 25,000 acres of muck for agriculture. The project was claimed to be the largest drainage job ever in that part of the country.

GRANT PUBLIC LIBRARY 1975.

FIGURE 10. The dredging and destruction of Rice Lake and its wild rice bed, 1917.

In 1917, the Rouge River Drain was constructed, and Rice Lake and its marsh were completely drained, destroying the historic wild ricing grounds (figures 9 and 10). The result of that effort exposed 3,000 acres of muck soils 25 feet deep. The old lake bottom, known as the island, produced well. The average harvest of onions was about 900 bushels per acre, and farmer Fred VanderHogg set a record harvesting 1,140 bushels of onions on one of his acres. In 1922, there were 1,000 acres under the plow, another 1,000 were ready to be plowed, and 3,000 more were being reclaimed. The Rouge River and its lateral branches continued to drain the water.

Mr. Kincaid was ninety-four years old when he wrote his story for a 1968 Michigan State University booklet for the Michigan Muck Farmers Association:

After these roads and additional drains were built, I had no trouble in selling all of the land I owned and some of it at what I considered a high price. However, the most I ever got was $450 per acre. Since then several parcels of land have resold for as much as $1,000 per acre—all from land that once was thought useless.

At the time I came to Grant, the population was 200. It has increased to about 700 present, and there is a fringe of population of several hundred who have built around the town, but outside the village limits. The majority of the increase in population can be attributed to the Rice Lake marsh and the wonderful crops of onions, celery, carrots, beets, and mint grown there.

Rice Lake and its beautiful marsh were no longer visible on the 1950 Newaygo County map. And that was the year that Rice Lake Farms was created. The farm is still in operation today as a second-generation family business, growing turnips, beets, parsnips, onions, squash (acorn, buttercup, spaghetti, butternut), and late season jumbo carrots in the rich muck called "the best onion, celery, and peppermint land in the state" by the *Muskegon News Chronicle* in 1913. Grant has some of the largest muck farms in the nation, including the Van Single and Brink Farms, which also grow a variety of muck-loving crops.

Perhaps as the muck farmers sit on their porches at the end of the day, they hear the sounds of cedar sticks and sora rails coming from the onion patch, formerly one of the largest wild rice beds in Michigan.

CHAPTER 5

The Dam at Getegitigaaning

THE WILD RICE I ONCE KNEW

I tell this story to my daughter, giiwegiizhigookway Martin. These comments, based on first-hand knowledge, come from me, and I am the eldest living tribal member here at Getegitigaaning. I was born here, raised here, and never moved away.

The information I share is not a study, nor is it scientific evidence; this is the knowledge I have of my life growing up watching the rice grow. Watching the rice being harvested, watching the rice being processed by both my mother and my Grandmother—So when I tell you things, I am telling you that of my life.

I speak today only of the rice beds on our homelands and lake at our Old Village. My name is Rose Polar Martin. I am 90 years old. I was born and raised right near the rice beds at Getegitigaaning. I was born during the Ricing Moon, on the banks of the Wisconsin River. This is where my mother Minnie White Polar was ricing. I am therefore a child of the rice.

Wild rice is sacred to the Anishinaabe. It is the center of the traditional and cultural life to us. To lose the rice would be to lose a vital part of who we are. Ojibwa people believe in life as a cycle which begins and ends with mother earth. Wild rice is part of this cycle. Hundreds of years ago the wild rice was abundant in this area and no one had to worry about where their rice came from. And as long as we did things in a good way, that Manoomin would be there for us.

Our members knew how to regulate the rice and had their own techniques to preserve the rice for the future generations while still sustaining the people in the present. Just like our wild game and other crops that were part of the life of the Getegitigaaning Nation the rice is becoming scarce. The people seem to be forgetting who we are and where we come from and what our responsibility is to the earth and to our future generations.

I am recalling through my memories the rice beds and the size of them and the amounts of rice produced in these beds. The beds were enormous. Now as you stand by the edge of our waters and look at the rice beds, they look fragile and sick. The rice beds I knew as a little girl were strong, healthy and thick. Our people came across those waters with their boats easily half full of rice. Many trips each day were made during the ricing season. The rice was plentiful and there was always enough rice for everyone living at the village. There were only a few times in my life when I saw the rice not produce, and those were sometimes natural things such as bad weather during the ricing stages. I also know for a fact that my Dad Henry Polar Sr., tells me there was a time when the rice almost disappeared because of the dam. He also said that the water fowl became less abundant, the fur bearing animals were scarce, and our cranberries completely disappeared.

During all of the years I lived at the village, I only remember a few times when ricing did not take place. This rice was our life. This food sustained us through the many winters of our lives. Many would have perished without it. I remember when rice is all we had to eat and it kept us alive.

In the early 50's with the re-location period, our members moved away. A small handful remained and held onto their homelands and way of life. When that happened, all the families moved away from the rice beds and stopped passing down the teachings of the rice and the gathering stopped. Some do remember and do know that the only way to truly be Anishinaabe and to continue to survive we must go back to the old ways. Our mother earth is sick and we can see that by the loss of this rice. Manoomin, our sacred food, must be protected for the people and all living things that depend on it as well. We were put here on this earth and blessed with "Bimaadiziiwin"—To Live a good long life. With that come our responsibilities—Keeping the earth, air and water pure is a responsibility we must all accept. Thank goodness our teachings were kept alive and the circle is once again being connected by our people. But to me what is sad is the size of our once rich rice beds. They have become pitiful and I fear that they will be gone completely.

Today, after much effort to re-seed our waters I finally see the beds slowly coming back. They are nowhere near our original rice beds size, but to change things now could be potentially deadly to our Manoomin. To try to measure or quantify the importance of the wild rice is nearly impossible—"How do you measure a gift given to you by the Creator?" Our sacred Manoomin was a gift from the Creator, therefore, it must be protected at all costs.

—Respectfully told by Rose Polar Martin, Elder, Getegitigaaning, 2016

A serene mist floats up from Getegitigaaning, floating in tandem with the rising sun. The water is as smooth as glass, and from its shore, the call of the eagle echoes across the bay. Her favorite perch is a sturdy branch in an old dead tree that overlooks the lake, and every morning after calling a greeting to the sun, the sacred eagle takes flight, white head and tail standing out against the dawn sky. To find this place, one must travel west across the Upper Peninsula to the town of Watersmeet, then south for nine and a half miles as the crow flies (map 6). There you will find the shallow lake that straddles the Michigan/Wisconsin border. It is the headwaters of the Wisconsin River, one of the most heavily worked rivers in the United States.

The Anishinaabemowin word "Getegitigaaning" is the original name for Lac Vieux Desert, and means old planted place or old garden. The lake received its current name in the 1700s from early French explorers, who translated the original one to the mongrel French name "Lac Vieux Desert." But this lake is no desert. It is rich, full of life, simply beautiful, and there is no better way to experience it than to sit quietly in a canoe in the middle of Rice Bay. The smell of fresh lake water drifts into your soul. Rice hens (sora rails) and ducks serenade you from within the tall wild rice plants. Bald eagles soar overhead, dancing and tumbling through the sky. Every once in a while you hear a splash as one of the many fishes that thrive in this incredible lake jumps for a tasty meal. But at no time is the lake more beautiful than at night. The call of the loon hangs in the air, and above, millions of stars blanket the black northern sky. The Milky Way stretches from shore to shore and is so magnificent it takes your breath away.

Getegitigaaning is an example of how changes to water levels can negatively impact Manoomin beds. This site is especially important because of the historical significance of the lake to the Getegitigaaning Ojibwe Nation (Lac Vieux Desert Band of Lake Superior Chippewa), who have riced here for generations. Not only did the changing water levels affect the Manoomin, it has also affected an entire tribe.

The story begins around the year 1870, when a wooden logging dam built of timber and sand was constructed on the Wisconsin River for the purpose of raising lake levels during times when head build-up was required to run logs. About twenty years later, the Vieux Desert Improvement Company was organized and a second log dam was constructed to replace the old one. The Wisconsin Valley Improvement Company (WVIC) purchased the second logging dam in 1907 for the purpose of supplying water for the nearest hydropower dams on the Wisconsin River. This was accomplished by adjusting the dam's gate to restrict the flow in the springtime as soon as the natural flow of the river was sufficient to supply the needs of the closest hydropower plants downstream. During the summer drought, the gate was opened slightly, and the release of the stored water increased the flow rate of the river. Because higher rainfall in autumn increased the natural flow of the river, the gate would be partially closed and the lake partially refilled.

Crystal
Lake

Mickey Creek

MICHIGAN

Lobischer Creek

Lac
Vieux
Desert

MICHIGAN
WISCONSIN

Copyright ©2013 Esri DeLorme NAVTEQ

MAP 6. Map of Getegitigaaning.

FIGURE 11. Original timber dam at Getegitigaaning, early 1900s.

That water was gradually used during the late fall months and in winter. The original timber dam was repaired numerous times and rebuilt in 1917 and again in 1924 (figure 11). In 1937, WVIC finally tore down the wooden logging dam and replaced it with a reinforced concrete and steel structure.

Evidence in the form of submerged stumps off Everest (Big) Island and Knuth's Peninsula (Desolation Point) indicated that water levels at Getegitigaaning were one to two feet lower than before 1928 (the beginning of available lake stage records) according to a 1956 engineering report by the Michigan Department of Conservation. The 1911 *Preliminary Report on Storage Reservoirs at the Headwaters of the Wisconsin River and Their Relation to Stream Flow* presented WVIC's proposed high and low water levels for Getegitigaaning, and high water levels during both winter and summer were 10 inches higher than the previous log dam, at 3'0" for both summer and winter seasons. The original dam had a high water mark set at 4'0" to facilitate winter water storage for running logs.

Prior to the placement of these water control structures, the Manoomin beds were vast on Getegitigaaning, covering the shallow bays. The higher water levels caused by the dams impacted the Manoomin, and its decline would continue for the rest of the twentieth century. No one asked the people of Getegitigaaning, who had lived there for several hundred years, what they thought of the dams or if they even wanted them. They were simply built.

The dam and its impact on lake levels has always been a source of controversy for both tribal and nontribal people at Getegitigaaning. A 1981 Bureau of Indian Affairs survey of several band members provided valuable insight about the decline of Manoomin after the construction of these dams and how it impacted their community (figure 12). When asked what time period their tribe had stopped harvesting Manoomin, responses varied from the late 1930s to the 1950s. One member said harvesting stopped in 1918. All blamed the rising water levels from the dams for the decline, and it was reported that "lake levels rose right when the Rice was just starting to come up," which would have dislodged the plants before they had time

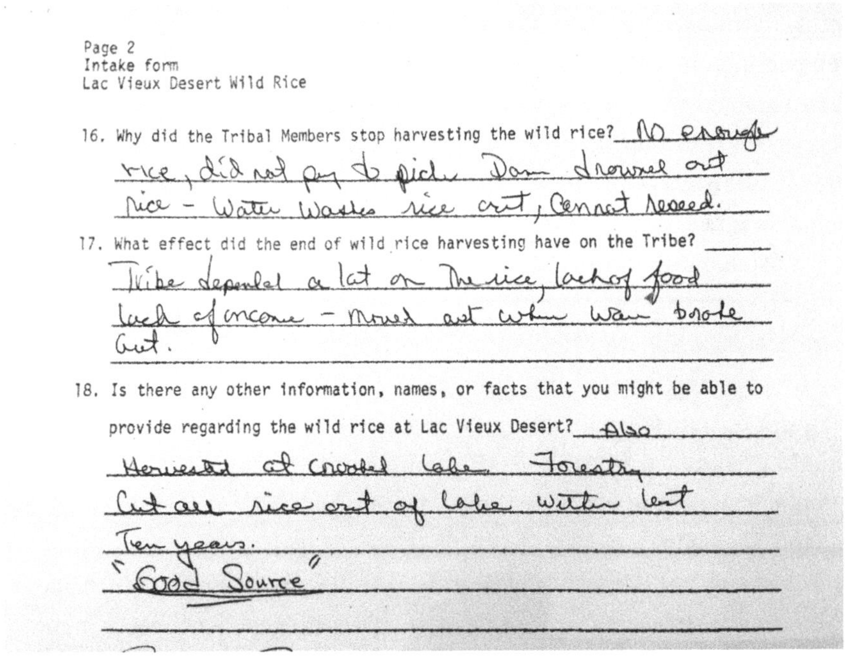

Page 2
Intake form
Lac Vieux Desert Wild Rice

16. Why did the Tribal Members stop harvesting the wild rice? _No enough rice, did not pay to pick. Dam drowned out Rice - Water Washes rice out, Cannot reseed._

17. What effect did the end of wild rice harvesting have on the Tribe? _Tribe depended a lot on the rice, lack of food lack of income - Moved out when War broke out._

18. Is there any other information, names, or facts that you might be able to provide regarding the wild rice at Lac Vieux Desert? _Also Harvested at Crooked Lake Forestry Cut all rice out of lake within last Ten years. "Good Source"_

FIGURE 12. Survey form used by the Bureau of Indian Affairs in 1984 to assess wild rice harvesting by Getegitigaaning band members.

to set roots. One member stated that "the reason many folks moved into town [Watersmeet] was because of the loss of wild rice from the lake." They stopped going to Slaughter Bay in the 1940s because "there was not enough rice to pick."

The amount of Manoomin harvested by the band members varied, depending on whether they sold the rice. "Two large barrels for the winter" were all one family needed for the year. The family of John Pete, a well-respected Elder and the last person to have remained at the Old Indian Village, harvested 1,000 pounds each year. John himself sometimes harvested 100 pounds a day.

There simply wasn't enough Manoomin left on the lake to sell or save for their own use. People had a hard time finding other places close to Getegitigaaning to pick. One woman claimed that she "tried to rice in other lakes in Wisconsin and [they] were fined by Game Wardens, they took [our] rice—Big Portage [Lake], 1968." Some tried ricing at nearby Crooked Lake in the Sylvania Wilderness Area, but said the "DNR has terminated." Fewer folks continued to rice, and when they stopped practicing the old traditions, the passing on of these teachings to the next generation was interrupted. A cultural shift was happening to the people of Getegitigaaning. A serious threat to a tradition that had been part of their cultural identity for hundreds of years was growing. All because of a small dam that you could almost spit across.

Unstable water levels were causing serious damage to the shoreline of Getegitigaaning due to severe wave action and ice shove damage that undermined lakeside installations and natural vegetation. The shoreline was eroding and trees were being uprooted and toppled, creating barren areas stripped of natural vegetation and replaced with riprap seawalls. Everett Island was eroded so badly in the center of its mass that it became two smaller islands. And of course the Manoomin beds diminished to remnants of what they once were.

It wasn't just the people of Getegitigaaning who were concerned about the rising lake levels in those days. Nontribal lakeside property owners made their voices heard about the damage the high water was causing to their property, prompting the authorities to act on their behalf. The following is an excerpt from the Department of Conservation's engineering report (Foster 1956):

> Because of protests from riparian property owners about property damage from high water levels, the Prosecuting Attorney of Gogebic County in 1951 requested information from the Department of Conservation as to whether some measures of relief could be initiated. The matter was referred to the office of the Attorney General since the control dam is located in Wisconsin, and since no inter-state agreement exists between Wisconsin and Michigan with regard to inland lake level control.
>
> In 1952 the Board of Supervisors of Gogebic County made a formal request for an engineering investigation of lake level control. In response to this request, reconnaissance surveys were begun the same year and continued in 1953. By this time the Board of Supervisors had requested the Prosecuting Attorney to start suit in Federal Court to prevent the Wisconsin Valley Improvement Company from allowing the lake to rise above 16 inches of gage height or elevation 1680.86, mean sea-level datum. In January 1954, the Michigan Department of Conservation attempted to arrange a meeting with Wisconsin authorities, but the effort was fruitless, and to date, no conference has been held.
>
> Now pending before the Federal Power Commission is an application from the Wisconsin Valley Improvement Company for approval of its present operational schedule. Opposition to a continuance of past methods of operating the control dam is expressed by riparian property owners both in Wisconsin and Michigan. (2)

In 1959, the WVIC acquired a fifty-year license from the Federal Energy Regulatory Agency's (FERC) predecessor, the Federal Power Commission, to operate the dam. The license was issued in 1959 but was retroactive to 1943. No fees were charged to the company for "using, enjoying, or occupying" the nearby federally owned lands that the reservoir overflowed onto. It was the Manoomin, the People of Getegitigaaning, and landowners around the lake who paid the price.

While the Manoomin was disappearing from the lake, the number of band members living at the lake diminished greatly. In 1942, John Pete and his sister chose to stay while the rest of the village moved to Watersmeet, where the men could find work. Later, the Urban Indian Relocation Act of 1952 scattered many of them to major cities in the Midwest with a promise of jobs. They left the rice beds and sugar bushes and headed to Detroit and Chicago looking for work. However, some people still remained at the Old Indian Village during this time, ricing and fishing where they could. Things started to turn around in the 1970s when many who left Getegitigaaning began to return home, moving to nearby Watersmeet for employment opportunities. Some even moved back to the Old Indian Village.

The people of Getegitigaaning did not forget the vast beds of Manoomin, and they worked hard to try to get the water levels lowered. The leader of the band at that time was John McGeshick, and he worked tirelessly trying to get the Bureau of Indian Affairs (BIA) to force the Wisconsin Valley Improvement Company to lower the lake levels so that Manoomin would return. At that time, the people of Getegitigaaning were handicapped legally by the fact that they were not officially designated as a Tribe by the U.S. government, as the members had been folded into the Keweenaw Bay Band after the Indian Reorganization Act of 1934. However, during the 1960s the People began to reorganize as a distinct band, and after years of hard work, they finally became federally recognized in 1988 as the Lac Vieux Desert Band of Lake Superior Chippewa.

Archie McGeshick, whose Spirit name "Naganash" means "one who leads," was born and raised in the Old Indian Village but left Getegitigaaning when the Manoomin disappeared (figure 13). He relocated to the Sokaogon Band's reservation near Crandon, Wisconsin, to be near their traditional ricing lakes. But as the years went by, Naganash began to feel a spiritual calling to transform his life. He entered the Midewewin Society and returned to his home at Getegitigaaning to work on behalf of his community and restore Manoomin to the lake.

Soon after Naganash moved back to Getegitigaaning, an important event occurred that began to turn the tide in favor of Manoomin. A ruling known as the Voigt Decision affirmed that the Ojibwe tribes that signed the

COURTESY OF THE FAMILY.

FIGURE 13. Archie McGeshick, Wild Rice Chief until his death in 1999.

1837 and 1842 treaties had retained the right to hunt, fish, and gather from the lands ceded in those treaties, under their own regulation.

The following year (1984), the eleven Ojibwe Nations in Michigan, Wisconsin, and Minnesota that were signatories of those treaties created the Great Lakes Indian Fish and Wildlife Commission (GLIFWC). GLIFWC was formed to help the tribes exercise their treaty rights and increase their involvement in the protection and stewardship of off-reservation resources. Getegitigaaning was one of those Ojibwe Nations, and Naganash became the first representative from his tribe on GLIFWC's "Voigt Task Force," the body that addresses inland fish and wildlife issues within the organization.

Every fall Naganash would head out in his boat to plant Manoomin. As the vessel slowly crept through the cold water, he would stand and reach into the weathered white grain sack, grab a large handful of seeds, and toss them out into the water in a sweeping motion. Concentric circles would form and overlap as the long-tailed grains hit the water, and once breaking the surface, would jet to the bottom and embed in the soft muck. Year after year Naganash planted. But the Manoomin would not grow. The water level was simply too high.

In 1991, WVIC sought to renew its fifty-year license, but those who cared about Manoomin and the treaty rights of the tribe had been preparing for it. The U.S. Forest Service and U.S. Department of the Interior (supported by the tribe and other federal and state agencies) requested a number of conditions that would restrict the manner in which the company operated the dam in order to return Manoomin to the lake. Just what were those conditions? The most important one for the Manoomin and the people of Getegitigaaning was Article 114, which required WVIC to implement an enhancement plan that included lowering of water levels by about 9 inches and a financial contribution by WVIC of $200,000 toward a seeding and monitoring program.

WVIC's license was granted on July 18, 1996, and it included the conditions requested by the federal agencies. WVIC unsuccessfully challenged several of the conditions in court and finally, after several years of litigation, the ten-year trial period for wild rice restoration and monitoring commenced in 2002. The amount of Manoomin that successfully grew during the test period varied year by year, but over 90 acres of wild rice were restored to Misery and Rice Bays by the end. While this was much less than the hundreds of acres that once covered the lake, it was a welcome beginning.

In 2014, an adaptive management plan was drafted by the U.S. Forest Service and other cooperating agencies for the long-term management of Manoomin on Lac Vieux Desert as part of WVIC's requirements for the remainder of the licensing term through 2026. On June 2, 2015, WVIC submitted the Wild Rice Adaptive Management Plan to the Federal Energy Regulatory Commission and requested its approval as the proposed operating plan for the duration of their license (2015-2026). The plan called for water levels to be maintained at depths favorable to the growth of wild rice. The plan was accepted and a license issued to WVIC by FERC in 2016. Naganash's dream of Manoomin returning to Getegitigaaning forever is now one step closer to reality.

In 1994, Naganash called his nephew Roger LaBine and told him he had cancer. He would not be able to do all the things he had wanted to do for Manoomin and for his tribe. So he asked Roger to carry on the work and began sharing teachings with him. For the next several years Roger spent many hours learning the knowledge carried by his uncle. In 1999, Naganash walked on and was laid to rest in the traditional cemetery at Getegitigaaning. He never saw the return of Manoomin to his lake, at least not from this world. But because of his initial work and the efforts of others, Manoomin has come back.

Rose Martin's daughter, giiwegiizhigookway Martin, is a passionate woman who has served as Getegitigaaning's Tribal Historic Preservation Officer from 2000 to 2016. Giiwe is a keeper of the tribe's history and, like Roger and Naganash, has dedicated her life to working for her People. Giiwe comes from a traditional ricing family and her love of Manoomin runs deep. The journey of one of her greatest accomplishments began in 2012, when she initiated an effort to gain recognition of the cultural and historical importance of Rice Bay to her tribe. For three long years, she and her staff gathered historical documentation and oral stories and built a case for the inclusion of Rice Bay in the National Register of Historic Places. It was no easy task to prove the long relationship between the band and Rice Bay, as was required to achieve recognition. Tribal history is passed on in the oral tradition, and the non-Indigenous world requires documentation in the form of written historical accounts rather than oral history, a requirement that totally discounts the cultural norm of Indigenous cultures. Giiwe combined both forms of historical representation, and her hard work was rewarded on December 2, 2015, when Rice Bay in Watersmeet Township, Gogebic County, Michigan, was listed in the National Register of Historic Places under National Register Criterion A for its traditional cultural significance. This is the first Manoomin bed ever recognized in the Register, and its inclusion shows how far we have come in the past few decades.

We sat around the roaring fire, several generations of McGeshicks, Charlie Fox, five hungry raccoons, and me. They are one of the last families to actively maintain the tradition of ricing at Getegitigaaning. It was the middle of ricing season. In the glow of the fire, we laughed, told stories, and talked of days gone by. Terry remembered her grandmother carrying large bundles of sticks on her back, using a leather strap around her head to help support the load. Beatrice, the eldest, spoke of her grandmother going to the woods to pick medicines for the family, but said she never learned those medicines from her *Nokomis*. The stories went on into the night.

I looked over at the children and realized what a great responsibility they have resting on their young shoulders. They are the carriers of this tradition. These children have grown up on the shores of this beautiful lake; they have played at rice camps and sung with their elders. They have made their ricing sticks. Manoomin is calling them home. They will listen. And thanks to people like John, Naganash, Roger, giiwe, Rose, and others, the Manoomin will be there to welcome them.

CHAPTER 6

Restoring Manoomin

I think restoration is all about hope. The Manoomin seed isn't the only gift the plant has to offer, and there's a few of us that have learned this lesson in our lives. Rice isn't just delicious to taste, it is also food for our Spirit.

The journey from going to look for the rice to the moment when we get to put it on the table . . . that whole journey is about the rice, it teaches us all along the way. Our blood memory remembers where that rice belongs in our lives today just as rice has a memory of where it belongs. The big obstacles come in when we have dams, draining of lakes, population explosion, boating, heavy tourism; with the changing times rice got in their way. Because of our relationship with our Mother and her life blood, the water and everything it needs to stay clean and pure, it is not only our right, it is our responsibility to put that rice back where it belongs. She needs that.

—Renee "Wasson" Dillard, Waganakising Odawa ndodabendaagwaz Citizen
of Little Traverse Bay Bands of Odawa Indians, as told to the author.

M anoomin is an annual plant that reseeds itself every year. It may be helped or hindered by the wind and the rain, which knocks ripe grains into the water gently or with force. Even ricers contribute to its replanting as grains fall off the plants while they are being pulled over the canoes for knocking. And of course, a certain percentage of the harvest should always be planted in areas that don't have rice, to expand the beds.

The planting of Manoomin has been done for hundreds of years by the Anishinaabek, and this was certainly true in Michigan based on tribal stories, although Chief Pokagon had no knowledge of his Pokagon Pottawatomie Band "sowing or caring for rice" in southwest Michigan (Pokagon 1898b). European newcomers also started planting Manoomin after wiping out most of the wild rice beds. One of the earliest written accounts of seeding was printed in 1875, where Manoomin was planted in the Sebewaing River as part of a channelization project by the U.S. Army Corps of Engineers. Pressure was being exerted by local businesses to deepen the river to allow for small vessels to navigate the channel and bring their goods to town. Captain Engineer A. N. Lee, in the *Annual Report of the Chief of Engineers for 1875*, suggested:

> Let the dredged earth, instead of being carried away in scows, be deposited by the dredge on either side of the cut, and distributed as evenly as possible. In the case in question it would give a depth of water, on either side, of about 3 feet. On these banks sow wild-rice seed. It will grow and flourish in as great a depth as 6 feet, and when it reaches maturity, it will be found, I think, sufficient to prevent the cut from filling up in the least. It will also serve the purpose of making the channel-banks much more accurate than could be done by placing buoys. The expense of trying this experiment would be little or nothing, compared to the advantages to be gained if it should succeed.

The project was funded and Manoomin planted, not for wildlife or human consumption, but rather to stabilize dredged material and prevent sediment from flowing back into the cut. It can still be found growing on both sides of the river channel to this day. As many of the state's marshes

Muskegon News Chronicle   November 25, 1910

Michigan in a Nutshell

KALAMAZOO—It is planned by the officials of the Chicago, Kalamazoo and Saginaw railroad to send out several men along the line of their road in the near future to plant quantities of wild rice in the various lakes, hoping to secure a permanent growth of the grain which is the principal food of the wild ducks. As soon as the weather conditions are favorable the planting will begin.

had been lost due to logging and other activities, interest in planting Manoomin to increase waterfowl habitat started to build. Sportsmen noticed the number of ducks declining in the 1800s and believed it due to the lack of good duck food, rather than their unregulated shooting. They planted Manoomin all across the state in hopes of increasing the number of ducks in their bags. Even the railroad jumped on board as officials of the Chicago, Kalamazoo, and Saginaw Railroads sent out several men along their rail lines to plant quantities of Manoomin in various lakes, with a goal of increasing duck habitat. A survey of historic newspapers in Michigan provided wonderful accounts of these efforts in the later 1800s and early 1900s (appendix 2).

Michigan's State Game, Fish and Forest Fire Department (later known as the Department of Conservation, then Department of Natural Resources) promoted these efforts by providing seed to sportsmen and hunting clubs. In 1916, twenty-two barrels of rice from Monroe Marsh were distributed to fourteen individuals (table 2). In 1917, rice was distributed to thirty-two individuals, and in 1918 to sixteen individuals (tables 3–4). The source of the rice in the latter two years is unknown, although it may have come from Wildfowl Bay. And they gave out even more. There were sixty-seven new dedications of private lands as game refuges between 1916 and 1919, and the department incorporated festivities and educational programs at these events, freely giving wild rice to the attendees to increase waterfowl habitat.

Table 2. Individuals Who Received Manoomin Seed from the Michigan Department of Conservation in 1916

DATE	AMOUNT	RECIPIENT	PLANTING LOCATION
9/4/1916	1 barrel	Olaf Nordum	Charlevoix Lakes
9/4/1916	1 barrel	John Doelle	Houghton Lakes
9/6/1916	3 barrel	A. L. Phelps	Crawford Streams
9/6/1916	2 barrel	John Doelle	Houghton Ponds
9/7/1916	2 barrel	Olaf Nordum	Charlevoix Ponds
9/7/1916	2 barrel	Ben Elms	Ludington Lakes
9/8/1916	2 barrel	A. L. Phelps	Grayling Lakes
9/8/1916	1 barrel	R. Condon	St. Joseph Lakes
9/9/1916	2 barrel	P. Yeider	Kalamazoo Ponds
9/9/1916	1 barrel	E. S. Long	Emmet County Ponds
9/9/1916	1 barrel	W. C Kidder	Tustin Lakes
9/9/1916	1 barrel	D. D. Tufts	Kalkaska Lakes
9/12/1916	1 barrel	J. W. Ireland	Wayne Lakes
9/12/1916	2 barrel	J. Stephenson	Boyne Lakes
Total	*22 barrels*		

Table 3. Individuals Who Received Manoomin Seed from the Michigan Department of Conservation in 1917

AMOUNT	RECIPIENT	RESIDENCE	AMOUNT	RECIPIENT	RESIDENCE
10 lbs.	Myers Peterson	Ludington	basket	Chas. Ingram	Boynce City
16 lbs.	Wm. H. Ross	Flint	carton	Chas. P. Downey	Lansing
10 lbs.	Wm. Hodgson	Metamora	carton	A. F. Brackett	Norway
9 lbs.	A. L. Ely	Ellsworth	carton	Wm. J. McDougal	Alpena
9 lbs.	B. J. Lasley	Gould City	carton	C. A. Button	Lansing
9 lbs.	A. J. Kroenike	Covington	carton	R. W. Darymple	Buchannan
9 lbs.	Harry Kress	Lake George	carton	Chase S. Osborn	Soo
10 lbs.	P. H. Wilson	Chassell	carton	G. G. Scronton	Harbor Beach
11 lbs.	C. R. Fisher	Rogers City	carton	J. A. Doelle	Houghton
11 lbs.	Dr. H. A. Muzzell	Coopersville	carton	Fred H. Loud	St. Ignace
11 lbs.	Wm. Burnett	Baldwin	carton	T. Oliver	Lincoln
10 lbs.	J. F. Cox	Lansing	carton	F. Bisonette	Bisonette's Station
basket	H. K. Gustin	Alpena	carton	C. Malott	Comins
basket	Ben Johnston	Alpena	carton	F. Merkell	Oscoda
carton	H. L. Stevens	Port Huron	carton	H. Masterson	Loon Lake
basket	Mark Cury	Lapeer	carton	A. Schrieber	Cook Development

Table 4. Individuals Who Received Manoomin Seed from the Michigan Department of Conservation in 1918

AMOUNT	RECIPIENT	RESIDENCE	AMOUNT	RECIPIENT	RESIDENCE
1 bag	Joe Lane	Elby	3 bags	C. J. Phelps	West Branch
1 bag	Mark Carry	Lapeer	3 bags	Wm. Huber	Battle Creek
1 bag	Harry Larson	Metamora	2 bags	Christ Millenbacker	unknown
1 bag	Charles B. Flanders	Lapeer	2 bags	P. H. Willision	Chassell
1 bag	Charles Lane	Metamora	3 bags	J. J. Titus	Grant
3 bags	L. O. Bloomer	Alden	4 bags	Elmer Croul	Trout Lake
5 bags	Otto Rohn	Ann Arbor	3 bags	Wm. Kidder	Tustin
3 bags	J. Ellison	Balair	*39 bags*		
3 bags	Ed. A. Nowask	Kalkaska			

There was great enthusiasm in the department at that time to try and restore Manoomin to Michigan's marshes. John Baird, State Game, Fish, and Forest Fire commissioner in the *Michigan Game, Fish and Forests Biennial Report, 1917–1918* recommended that all available Michigan waters should be stocked with wild rice, wild celery, and other duck and fowl foods. Indeed, between 1917 and 1918, the department seeded forty-eight separate waters with wild rice.

But unfortunately, it appeared that little was known or understood about suitable conditions or methods of restoration at the time by the nontribal people, and thus many efforts failed. In the 1940s, the Michigan Department of Conservation attempted to review these earlier plantings and determine their success, but reported that they had great difficulty due to the lack of detailed records, or any records at all, and thus randomly surveyed only a portion (tables 7–9). In addition to the twenty-seven sites they found records for, they reported on fifty additional miscellaneous projects. Hiawatha National Forest conducted twenty-six additional plantings, but their success or failure was not ascertained. The report's author (believed to be Herbert Miller, but no author is listed) concluded that all these efforts were unsuccessful and recommended that the seeding of Manoomin be discontinued because of these failures and the abundance of other food sources for waterfowl. He reminded us that some of Michigan's most important waterfowl concentration areas, such as Lake St. Clair, Sebewaing,

Table 5. Summary Chart of the 1918 Manoomin Planting Project by the Michigan Department of Conservation

NAME OF COUNTY	NAME OF LAKE OR RIVER PLANTED	BUSHELS PLANTED	TYPE OF BOTTOM SOIL			
			SILT SAND	SANDY CLAY	SALTY MUCK	PEAT
Charlevoix	Boyne Falls Pond and Deer Lake	6			x	
Cheboygan	Indian River	4			x	
Chippewa	Mud Lake	5				x
Crawford	Lake Margrethe	21	x			
Houghton	Portage Lake	4	x			
Livingston	Whiteford Lake on Huron River	2		x		
Newaygo	Blanche Lake	5			x	
Ogemaw	Piper, Ambrose, Clear, Grass Lakes	5			x	
Roscommon	Houghton Lake	66			x	
Washtenaw	West Lake	4				x
Washtenaw	Pinckney Creek	2			x	

Source: Michigan Department of Conservation, Survey of Wild Rice Plantings in Michigan, report no. 1022 (Lansing: Michigan Department of Conservation, n.d.).

and Wildfowl Bay, were almost entirely lacking wild rice in 1943. That would make sense given that water levels in those lakes were on the upward side of the high-water cycle that peaked around 1950. Manoomin was likely much more abundant around the low-water period of 1935.

The research project did not include funding to study why these restoration attempts succeeded or failed, but the author did offer some personal observations on water-level fluctuations. He noted that changes in water levels of lakes controlled by dams affected the Manoomin, and this could be seen at Lake St. Helen in Roscommon County. As the water levels changed, the size and density of the wild rice also changed, a phenomenon he also noticed in the Great Lakes rice beds, although he did not attribute the absence of beds in 1943 to this phenomenon. He claimed that just how these changes affected the Manoomin were not understood, but he correctly suspected that Manoomin in the floating leaf stage was particularly vulnerable. The author also stated that it was reported that hydrological changes prevented fertilization, although it hadn't been proven. Unfortunately, had he consulted with Anishinaabek ricers, he and so many others might have

DEPTH OF WATER	DID SEEDS PRODUCE PLANTS?	IF SO, HOW MANY YEARS DID THEY SURVIVE?	DENSITY OF STAND	WERE PLANTINGS CONSIDERED SUCCESSFUL?
1–3"	yes	1	sparse	no
1–4"	yes	present	abundant	yes
1–4"	yes	1	sparse	no
1–4"	?	?	?	no
1–2"	yes	2	good	no
1–2"	yes	present	good	yes
1–3"	yes	present	good	yes
1–4"	yes	2	sparse	no
1–4"	yes	present	abundant	yes
0.5–1.5"	yes	1	sparse	no
1–2"	yes	1	didn't produce seed	no

learned a great deal about the requirements of Manoomin. These were the people who had been planting and living with wild rice for hundreds of years. But such were the times. Had communication occurred, perhaps the outcome might have been different for the restoration projects so earnestly undertaken.

Based on historical documents, there appears to be a lull in any programmatic efforts to plant wild rice by nontribal groups or organizations from the 1950s through the 1990s. This was likely due to failures of previous attempts by the Department of Conservation, which resulted in the recommendation to stop seeding efforts. In that time span, wild rice continued to decline in Michigan and soon was no longer in the memories of people involved in habitat management and restoration, and a kind of "ecological amnesia" developed. Of course, older duck hunters remembered the beds of Saginaw Bay, and some tribal elders and members of the Midewewin Societies still had stories of ricing. And there were still people ricing in the western UP when they could find beds. But for the most part, it seemed Manoomin was quietly slipping into history.

Table 6. Success of Miscellaneous Manoomin Plantings in Michigan as of January 1943

NAME OF COUNTY	NAME OF LAKE OR RIVER PLANTED	YEAR OF PLANTING	BUSHELS PLANTED*	TYPE OF BOTTOM SOIL			
				SILT SAND	SANDY CLAY	SILTY MUCK	PEAT
Alger	Iland Lake	1939	?			x	
Allegan	Mill Pond, Kalamazoo River	1939	?			x	
Alpena	Squaw Bay	1941	1		x		
Alpena	Devils Lake	1941	1				x
Alpena	Devils Lake	1942	3				x
Alpena	Thunder Bay River	1940	5			x	
Alpena	Thunder Bay River	1941	5			x	
Baraga	Delene Lake	1941	?			x	
Charlevoix	Deer Lake	1938	1			x	
Charlevoix	Boyne River	1938	1			x	
Charlevoix	Lake Charlevoix	1938	1			x	
Chippewa	Mud Lake	1922	3				x
Chippewa	East Lake	1923	3				
Chippewa	Carp Lake	1922	3				
Chippewa	Little Trout Lake	1922	3				
Emmet	Crooked River	1910	25			x	
Gladwin	Wixon Lake	1930	1			x	
Gogebic	Middle Branch Ontonagon River	1938	2			x	
Gogebic	Presque Isle River	1938	4			x	
Gogebic	Carlson Lake	1938	2			x	
Hillsdale	Bird Lake	1924	?		x		x
Hillsdale	Bird Lake	1925	?		x		x
Houghton	Upper Dam Lake	1938	2		x		
Huron	Sebawaing Bay	1939	1		x		
Huron	Sebawaing Bay	1940	3		x		
Huron	Middle Grounds	1931	3		x		
Iron	Paint River	1938	1		x		
Iron	Winslow Creek	1938	2		x		
Iron	Mallard Lake	1938	2		x		
Iron	Martin Lake	1938	1		x		
Iron	Clear Lake	1938	1		x		
Iron	Lake Emily	1938	2.5	x	x		
Iron	Sargent Lake	1925	2		x		
Iron	Diver Lake	1920	9		x		
Mackinac	Flower Bay	1926	10		x		
Menominee	Hayward Lake	1929	60		x		

DEPTH OF WATER (FEET)	DID SEEDS PRODUCE PLANTS?	IF SO, HOW MANY YEARS DID THEY SURVIVE?	DENSITY OF STAND[†]	WERE PLANTINGS CONSIDERED SUCCESSFUL?
2	no	0	—	no
1–4	no	0	—	no
1–3	yes	0	—	no
1–4	no	0	—	no
1–4	yes	1	sparse	no
1–3	no	0	—	no
1–3	yes	1	sparse	no
2–7	yes	1	good	yes
0.5–1.5	yes	2	sparse	no
0.5–2	yes	2	sparse	no
0.5–2	yes	2	sparse	no
0.52–2	yes	present	sparse	yes
0.5–2	—	—	—	no
0.5–2	yes	present	sparse	yes
0.5–2	yes	present	sparse	yes
1–3	yes	present	abundant	yes
1–6	no	0	—	no
1–3	yes	1	sparse	no
1–3	yes	1	sparse	no
1–2	no	0	—	no
2–3	yes	1	sparse	no
2–3	yes	1	sparse	no
1–2	no	0	—	no
1–3	yes	1	sparse	no
1–3	no	0	—	no
1–3	yes	1	sparse	no
1–2	yes	1	sparse	no
1–2	yes	1	sparse	no
1–3	yes	5	good	yes
1–2	yes	?	sparse	no
1–3	no	0		no
3–?	yes	5	abundant	yes
3	yes	17	abundant	yes
3	yes	22	abundant	yes
1–4	yes	present	good	yes
2–6	yes	3	sparse	no

NAME OF COUNTY	NAME OF LAKE OR RIVER PLANTED	YEAR OF PLANTING	BUSHELS PLANTED*	TYPE OF BOTTOM SOIL			
				SILT SAND	SANDY CLAY	SILTY MUCK	PEAT
Menominee	Shaky Lakes	1929	250	x			
Menominee	Menominee River	1929	30		x		
Menominee	Lake Michigan Shore	1929	25		x		
Ottawa	Bruce Bayou on Grand River	1937	1		x		
Schoolcraft	Seney Refuge N.W. Refuge	1936	6	x	x		
Schoolcraft	Seney Refuge Holland Ditch	1937	1	x			
Schoolcraft	Seney Refuge	1938	68		x		
Schoolcraft	Seney Refuge	1939	100			x	
Schoolcraft	Seney Refuge	1940	34.5	x		x	
Schoolcraft	Seney Refuge	1941	104	x		x	
Schoolcraft	Seney Refuge	1941	8			x	
Van Buren	Unknown Lake	1938	0.25				
Van Buren	Paw Paw River	1942	1			x	
Washtenaw	West Lake	1942	1				x
TOTALS			793.25 bushels				

*Conversion factors used 25# equals 1 bushel.   †Density of stand described in terms of sparse, fair, good, and abundant.
Source: Michigan Department of Conservation, Survey of Wild Rice Plantings in Michigan, report no. 1022 (Lansing: Michigan Department of Conservation, n.d.).

In the 1990s, while Getegitigaaning was fighting to get Manoomin back on their lake, other tribes also began planting Manoomin. Today, the effort to restore Manoomin is revitalized, with projects underway in Indian Country and across the state. The cultural and ecological importance of Manoomin is being reborn, and people are responding with a unified voice.

Presented below are historical wild rice seeding projects located in the literature. They paint a picture of enthusiasm and failure in the attempts to replace the wild rice beds lost to the development of the land. Following these are accounts written by dedicated people directly involved in seeding projects in Michigan today. The interest in and commitment to preserving Manoomin now cross cultural boundaries, and there is a strong movement growing to ensure that Manoomin will survive for the next generations.

DEPTH OF WATER (FEET)	DID SEEDS PRODUCE PLANTS?	IF SO, HOW MANY YEARS DID THEY SURVIVE?	DENSITY OF STAND[†]	WERE PLANTINGS CONSIDERED SUCCESSFUL?
1–2	yes	5	sparse	no
1–2	yes	1	sparse	no
1–2	yes	10	abundant	yes
1–3	no	0	—	no
2–3	yes	1	sparse	no
1–3	no	0	—	no
2–3	yes	2	sparse	no
1–3	yes	2	sparse	no
1–3	yes	2	sparse	no
1–3	yes	2	fair	yes
2	yes	1	sparse	no
1–3	no	0	—	no
1–4	no	0	—	no
0.5–1?	yes	10	sparse	yes
	13 no, 36 yes			*37 no, 13 yes*

Historical Restoration Projects

There were many restoration projects across the state undertaken by the newcomers beginning in the 1800s, and many of these were reported in the local newspapers, alongside stories of jailbreaks and failed crops. Indeed,

(Cass City, MI) Tri-County Chronicle   October 16, 1903

The Department of Agriculture is investigating the usefulness of wild rice as a food, notwithstanding the fact that threats of lynching, white capping, etc., have been made against anyone who would introduce any more new breakfast foods. Wild rice has an extended habitat and it is stated was probably the chief starchy food of about 30,000 American aborigines.

Table 7. Manoomin Plantings of Undetermined Success

| NAME OF LAKE OR RIVER | LOCATION OF PLANTING | | | | TIME OF PLANTING | POUNDS OF RICE PLANTED |
	SUB'D	SEC	T.N.	R.W.		
Autrain River	SW SW	17	46	20	F/'36	154
Autrain River		31-2	47	20	F/'36	20
Autrain River		18	46	20	11/'37	50
Autrain Lake	SE SE	5	46	20	11/'37	50
Autrain Rriver	S1/2 31	31	47	20	11/'39	150
Bar Lake	SE SE	2	44	19	F/'36	25
Boot Lake	NW SW	28	45	17	11/'37	35
Hartney Lake	SW NW	27	45	19	11/'38	67
Hovey Lake	NW SE	17	45	19	11/'38	20
Hovey Lake	SW SE	17	45	19	F/'36	10
Johnson Lake	SW SW	9	46	21	F/'36	30
Lower Indiana River	SE NW	4	44	18	F/'36	25
Lower Cold Springs	SW NE	24	45	19	11/'37	35
Lake 17	SW NE	17	45	20	11/'38	15
Lake 17	Center	17	45	20	11/'39	30
Lilly Lake	SE SE	21	45	17	F/'36	14
Miners Lake	SW SE	10	47	18	F/'36	12
Sand Lake	NE SW	27	45	17	2/'36	75
Stutts Creek	NE NE	20	46	18	11/'38	35
Stutts Creek	NE1/4	21	46	18	11/'37	25
Trout Lake	NW NE	6	44	20	11/'38	7
Wetmore Lake	NE1/4	20	46	20	F/'36	25
Hovey Lake		17	45	19	11/'37	25
16 Mile Lake		13	45	20	11/'37	7
Stutts Creek	SW1/4	22	46	20	F/'36	15
Sturgeon River	NE SW	26	45	20	11/'38	

"Sec" denotes Section, "Sub'd" denotes Subsection, "T.N." denotes Township North, "R.W." denotes Range West
Source: Michigan Department of Conservation, Survey of Wild Rice Plantings in Michigan, report no. 1022 (Lansing: Michigan Department of Conservation, n.d.).

TYPE OF BOTTOM SOIL				DEPTH OF WATER	DID SEEDS PRODUCE PLANTS?	IF SO, HOW MANY YEARS DID THEY SURVIVE?	DENSITY OF STAND
SILT SAND	SANDY CLAY	SILTY MUCK	PEAT				
	x			2"	yes	2	unknown
x				1.5"	yes	2	"
	x			1"	yes	2	"
	x			2"	yes	3	"
	x		x	1.5"	unknown		
	x			2"	yes	3	"
x				1.5"	unknown		
	x			1"	yes	2	"
			x	2"	no		
	x			2.5"	yes	unknown	
			x	2"	unknown		
	x			1.5"	yes	2	"
			x	1"	unknown		
			x	2"	unknown		
	x			2"	unknown		
			x	1"	unknown		
	x			2"	unknown		
x				2"	unknown		
			x	1.5"	yes	1	"
			x	2"	yes	2	"
			x	1"	yes	1	"
			x		yes	2	"
			x	2"	yes	1	"
	x			1.5"	unknown		
			x		yes	3	"
			x	1"	unknown		

Table 8. Manoomin Locations That Have Been Seeded since the 1800s

PENINSULA	COUNTY	SITE NAME	DATE(S) SEEDED
LP	Berrien	Little Paw Paw Lake	1928
LP	Crawford	Simpson Lake	5/19/1881
LP	Emmet	Spirit Lake (Wycamp Lake)	2/11/1887
LP	Genesee	Long Lake	9/1/1913
LP	Grand Traverse	Arbutus Lake	1919
LP	Grand Traverse	Rennie Lake	1919
LP	Huron	Sebewaing River Mouth	1874
LP	Ottawa	N. Ottawa County Rod and Gun Club Seeded Site 1	1945
LP	Ottawa	N. Ottawa Rod and Gun Club Seeded Sites 2	1945
LP	St. Joseph	St. Joseph River Colon	1894
LP	Van Buren	Van Auken Lake	1928
LP	Wayne	Henry Ford Pond near Fairlane Dam	1911
UP	Alger	Au Train Lake	1925
UP	Alger	Echo Lake	1906
UP	Alger	Grimes Lake	1930
UP	Chippewa	Munuscong Bay	1928–30
UP	Chippewa	Pendills Lake	1928
UP	Chippewa	Potagannissing River	1930 8/26/1966
UP	Dickinson	O'Neil Lake	9/1/1914
UP	Houghton	Portage Lake (south part)	1923
UP	Iron	Otter Lake	1914
UP	Keweenaw	Deer Lake	10/12/1909
UP	Keweenaw	Lac Labelle	10/12/1909
UP	Luce	Hunters Landing Tahquamenon River	1935
UP	Mackinac	Brevort Lake	8/5/1942
UP	Mackinac	Hay Lake	9/25/1884
UP	Marquette	Lake Independence	1922
UP	Schoolcraft	A-1 Pool Seney National Wildlife Refuge	10/2/1954 9/24/1956 1957 9/14/1968

over forty historic newspaper articles referenced wild rice between 1877 and 1939 (appendix 2). Often details were scant; however, if the locations were clearly identified, they were included in our map showing seeded sites. Historical documentation was also found in government publications, sportsmen's magazines, and other journals. There were successes

UP	Schoolcraft	B-1 Pool Seney National Wildlife Refuge	9/25/1954 10/3/1956
UP	Schoolcraft	C1 Pool Seney National Wildlife Refuge	9/20/1954
UP	Schoolcraft	C-2 Pool Seney National Wildlife Refuge	1947
UP	Schoolcraft	C-3 Pool Seney National Wildlife Refuge	9/20/1956 9/21/1956 9/26/1958
UP	Schoolcraft	D-1 Pool Seney National Wildlife Refuge	1938 10/9/1954 9/20/1956 1957–1958
UP	Schoolcraft	E-1 Pool Seney National Wildlife Refuge	1938 10/3/1956 9/14/1968
UP	Schoolcraft	F Pool Seney National Wildlife Refuge	1938 9/17/1956 9/20/1956
UP	Schoolcraft	G-1 Pool Seney National Wildlife Refuge	1938
UP	Schoolcraft	H-1 Pool Seney National Wildlife Refuge	1938
UP	Schoolcraft	Indian Lake	1905
UP	Schoolcraft	Indian Lake	1925
UP	Schoolcraft	I Pool Seney National Wildlife Refuge	9/19/1956 9/26/1958
UP	Schoolcraft	J Pool Seney National Wildlife Refuge	1938 9/27/1951 9/23/1952 1953 9/10/1954
UP	Schoolcraft	McDonald Lake	1925
UP	Schoolcraft	Old Goose Pen (Seney Wildlife Refuge)	1938 1947
UP	Schoolcraft	Show Pool Seney National Wildlife Refuge	1938 1947 9/24/1956 9/14/1968
UP	Schoolcraft	T Pool Seney National Wildlife Refuge	1947

*Sites that have been seeded after 1990 were omitted to protect the locations.

and failures, protests by farmers against seeding and threats against those who would plant it, and many hunters' hopes for a sky full of fat ducks by autumn. Whether these sites took hold and the Manoomin beds withstood the test of time we may never know. To date we have documented forty-five historic locations where Manoomin has been seeded in the Upper and

MAP 7. Map showing seeded sites since the 1800s.

CARTOGRAPHY BY JASON TALLANT.

Lower Peninsulas (table 8, map 7). Of those, only three of the historically seeded sites have Manoomin today.

LIVINGSTON COUNTY LAKES

- Date: 1880s
- Description: Howell Shooting Club sowed wild rice in the shallow lakes of the county.
- Project lead: Howell Shooting Club
- Amount of wild rice seed: unknown

- Seed source: unknown
- Success: unknown
- Reference: Ellis 1880

ST. JOE RIVER, BETWEEN COLON AND MENDON
- Date: 1880s–1891 at least
- Description: Hunters seeded Manoomin in the St. Joe River near Colon Lake in the 1880s through at least 1891 to bait ducks per complaint by Dr. Edwin Steward, MD, health officer of the Village of Mendon. Seed worked its way downstream to Mendon and clogged the river, making locals unhappy. One reference described the once beautiful river as "practically a marsh."
- Project lead: local hunters
- Amount of wild rice seed: unknown
- Seed source: unknown
- Success: Successful during 1880s through at least 1891. Unknown after. No rice present today.
- Reference: Hungerford 1894, *Detroit Free Press* 1901a

LONG LAKE, GENESEE COUNTY
- Date: 1913
- Description: Wild rice planted by Genesee County Fish and Game Association in Long Lake and Forest Township.
- Project lead: Genesee County Fish and Game Association
- Amount of wild rice seed: 150 pounds Long Lake, 50 pounds Forest Township
- Seed source: Minnesota
- Success: Newspaper reported the following year that the rice was growing nicely.
- Reference: *Flint Daily Journal* 1913, 1914

STATEWIDE, 1916
- Date: 1916
- Description: The goal was to establish a continuous feeding route over

Michigan for migrating waterfowl. Michigan State Game, Fish and Forest Fire Department cooperated with sportsmen during the biennial period of 1916-1919. Wild rice seed was given out at game refuge dedications. Fourteen individuals received wild rice seed (table 2).

- Project lead: Michigan State Game, Fish and Forest Fire Department
- Amount of wild rice seed: 22 barrels total
- Seed source: Monroe Marsh
- Success: Low success
- Reference: Oates 1917

STATEWIDE, 1917

- Date: 1917
- Description: Wild rice was distributed to conservation officers and sportsmen's clubs for planting in local lakes and streams. Thirty-two individuals were listed as receiving rice (table 3).
- Project lead: Michigan Game, Fish, and Forest Fire Department
- Amount of wild rice seed: 125 pounds, 4 baskets full, and 16 cartons
- Seed source: Unknown
- Success: Low success
- Reference: Baird and Jones 1919; Department of Conservation n.d.

STATEWIDE, 1918

- Date: 1918
- Description: Wild rice was distributed to conservation officers and sportsmen's clubs for planting in local lakes and streams (table 5). Mr. J. Baird, State Game, Fish, and Forest Fire commissioner, stated that all available Michigan waters should be planted with wild rice and other aquatic food plants. Sixteen individuals were listed as receiving wild rice seed (table 4).
- Project lead: Michigan Game, Fish, and Forest Fire Department
- Amount of wild rice seed: 168 bushels (4,200 pounds). Also listed as 39 bags.
- Seed source: Unknown
- Success: The Michigan Department of Conservation looked at eleven

of these projects and only four still produced rice twenty-four years later (the time span was 1918–1941). Two of the successful sites had actually been replanted. Seven of the sites failed. He assumed the rest of the projects failed due to the absence of wild rice at the sites.
- Reference: Baird and Jones 1919; Michigan Department of Conservation n.d.

PENDILL'S LAKE, CHIPPEWA COUNTY
- Date: 1928
- Description: Pendill's Lake is a bog lake that was planted with Manoomin by several hunters from Sault Ste. Marie.
- Project lead: Hunters from Sault Ste. Marie
- Amount of wild rice seed: Unknown
- Seed sources: Unknown
- Success: Field review in September 1928 showed no plants survived.
- Reference: Baird and Jones 1919; Michigan Department of Conservation n.d.

WILDFOWL BAY
- Date: 1929–1930
- Description: The Michigan Department of Conservation's Game Division planted wild rice at various locations around Wildfowl Bay to establish more duck food.
- Project lead: Michigan Department of Conservation's Game Division
- Amount of wild rice seed: Unknown
- Seed sources: Unknown
- Success: Plants that grew on hard bottom were "sickly" and short. Planting did not produce extensive beds at that time. Areas where the rice was planted that had soft, mucky bottom had good success. From these results, the Game Division believed that there would be no success in planting Manoomin along the shores of Saginaw Bay due to the lack of large areas with soft bottom sediments.
- Reference: *Detroit Free Press* 1930

SENEY NATIONAL WILDLIFE REFUGE
- Date: 1938–1941, 1945, 1947, 1950–1954, 1956–1959, 1968
- Description: Seney conducted numerous wild rice plantings on the refuge in managed wetlands in order to increase waterfowl habitat. Seed was primarily acquired from refuges in other states (appendix 3).
- Project lead: Seney National Wildlife Refuge
- Amount of wild rice seed: Total amount of seed planted approximately 33,437 pounds.
- Seed sources: Rice Lake Wildlife Refuge (Minnesota), Tamarac Wildlife Refuge (Minnesota), Arrowwood National Wildlife Refuge (North Dakota), Mud Lake (Luce County, Michigan)
- Success: The rice beds waxed and waned with heavy browsing by muskrats, geese, ducks, and deer, particularly during the early stages of growth. Muskrat trapping was restricted in 1939 and this was a problem for the refuge. Nearly 11,000 acres of seed was planted in 1956, and in order to try and spare some of the seed from the hungry ducks, grain was mixed in with the Manoomin with the hope that the ducks would eat the grain first and bury the rice. The ducks moved from one pool to the next, following the sowing. The plants grew quite well the following season, but the seeds were browsed upon in the summer by geese. In the early 1970s, a 4-acre bed was well established in C-1, where the last planting was done there in 1955. The last seeding in other parts of the refuge occurred in 1968, and wild rice persisted until at least 1984, when the bed in C-1 was the only remnant artifact of this tremendous effort to establish Manoomin in the refuge.
- References: Seney National Wildlife Refuge Annual Reports, 1938–1984; Fjetland 1973

DEVILS LAKE, ALPENA COUNTY
- Date: Fall 1941, Spring 1942, Fall 1942
- Description: Experimental planting area, not known to have Manoomin prior to seeding. Bottom sediments were similar to Houghton and Tawas Lakes (which had wild rice at the time). Other physical conditions were also similar.

- Project lead: Michigan Department of Conservation, H. Miller, using Pittman Robertson funds.
- Amount of wild rice seed: *Zizania aquatica* (river rice, referred to as "giant rice")—one bushel planted in fall of 1941. In spring of 1942, twelve small plantings totaling three bushels of *Zizania palustris* ("northern variety").
- Seed source: Unknown
- Success: Only one small area about ½ acre in size produced a sparse stand. Seven plantings failed; four could not be checked due to inaccessibility by boat. Spots that did produce were reseeded in the fall of 1942. The only spot where Manoomin grew was where other aquatic plants grew.
- Reference: Michigan Department of Conservation n.d.

MIDDLE GROUNDS IN WILDFOWL BAY, PART OF SAGINAW BAY.
- Date: April 15, 1945
- Plot 1 Unit B—T16N R9S Sec 3
- Plot 3 Unit A—T16N R9S Sec 9
- Plot 5—T15N R9S Sec 6. From Sebewaing Sugar Factory water-intake channel south along bulrush bank to "Krutchfield Bar."
- Plot 6—location unknown
- Description: Seeding was done to hasten the reappearance of Manoomin after a high-water period in 1944. Seed was broadcast in water 1½ to 2½ feet deep in muck areas protected from waves. Rice naturally occurred there. Michigan Department of Conservation gave the Detroit Sportsmen's Congress and other organizations the opportunity to participate to any extent they wished. H. J. Miller from the department met with a committee from the Detroit Sportsmen's Club (which included Lloyd Eagen, Kendrick Kimbal, H. G. Colvin, and Ted Hannaford) and the Sebewaing Sportsmen's Club (Pete Halstead, Jack Jerow [sic], and Roland Roberts) to plan the project. On April 15, fifteen men from both clubs participated in the seeding. They included Detroit Sportsmen's Congress: H. G. Colvin, C. A. Frank, R. H. McClurg, Lloyd Hagan, Kendrick Kimbal, Art J. Best and Claude Carpenter;

Sebewaing Sportsmen's Club: William Kroll, Jack Jerow, H. C. Roberts, Ed Quick, Joe Fitcher, Carl Priene, Roland Rafner, and Clarence Grouch.
- Project lead: Thomas Osmer and Herbert Miller
- Amount of wild rice seed: *Zizania palustris subsp. palustris* (original taxonomy named as *Zizania aquatica variety angustifolia*), Plot 1: one bushel over one acre; Plot 3: 2¾ bushels over 2¾ acres; Plot 5: one bushel over one acre; Plot 6: assumed same as Plot 5.
- Seed source: Tarrell's Aquatic Nursery, Oshkosh, Wisconsin
- Success: June 4, 1945, no rice was found; June 29-30, 1945, a few plants in the floating leaf stage were found; October 5-6, 1945, a few clumps in Plot 3 Unit B were found. Grover Pitcher, a local commercial fisherman, observed lots of carp working the area in which Manoomin was planted in Plots 5 and 6. He felt that the carp were attracted by the seed, which H. J. Miller claims they eat.
- Reference: Miller 1946d

GRAND RIVER MARSHES, NORTH OTTAWA ROD AND GUN CLUB
- Date: Spring 1945
- Location: North Ottawa Rod and Gun Club, Ottawa County
- Description: North Ottawa Rod and Gun Club put in experimental plantings of Manoomin in three locations where it had formerly grown. Earlier beds were thought to have been planted by hunters long ago, according to the report's author, H. J. Miller. The wild rice had disappeared, hence the restoration effort.
- Project lead: Kenneth King and Mr. Dietz of the North Ottawa Rod and Gun Club—participants included J. Hyhof Poel, city clerk of Grand Haven; J. Welter Boyd; Kenneth King; and Mr. Dietz.
- Amount of wild rice seed: Two bushels of wild rice seed and 1,000 transplants.
- Seed source: Unknown
- Success: Only a few scattered plants at one location—it was reported that carp, fluctuating water levels, and high boat traffic may have impacted the plantings. Seeds were planted in 6 inches of water, which was also questioned as contributing to the lack of success.
- Reference: Miller 1946a

Restoration Efforts 1990s to 2010

HOUGHTON LAKE, ROSCOMMON COUNTY

- Date: 1996, 1997, 2008, 2010
- Description: Houghton Lake has historically contained large wild rice beds. Four restoration projects have been undertaken.
- 1996—Local rice was not found for this project, so it was purchased from the Great Lakes Indian Fish and Wildlife Commission (GLIFWC). Three ½ acre plots were selected in weed beds in Muddy Bay, North Bay, and Middle Grounds. These were chosen based on the presence of Manoomin the year before and for their suitable water depths. Seeds were stored submerged in 55-gallon drums until they were planted in September.
- 1997—The same sites were seeded in 1997, with planting occurring in October. The seeds were distributed equally between sites. They were again purchased from GLIFWC.
- 2008—Muskegon River Watershed Assembly partnered with the Houghton Lake Lake Association on this project.
- 2010—This project was spearheaded by the Houghton Lake Lake Association (HLLA). Seven members participated, including Craig Cotterman and Keith Stiles, as well as Dr. Scott Herron of Ferris State University. Three areas were planted in this effort: Middle Grounds, Houghton Lake Flats, and a spot near Ben Jeff Park on the Muskegon River.
- Project lead: 1996, 1997—Michigan Department of Natural Resources; 2008—Muskegon River Watershed Assembly and Houghton Lake Lake Association; 2010—Houghton Lake Lake Association.

AMOUNT OF WILD RICE SEED:

- 1996   112 pounds from Rice Lake (WI) were planted in North Bay, 117 pounds from Spur Lake (WI) were planted in Muddy Bay, and 300 pounds of Minnesota rice were planted in Middle Grounds.
- 1997—Attempt to harvest from the Dead Stream flooding but it took too much time, so 500 pounds were purchased from GLIFWC.
- 2008—Unknown.

- 2010—Unknown.
- Seed Source: *Zizania palustris aquatica* (old nomenclature)
- 1996—Rice Lake (WI), Spur Lake (WI), unknown Minnesota lake.
- 1997—Northern Wisconsin and northern Minnesota.
- 2008—Martiny Lake, Mecosta County, Michigan.
- 2010—Wildlife Nurseries, Oshkosh (WI).

SUCCESS:
- 1996—Plants did not advance past the floating leaf stage and their density declined during July and August. By September, none of the plantings produced mature plants with well-developed seed heads. A few mature plants were observed in the Middle Grounds but were believed to originate from the seed bank rather than the newly planted seeds.
- 1997—Success unknown.
- 2008—Success unknown.
- 2010—Rice is still present in Middle Grounds but it is unknown if it is from the 2010 planting effort.
- References: Bonnette 1998; *Houghton Lake Resorter* 2010, 2016; Muskegon River Watershed Assembly 2016a

MUSKEGON LAKE, MUSKEGON COUNTY
- Date: 2002–2005, 2006, 2007
- Description: This demonstration project funded by the U.S. Fish and Wildlife Service was developed to reestablish aquatic vegetation in the Muskegon Lake Area of Concern (AOC) and the lower Muskegon River estuary at the mouth of the river, and within the Muskegon State Game Area. The project also attempted to identify and determine the most successful methods of planting Manoomin. The U.S. Fish and Wildlife Service also provided oversight for the project.
- Project lead: 2002 through 2005: Gale Nobes, Muskegon River Watershed Assembly (MRWA). The following participated in the project: Kathy Evans (Muskegon Conservation District), Greg Mund (Natural Resource Conservation Service [NCRS]), Glen Lambert (NRCS),

Nichol Stout (Grand Valley State University), Nik Kalejs (Michigan
Department of Natural Resources), Roger Morgenstern (Consumers
Energy), Dr. Scott Herron (Ferris State University), Wayne Groesbeck
(Michigan Anglers and MRWA), Gary Noble (MRWA), Sharon Detz
(Native American Ministry), Liz Binoniemi (Little River Band of
Ottawa Indians), Jack Leonhardt (West Michigan Walleye Club),
Muskegon Lake Public Advisory Council, Grand River Band of Odawa,
and local, site-specific partners such as schools (Bunker, North
Muskegon High School, and Reeths-Puffer), the City of Muskegon,
Paperworkers Local 6-1015, Muskegon Conservation Club, and
Muskegon Environmental Research and Education Society (MERES).
These partners participated through volunteer assistance or provided
services to/for the project: 2006 October—Gale Nobes and Greg
Mundt planted at Grand Trunk; 2007 October—volunteers planted in
Muskegon Lake.

AMOUNT OF WILD RICE SEED:
• 2002: November 8—Grand Trunk (Car Ferry) dock (50 pounds);
  November 9—Meres Property (40 pounds), Consumer Energy (220
  pounds), Johnsons Point (50 pounds).
• 2003—600 pounds.
• 2004—600 pounds.
• 2006—120 pounds.
• 2007—175 pounds.
• Seed source: Kester's Wild Game Food Nursery, Omro, Wisconsin.
  Species uncertain but likely *Z. palustris*.
• Success: The project did not accomplish the goal of restoring
  Manoomin, although great effort was given to these projects. Lack
  of success was attributed to changes in Great Lakes water levels that
  affected the sites, heavy browsing by mute swans and muskrats, and
  boat traffic. The project was successful in providing many valuable
  lessons and also in the establishment of the other shoreline plants.
• References: Gale Nobes, MRWA personal communication, 2016;
  McVicar 2010

PLATE 1: River rice, *Zizania aquatica*, at Nottawa Creek.

PLATE 2: Lake rice, *Zizania palustris*, at Tawas Lake.

PLATE 3: Manoomin in the floating leaf stage.

PLATE 4: Flowers of *Zizania aquatica*.

PLATE 5: Roger LaBine and Charlie Fox seeding Manoomin on Getegitigaaning (Lac Vieux Desert) in 2012.

PLATE 6: Birch-bark
winnowing tray.

PLATE 7: Carving ricing sticks out of cedar.

PLATE 8: Charlie Fox, Mole Lake Band of Lake Superior Chippewa, measuring the day's harvest at Getegitigaaning.

PLATE 9: Freshly harvested Manoomin drying in the sun.

PLATE 10: Roger LaBine parching Manoomin in an old washtub.

PLATE 11: Dancing Manoomin at Getegitigaaning rice camp.

PLATE 12: Winnowing
the rice removes the
chaff.

PLATE 13: The final cleaning table at rice camp, Getegitigaaning, 2010.

PLATE 14: Charlie Fox putting Manoomin into his rice machine, "the Manoominator."

PHOTO BY BARB BARTON.

PLATE 15: Floating plants like water lilies shade out rice seeds. Manoomin growing in the open-water areas of Rice Bay at Getegitigaaning.

PLATE 16: The author crafted a shepherd's hook–style ricing stick to reach the tall river rice plants.

PLATE 17: Cooked Manoomin, the darker paddy-grown on the left, wild harvested on the right.

PLATE 18: Grinding Manoomin to make flour.

PLATE 19: Manoomin should be soaked overnight before cooking. The grains open and curl by morning.

Present Day Restoration Projects

The need for restoration is a story that we are familiar with. With every generation since the boarding school era, we have been in the process of reclaiming our traditional culture. In a way, we have been doing a cultural restoration at the same time. That is one of the gifts that we could call a byproduct of wild rice restoration.

Ricing was never meant to be a singular activity; it brings us together unlike the boarding schools which tore us apart. Some of our communities have had to travel long ways on old trading routes to get seed to bring back home. Our culture keepers have been called upon to offer ceremonies when rice is reintroduced to our area.

Homecoming ... at my age, it is hard to introduce something that I am not familiar with or have been around. It has been an honor to be used as an instrument for Mnomiin's journey home. Because of the outreach of another community, Mnomiin found its way back to our people. We had already been doing restoration for years, but because our elder community wasn't able to offer any passed down wisdom about Mnomiin, it had lost its place in our homes and practices. The Mnomiin helped us create a deeper sense of community by bringing us together to process it. Through that newfound practice, it was the Mnomiin that awakened the blood memory of our ancestors' wild rice traditions within us.

After the restoration had been going on for years and the community became aware of the efforts, that is when the Spirit of Mnomiin spoke to the Spirit of the community. The women ceremoniously fed our decision makers the sacred Mnomiin because it needed the security offered by regulations, funding, and support to continue being part of our lives. Our restoration continues at the time of this writing, although no one knows what the future will bring for Mnomiin, there is one thing that I believe is fact. That is, Mnomiin came home and Mnomiin is here to stay, and in that we have hope.

—Renee "Wasson" Dillard, Waganakising Odawa ndodabendaagwaz Citizen of Little Traverse Bay Bands of Odawa Indians, as told to the author.

There are many restoration projects underway today, and there are both old and new threats that make this work challenging. Carp are now widespread and, as they did in the past, continue to disrupt the growth of Manoomin in newly planted areas. Geese, swans, and muskrats put intense browsing pressure on these areas. Bigger and faster craft are speeding across the waters, which can dislodge Manoomin in the floating leaf stage or damage emergent plants through direct impact. Water quality continues to be an issue in today's world, although there have been great strides to clean up some of the most contaminated sediments.

The latest threat Manoomin faces is climate change, which brings with it a host of problems (Cherevulil and Barton 2014). Higher ambient temperatures can negatively impact germination by shrinking the cold dormancy period in winter (warmer water); cause a loss of ice cover, which protects the seeds during winter storm events; and reduce seed production due to hot, dry conditions, which negatively affect pollination. Increasing water temperatures can result in more contaminants and phosphorus released from the sediment due to greater decomposition and lower dissolved oxygen. This warmer water environment will likely increase carp, hydrilla, water hyacinth, and other invasive species detrimental to wild rice. Precipitation increases will alter hydrology by causing severe flooding events, increased sedimentation, and lower water levels resulting in habitat loss. Warm humid temperatures will increase the occurrence of brown spot fungus, which can devastate a rice bed.

Threats related to climate change offer few opportunities to protect the Manoomin, but that is not stopping many people from trying to restore Michigan's wild rice beds. Projects are being carried out by tribal and non-tribal governments, nonprofits, and hunting clubs, and there is a renewed sense of collaboration to share knowledge and techniques. Some groups are conducting research on habitat and water quality, and others are looking at new ways of enhancing populations such as transplanting. These narratives describe the wonderful work underway.

Little Traverse Bay Bands of Odawa Indians

"MANOOMIN RESTORATION BY THE LITTLE TRAVERSE BAY BANDS OF ODAWA INDIANS"

—Maxwell Field, biologist, LTBB

"The Little Traverse Bay Bands of Odawa Indians (LTBB) considers Manoomin to be a culturally significant species and a sacred gift from the Creator. Manoomin provides a major food source for migrating and nesting waterfowl, muskrats, deer, and other migratory birds. Manoomin provides both fish and wildlife habitat by providing nursery areas for larval fish and fry as well as providing a muskrat food-cache source for overwinter survival.

The goal of the LTBB Natural Resource Department (NRD) since 2002 has been to seed Manoomin green seed into inland lakes on and adjacent to the LTBB Reservation located in the tip of Michigan's Lower Peninsula. This effort takes place every fall, and it is the hope of the LTBB community that Manoomin establishes itself in these lakes over time and eventually produces a

Table 9. Manoomin Monitoring Efforts by the Little Traverse Bay Bands of Odawa Indians

PICK UP DATE	LOCATION	PRICE PER LB.	TOTAL WEIGHT	TOTAL COST	# INLAND LAKES SEEDED
9/10/2002	White Earth	unknown	4 lbs	unknown	1
9/3/2003	Leech Lake	unknown	1,300 lbs	unknown	1
9/16/2004	Leech Lake	$1.50	1,500 lbs	$2,250.00	1
9/22/2005	White Earth	unknown	1,500 lbs	unknown	2
9/6/2006	Leech Lake	unknown	1,800 lbs	unknown	3
9/5/2007	Leech Lake	$1.75	1,500 lbs	$2,625.00	4
9/8/2008	Leech Lake	$2.50	1,500 lbs	$3,750.00	3
9/9/2009	Leech Lake	$3.00	1,500 lbs	$4,500.00	4
9/1/2010	Leech Lake	$2.50	1,500 lbs	$3,750.00	4
9/7/2011	White Earth	$1.50	1,500 lbs	$2,250.00	4
8/29/2012	Leech Lake	$1.75	2,000 lbs	$3,500.00	4
2013	Leech Lake	$1.75	2,000 lbs	$3,500.00	3
9/8/2014	Leech Lake	unknown	2,500 lbs	unknown	2
9/8/2015	Leech Lake	$2.00	3,500 lbs	$7,000.00	3

harvestable and sustainable food resource. Since 2013, LTBB has taken a more proactive role in the monitoring and management of Manoomin by starting the Manoomin Project with the goal of reestablishing this important native keystone species not only for the LTBB community but for the natural community as well. Aside from the seeding efforts, LTBB Manoomin monitoring efforts include mapping out current Manoomin stands by creating ArcGIS shapefiles to measure acreage and location (table 9). With this data, LTBB can compare Manoomin stand size and stand location through time. This will allow LTBB to evaluate Manoomin planting success and status on an annual basis and will aid with the identification of suitable target water bodies for future Manoomin seeding efforts. The LTBB NRD has also taken a direct approach to engage its citizens by hosting community gatherings where Manoomin has been reintroduced for healthy consumption and lifestyles. Also, the LTBB Education Department has built a curriculum around Manoomin for LTBB youth and community citizens. The LTBB NRD has spread seed in local inland lakes just as they have spread the word about how culturally important Manoomin is to all Anishinaabek."

Houghton Lake

"HOUGHTON LAKE'S WILD RICE TODAY"

—Keith Stiles, past president, Houghton Lake Lake Association, 2007 to 2014

"As past President of the Houghton Lake Lake Association (H.L.L.A.), the one goal/project that we did not succeed at was some increase in the wild rice. It was on the top of our list. It was the most frustrating as well. Historically, the wild rice thrived in vast areas in the lake for decades until the late 1980s.

In working with the Michigan Department of Natural Resources, Michigan Department of Environmental Quality, Muskegon River Watershed Assembly, and the Native Wild Rice Coalition we planted well over 30 bushels of Wisconsin seed. We tried seeding in the spring and fall over a few years. Many of these seedings were blessed by Dr. Scott Herron.

The H.L.L.A. has put this project on hold but has not given up on it. All benefit from the wild rice, birds, animals, fish, and mankind. I would classify the rice as endangered in Houghton Lake. A few stems show up every year in the old beds. Many factors have been blamed on its disappearance. All have some degree of contributing, some more than others."

Pine Creek Reservation

"WILD RICE PROGRAM"

—John Rodwan, environmental director, Nottawaseppi
Huron Band of the Potawatomi

"No program within the Nottawaseppi Huron Band of the Potawatomi Indians' (NHBPI) Environmental Department influences more community, cultural, and natural resources than the Wild Rice Program. Recognizing the deep historical connection the tribe has with wild rice, its protection and restoration has been a high priority since the tribe's Federal Re-recognition in 1995. However, with much of the traditional lifestyles associated with wild rice and a myriad of factors negatively influencing its habitat, it was a significant challenge to bring it to the current point that it is considered a managed natural, cultural and community resource. Drawing upon a strong network with local, state, federal and tribal partners, along with a dedicated and compassionate staff, the Department has successfully brought wild rice into its rightful position as a significant tribal resource and source of pride. Getting to this point was fraught with challenges and is an interesting story in itself. It took dedication, traditional ecological knowledge, science, funding; partnerships, and a supportive community. If any of these elements were not included, the Wild Rice Program might still have been a concept rather than a reality.

Although harvesting and processing of wild rice has not occurred on the Pine Creek Reservation in recent memory, it remained in the tribal collective memory through traditional teachings. Through decades of dredging, draining, and disfigurement of our fragile riverine waterways, the native rice populations had all but disappeared. These stresses were conducive to introduction of invasive species such as narrow leaf cattail, purple loosestrife, and phragmites, which displaced the native populations of wild rice. Despite the physical loss of the wild rice resources, they remained deeply within the tribal traditional values. Soon after NHBPI was Federally Re-recognized in 1995 they formed an Environmental Department that soon thereafter initiated wild rice surveys and began compiling knowledge of wild rice. At this point it was discovered that there were several varieties, with the Southern Michigan variety being the threatened variety known as Wild River Rice (*Ziziana aquatica*, later elevated to full species). Not only is Wild River Rice threatened and scarce, it bears a smaller seed and is more difficult to harvest and process. These harvesting and processing methods had largely been lost to time, requiring a rediscovery of specialized techniques.

As rice program funding resources became more available to NHBPI, staff was able to conduct more research and engage knowledgeable traditional tribal leaders. Inventorying rice beds and identifying rice habitat was the first step. Much of this was accomplished through annual high resolution multispectral aerial photography followed by field verification.

Once the signatures of wild rice were obtained, we were able to search further afield and identify other rice beds with less effort. These rice beds were then monitored using GIS technology. Through these efforts, the health and vigor of the rice beds were determined. The next step was to determine the methods of expanding and restoring the beds, which is proving to be challenging given the history of stream modifications and resultant introduction of invasive species. Through additional funding these challenges are currently being addressed. Success has been incremental and at times challenging, but traditional ecological knowledge coupled with Western science is proving to be a workable approach.

Annual ricing camps, community outreach, knowledge sharing between tribes is now reinvigorating the tribal diet, habitat, language, food sovereignty, and community cohesion. Much attention is being placed on the early success of the program, which is generating momentum and a broader community interest."

St. Joe and Kankakee River Watersheds

"WILD RICE"

—Dr. Jennifer Kanine, director, Department of Natural Resources,
Pokagon Band of Potawatomi Indians

"Mnomen, or wild rice, has always been a part of the Neshnabé culture. Mnomen is part of the Neshnabé migration story. It is the way that the Potawatomi knew where to settle during their migration from the eastern seaboard. They were told to go to the place where 'food grows on water,' and this is what they did. When they arrived in the Great Lakes region, the Neshnabé came across an abundance of 'food growing on the water.' This food was mnomen.

Within the state of Michigan there are two recognized forms of rice, 'Northern' lake rice and 'Southern' river rice. Lake rice (*Zizania palustris*) is typically found where there is less flowing water and tends to grow shorter than river rice with larger grains. River rice (*Zizania aquatica*) typically grows where there is some flow to the water. This can include rivers, streams, and inlets and outlets of lakes. River rice tends to grow much taller, has a firmer stalk, and has smaller grains. Both forms of rice are sensitive during their early growing phases to fluctuating water levels and flashy water systems. Mnomen can be damaged and/or destroyed if flooding events and significant storm events occur during the early growing phases. The Potawatomi in the lower Great Lakes region were fortunate to have found both varieties of rice growing in their homelands.

Although over time wild rice has been lost in many areas due to multiple factors, mnomen has always been a staple and traditional food for the Potawatomi. Most notably, there have not been any rules or regulations within the state of Michigan or Indiana to protect mnomen from over-harvest, removal, or destruction. Many of the factors that negatively affected mnomen were neither approved nor desired by the Potawatomi. One such reason mnomen declined dramatically over time was due to the dredging and straightening of many rivers in the later part of the nineteenth century and earlier part of the twentieth century. So much of the river rice has been lost in the state of Michigan that this plant is now considered state threatened and a permit is needed to collect any grains in the state. Lake rice habitat declined through time as more individuals moved into the area and established housing around lakes. Most typical landowners value their view of the lake and take pride in not having a 'weedy' appearance in front of their homes. This meant that home owners sought to remove wild rice through mechanical and chemical means. It's not known whether they realized the importance of wild rice to the Neshnabé culture and wildlife. Over time, influxes of sedimentation, increased levels of pollution, and additional forms of human impact have resulted in the decline of mnomen.

Restoration on tribal properties has taken multiple forms over the years. It has been said that mnomen will grow when it is planted in a good way and with good intentions. Mnomen seeds are designed to fall to the bottom of the water body, with hairs and 'tail' that helps to drive mnomen seeds into the sediment. Pokagon Band first acquired all mnomen used for restoration purposes from White Earth in Minnesota. However, this mnomen has not been successful over multiple years of planting. This rice was planted both through mud balling and hand throwing. It was unknown if the lack of success was due to mnomen being suited for a Northern Minnesota climate and trying to grow it in a Southwestern Michigan climate or if it was a competition from other plants or wildlife. To better understand the possibilities of competition and growth, Pokagon Band Department of Natural Resources (PBDNR) developed a pilot project to determine if there was any immediate differences in multiple treatments. PBDNR set up plots within two lakes with temporal and treatment differences. Plots were either cleared of all aboveground vegetation or were left uncleared. Of these two treatment types, mnomen was then planted in half of the plots in the fall and half of the plots in the spring. Furthermore, Mnomen was harvested from Michigan and planted for recruitment abilities versus historically planted Minnesota mnomen. It is quite clear, as of July 2016, that mnomen is not able to compete very well, if at all, with spatterdock and water lilies. In plots that were left uncleared, mnomen development is few and far between, with some areas having no mnomen growth. Furthermore in the uncleared areas, some mnomen got as far as floating leaf stage before being crowded out by the spatterdock and lilies. In plots that were cleared, there is a lush growth of aerial leaf mnomen in multiple lakes. This mnomen was planted in the fall, free thrown, and is of the Minnesota and Michigan varieties. Tribal waters haven't experienced such an abundance of growth from mnomen seed in generations.

Recently, PBDNR began a multi-year project to survey for aquatic and terrestrial invasive plant species within and adjacent to tribal waters, partly in an effort to create a baseline survey of an invasive species that may be on tribal properties, but also as a means to determine if there are plant species that may be competitive with mnomen. Since it is apparent, from the test plots, that mnomen is not able to compete with an overabundance of growth of spatterdock and lilies, surveying for competitive and invasive species will be beneficial to providing information for future restoration efforts. If mnomen is to be established in tribal waters in sizeable, eventually harvestable beds, the removal of competitive species will be necessary. An additional aspect of the project during year one is to survey tribal waters for mnomen. This will provide valuable insight if there are tribal waters that still contain mnomen that has not been restored through tribal means. If mnomen is found during survey efforts, rice locations will be marked via GPS and mnomen measurements will be taken which include: plant stalk density, plant height, mnomen health, water depth, associated plants, as well as soil type and water clarity. During year two, PBDNR will begin to survey rivers, streams, and lakes that are located within the band's ten-county service area in Southwestern Michigan and Northern Indiana. Preliminary searches within the service area will be determined based on historic and citizen accounts as well as current knowledge. PBDNR is currently working with multiple watershed groups to spread the word so when groups are out within the watersheds they are reporting possible mnomen areas they may come across.

The year 2016 was productive for mnomen growth. With the test pilot showing positive results, Pokagon Band Department of Natural Resources plans to establish more test plots of more varieties of rice to determine if there is a variety that grows better in tribal waters. Through collaboration with multiple tribes and state and federal agencies, Pokagon Band is pursuing collection of lake and river rice from multiple sources. Collected mnomen will be planted in tribal waters, and river rice may begin to be established through transplanting as well. PBDNR is working to restore the original meanders of the Dowagiac River, a long-term project; it is hoped that once the river's sinuosity is restored and the river is reconnected to the floodplain, river rice can retake its rightful place in the river. Mnomen harvesting and rice camps will continue for the foreseeable future; the community truly enjoys coming together and immersing themselves in the experience of processing rice. During harvesting season 2016, citizens followed in the footsteps of their ancestors by assisting in the collection of mnomen through traditional methods. In the future, Pokagon Band hopes to have mnomen beds established on tribal properties so citizens can harvest and process mnomen entirely within their own tribal lands. As it was, so shall it be again, through much hard work and collaboration between multiple departments and many citizens."

Little River Band of Ottawa Indians

"WILD RICE RESTORATION"

—Allison Smart, environmental coordinator

"The story of mannomin restoration at the Little River Band of Ottawa Indians (LRBOI) started shortly after the tribe was reaffirmed on September 21, 1994, via the Little Traverse Bay Bands of Odawa Indians and the Little River Band of Ottawa Indians Act, Pub. L. 103-324, 25 U.S.C. 1300k et seq., signed by President Clinton. Eight years after reaffirmation, in 2002 the Little River Band of Ottawa Indians developed a local restoration plan to reintroduce the non-threatened species to two areas within the historical 1836 reservation boundary. Seed gathered from Minnesota was planted in the fall of 2003, 2004, 2005, and 2007 in the Manistee Marsh and the backwaters of Tippy Dam Pond at approximately 50 pounds of seed per acre. These restoration attempts were monitored throughout the time, and several enclosure studies were undertaken to determine the waterfowl predation on these newly planted populations. Seed was also planted in three other locations in the greater Manistee area. In these three locations the wild rice did not take for longer than one growing season.

By 2009, the Manistee Marsh and Tippy Dam Backwaters populations were existent, but not in the density and acreage the original plan had hoped for. At this point the Little River Band of Ottawa Indians Natural Resources Department elected to take a different approach to wild rice restoration. With the recently signed 2007 Inland Consent Decree, LRBOI was able to expand their work to areas outside of Manistee, and this new approach would involve collaborative research with universities and time.

In the fall of 2009, the aquatics branch of the Little River Band of Ottawa Indians Natural Resources Department (LRBOI NRD) started having conversations with faculty at Central Michigan University. A graduate student was determined to investigate the ecological and environmental indicators of habitat for wild rice in Michigan. This student undertook a two field-season study of eighteen wild rice beds and eighteen similar sites that did not have wild rice present to determine if there were abiotic habitat differences between where wild rice was present and where wild rice was absent. This study also compared abiotic habitat parameters between sites with *Zizania palustris* and sites with *Z. aquatica*. Information gained from this study changed a lot of the planning for the Little River Band of Ottawa Indians. First, LRBOI now has to pay attention to species and areas where each species are determined to grow based upon abiotic habitat parameters. Second, there was no statistically significant difference between sites with wild rice present and sites with wild rice absent. At the end of the day, this study left LRBOI with more questions than answers.

In the fall of 2012, LRBOI began working on a genetic project with Central Michigan University looking at the population genetics of wild rice populations in the Lower Peninsula of Michigan. This study determined that there are several genetically distinct populations of *Z. palustris* in Michigan. This study led to the current LRBOI/Central Michigan University study that is looking at the influence of anthropogenic plantings on Lower Michigan population genetics of wild rice. All of these studies will clarify seed source selection for the next round of wild rice restoration performed by the LRBOI Natural Resources Department.

From 2012 onward, LRBOI has continued to monitor and observe local wild rice stands. We collect data on bed area size, stem density, and water depths at four different locations each year. This data collection has recently been standardized with the tribal regional wild rice monitoring network. We plan to continue to monitor this information to determine changes in wild rice bed populations over time in each of these locations. LRBOI has also started to identify future restoration sites, and continues to perform surveys to identify and document wild rice locations throughout the 1836 ceded territories. As populations are found, some are added to the monitoring list. Others are small populations that are documented and revisited at later dates to determine if wild rice is still growing successfully. During this time period we have knowledge of an increased harvest effort by membership at several lakes within the 1836 Ceded Territories. LRBOI hopes to be able to restore both species, the state-listed *Z. aquatica* and the non-listed *Z. palustris*, to areas near Manistee in the near future to increase opportunities for members to harvest. The mannomin program is able to be success-ful because of support from our tribal government and multiple partner-ships with Central Michigan University, U.S. Fish and Wildlife Service, the Michigan Department of Natural Resources, and funding from the Bureau of Indian Affairs' Circle of Flight and Great Lakes Restoration Initiative programs."

Shiawassee National Wildlife Refuge

"WILD RICE PROJECT PROVIDES SEED FOR THOUGHT"
—Patrick J. Rusz, PhD, director of Wildlife Programs,
Michigan Wildlife Conservancy

"A wild rice project at the Shiawassee National Wildlife Refuge in Saginaw County, conducted by the Michigan Wildlife Conservancy (MWC), is point-ing out the need for some rethinking about the potential to restore the unique plant species. All three areas (totaling 5 acres) planted by the Con-servancy in fall of 2014 or the following spring grew some wild rice, and one area had very dense stands with seven-foot stems and plenty of seed heads by mid-August 2015. The same test areas were reseeded and also yielded interesting results in 2016.

The MWC started its wild rice project with the cooperation of the U.S. Fish and Wildlife Service that manages the refuge, and seed obtained through Roger LaBine of the Lac Vieux Desert Band of Lake Superior Chip-pewa. The aim was to better understand the factors that influence rice-planting success. Seed was planted in three types of habitats that had various limiting factors for wild rice establishment, and in one area, twelve fenced plots were used to gauge the effect of browsing by waterfowl, musk-rats, and other animals on rice seedlings.

I think we are a long way from analyzing all the factors, or from declar-ing the project a success, but we know that some wild rice grew in all types of micro-habitats—soft and firm bottoms, shallow and deep water, clear and turbid water—and where there were high densities of carp and potential browsers such as muskrats and geese. Browsing has affected the rice growth, but even where it was severe, the plants produced some seed heads.

Based on the results to date, I think that under certain conditions, wild rice can 'bounce back' from somewhat severe muskrat browsing. Water level draw-downs after the floating leaf stage may help with this. I also suspect that movement of water (slow flow) is not as important to wild rice as some of the literature seems to suggest.

Future plans are to continue to seed the areas on the National Refuge for the next three years, consistent with published guidelines for wild rice restoration. Annual monitoring will also continue, and trail cameras may be employed to obtain more information about the nature and timing of browsing. The Shiawassee Flats Citizens and Hunters Association is now supporting the work with funds and volunteer labor. In fall of 2016, an additional six areas (totaling 8 acres) will be seeded at the Shiawassee River State Game Area, adjacent to (east of) the National Refuge. Each area will have at least two fenced plots (twelve total) to help assess browsing impacts.

The work at the State Game Area will be done in cooperation with the Michigan Department of Natural Resources and will help determine whether diked-in areas with reliable water-level control—availability of control gates and pumps—have potential for growing enough rice to attract waterfowl in mid-Michigan. Together, the efforts on the adjacent federal and state managed sites will provide a lot of seed for thought over the next five years."

Ottawa National Forest

"SUMMARY OF WILD RICE RESTORATION ON THE OTTAWA NATIONAL FOREST"

—Lauren Romstad, Ottawa National Forest biologist, August 17, 2016

"The Ottawa National Forest has been actively engaged in wild rice restoration since the 1990s when collaboration began with several local tribes, including two in Michigan (Lac Vieux Desert Band of Lake Superior Chippewa

Table 10. Manoomin Seeding Efforts in the Ottawa National Forest, 1938–1999 (in pounds)

WATER BODY	COUNTY	1938*	1990	1991	1992	1993	1994	1995	1996	1997	1998	1999
Albino Lake												
Bobcat Lake	Gogebic											
Bonifas Creek	Gogebic											
Brule Lake	Iron										446	
Brush Lake	Gogebic											
Crooked Lake	Gogebic				400	765	630	275	700	500	440	
Erikson Lake	Gogebic											
Kunze Lake	Houghton											
Lac Vieux Desert	Vilas		200	900	400	300	1,500	670	903	300	560	302
Lake 13	Houghton											
Lake St. Kathryn	Iron, MI											
Lobischer	Gogebic											
Mallard Lake	Iron	76										394
Martin Lake	Iron	38										
Middle Branch Ontonagon River	Gogebic	76										
Mink Lake	Gogebic											
Paint River (unknown location)*	Iron	38										
Perch Lake	Gogebic								207			
Perch Lake	Iron										555	
Paulding Pond	Gogebic											
Presque Isle River Flowage	Gogebic	152								120	225	
Robbins Pond	Gogebic											
Stone Lake	Gogebic								207			
Sucker Lake	Gogebic							440	660	598		
Sun Lake	Gogebic											
Winslow Creek (unknown location)	Iron	76										

*The 1938 records of plantings reported bushels; there was no clear description of how many pounds per bushel, except possible 25 pounds, but then in the report it claimed a total of 795 bushels were planted that came to 29,875 pounds, which when converted equals 38 pounds.

Disclaimer: Some of this data is from Great Lakes Indian Wildlife Commission and is accurate. Some data is our best estimate since information was missing (such as exact pounds seeded) particularly on Lake 13, Kunze, and Lake St. Kathryn, Bonifas Creek, and Lobischer Ck. In recent years some records were not shared and therefore are missing. Most recent update was on August 15, 2016.

and the Keweenaw Bay Indian Community) and one in Wisconsin, and the Great Lakes Indian Fish and Wildlife Commission (GLIFWC) (table 10). Prior to the 1990s, it is unknown whether any wild rice seeding occurred because no records were found. One historical document summarized seeding projects in the Upper Peninsula from 1918 through the 1940s (Michigan Department of Conservation n.d.). Two of the wild rice beds noted in this document were seeded in 1938—the Presque Isle River and the Middle Branch Ontonagon River (located in Gogebic County, within the Ottawa National Forest). Both sites were restored in the 1990s through this collaborative effort, though whether the beds are located in the same location is unknown.

In 1997 the Great Lakes Indian Fish and Wildlife Commission completed an inventory and report 'Results of the 1997 Wild Rice (Manoomin) Survey in the 1842 Ceded Territory of Michigan' (Falck 1997). This report summarized a field review and inventory of numerous sites across the Western UP, which included several on the Ottawa National Forest. Results found that the majority of sites were considered poor due to hard bottom substrates and competing vegetation. A few sites had potential suitability for wild rice and were seeded, including the Presque Isle River Flowage and Brule Lake in Iron County. Falck suggests many sites in the Western Upper Peninsula do not have the flowing water and organic substrate necessary to support wild rice.

During the 2006 revision of the Ottawa National Forest's Plan, a new objective was included to 'maintain and/or expand the quantity and ecological health of wild rice beds.' This objective helped lend additional support to fund and participate in wild rice restoration.

Despite the several decades of seeding following the 1990s, the majority of seeding efforts have not been promising. As of 2016, only five wild rice beds have been successfully established that can provide harvesting opportunities. The remaining twenty-three sites were seeded at least once since 1990; however, many did not respond or seeding was stopped because sites did not have optimal conditions. While some smaller lakes produced some wild rice growth, the density and conditions of plants varied greatly (Robbins Pond, Lake 13). The smaller sites also are more difficult to restore because environmental pressure, like waterfowl, can quickly impact the

Table 11. Manoomin Seeding Efforts in the Ottawa National Forest, 2000–2014 (in pounds)

WATER BODY	COUNTY	2000	2001	2002	2003	2004	2005	2006	2007	2008	2009	2010	2011	2012	2013	2014
Albino Lake	Gogebic														302	
Bobcat Lake	Gogebic						47									
Bonifas Creek	Gogebic														520	
Brule Lake	Iron	130														
Brush Lake	Gogebic								153						214	
Crooked Lake	Gogebic														743	
Erikson Lake	Gogebic															92
Kunze Lake	Houghton								30	56	50 (est.)		60	35		
Lac Vieux Desert	Vilas	1,135	2,820	3,053	3,908	3,892	3,123								575	
Lake 13	Houghton								142	315	315 (est.)		167	136		
Lake St. Kathryn	Iron, MI								79	138	150 (est.)		174	94		
Lobischer	Gogebic														400	
Mallard Lake	Iron	727							251		515					
Martin Lake	Iron															
Middle Branch Ontonagon River	Gogebic															
Mink Lake	Gogebic															157
Paint River (unknown location)*	Iron															
Perch Lake	Gogebic			1												117
Perch Lake	Iron															
Paulding Pond	Gogebic															
Presque Isle River Flowage	Gogebic	700	506				1,030	981	478	192					325	230
Robbins Pond	Gogebic														225	
Stone Lake	Gogebic															
Sucker Lake	Gogebic			65											1,374	
Sun Lake	Gogebic			65												
Winslow Creek (unknown location)	Iron															

new growth. Overall, it appears that most lakes on the Ottawa lack optimal growing conditions for rice, confirming the results from Great Lakes Indian Fish and Wildlife Commission's 1997 survey. Furthermore, while some smaller lakes have shown potential conditions for rice, the impacts from environmental factors, like waterfowl, seem to severely hinder their success. Another issue with wild rice restoration in general has been that private ownership on some larger lakes has limited the opportunity because of public opposition. For this reason alone, a few lakes have been dropped from consideration.

In 2011, an effort began to improve our record keeping. A spreadsheet was created to document seeding on the Ottawa National Forest (table 11). Unfortunately, many older records were from handwritten notes or partial memos and are incomplete. In 2016, a map was created to show all existing locations of wild rice and the condition of each bed. In 2016, a five-year formal partnership agreement was established with Lac Vieux Desert to continue collaboration and help fund the tribe to continue seeding. Because of the successful partnership and efforts of the local tribes, wild rice restoration will likely continue, and only be limited by the sites themselves."

•   •   •

In addition to the projects listed above, the Keweenaw Bay Indian Community, Match-E-Be-Nash-She-Wish Band of Pottawatomi Indians (Gun Lake Band), Grand Traverse Band of Ottawa and Chippewa Indians, Saginaw Chippewa Tribe, and the Bay Mills Indian Community have been involved in Manoomin work to varying degrees, but did not provide information for inclusion in this book.

CHAPTER 8

Harvesting and Processing Manoomin

NiiMaamaa Meshkowewe ausanookwe (Strong Wind Lady/aka Rose Martin) remembers her days on these very lands. She stands now today 92 years old and looks out over the water on Lake Lac Vieux Desert/Getegitigaaning, and recalls her memories of the Rice Harvest at the Old Village. She was born and raised right here at the Old Village.

She said, "I am old now, but I clearly remember my days running around, being excited, and looking forward to the Ricing Season. Our people continue to do this process in the same way that our ancestors did hundreds of years ago. Seems like people are too busy today with the world's hectic life, and the rice camps don't take place anymore. It was always at least one whole week that this camp would take place when we were young." She looks over towards Rice Bay and says, "this is the same spot I stood waiting and watching for my mother and my grandmother to come across the lake with the boat full of rice. Then it was another boat full, and another. There was an abundance of rice out there.

"In the old days, this was a community wide event, and even further somewhat of an inter-tribal event. When the Rice Chief said it was time to harvest, it was time to begin. Rice camp began. We also went to other communities for weeks at a time. I remember the feast that took place at the Community Hall that very evening to thank the Creator for our sacred manoomin and ask for a safe ricing season. Then the next day the boats were going steady. Off they would go in boats of different kinds. Several families had flat bottom home-made boats, several had canoes. The equipment of a push pole and cedar ricing sticks and the harvest begins. Once back at camp my dad and the men at the village would dry, roast, and fan the rice. My job was dancing the rice. My brother Henry and I had this job. The rice kept us alive many winters, as our only staple other than the meats they harvested.

"I so looked forward to the families from other reservations coming to set up camp at LVD. While my mother, and my grandmother did the harvesting, my dad would do the processing. To me as a child it was the socializing that I looked forward to. Our Village was remote and we saw very few people from the outside world, and I looked forward to seeing the other kids. They would come from Mole Lake and Lac du Flambeau. We would run and play, socialize with our friends and relatives from other places, and make new friends. This was the important part of the ricing season to us as children, and adults as well. Each person had a job, back then the women went after the rice, the men processed it, and the children often danced the rice. That was my job and my brothers'. Everyone had a job to do—that is just the way it was.

"My memories are beautiful reminders of the way it was back then, and I pray as I stand here today, that the generations up ahead are able to do these things that are so important to us as Anishinaabe people. The waters are being threatened 'world-wide.' That scares me, and I pray our water will be protected, in order to protect our sacred food that grows on water."

Mii oo—That is all.

—Transcribed by giiwegiizhigookway Martin, Getegitigaaning Ojibwe Nation

M embers of the Getegitigaaning Ojibwe Nation have been harvesting and processing Manoomin for generations. And they have held onto these traditions for hundreds of years, despite tremendous cultural oppression forced upon them. The methods they use are fairly consistent with the techniques of other tribes across the Great Lakes region.

The methods of harvesting and processing Manoomin remain mostly unchanged to this day at Getegitigaaning, except that modern machines now take the place of dancing and winnowing (although the traditional methods are still used when no machines are available). There are no assigned gender roles, unlike some tribes outside of Michigan, where females are not permitted to dance on the Manoomin. Both genders do whatever tasks need to be done. The only exception is when girls or women are on their Moon Time (menstruating); they are asked to refrain from working with the Manoomin, a practice rooted in their spiritual teachings.

Traditionally, Getegitigaaning had a wild rice chief who would monitor the health and progress of the beds and determine when they would be opened for harvesting. Archie McGeshick Sr. was the last individual rice chief for the tribe and he served until his death in 1999. At the present time, the duties of rice chief are fulfilled by a committee within Getegitigaaning's tribal government. Keweenaw Bay Indian Community also has a rice chief. Evelyn Ravindran, biologist and manager of the tribe's fish hatchery, described to me in 2016 how their chief is selected:

> Our first wild rice harvesting was done at Sand Point in 1999. In 2001, the Tribal Council named Sandy Dowd our 2nd wild rice chief and Alice Hadden was posthumously named our first wild rice chief in honor of her leadership in organizing the first harvest. In 2004, after the death of Sandy Dowd, ricers met to discuss who should be the wild rice chief before going to the Cultural Committee. Then the suggestion was taken before the Tribal Council for approval. Ricers met to discuss amongst themselves who would be willing to accept the honor and responsibility of becoming the wild rice chief before going before the Cultural Committee. The Cultural Committee discussed the suggestions made by the ricers and when there was agreement, then the

ricers went before the Tribal Council for approval. Eleanor Moede was named the wild rice chief and Evelyn Ravindran (myself) was named the assistant wild rice chief. The Cultural Committee thought the wild rice chief should be a woman elder willing to accept the honor and responsibility of being a wild rice chief. (pers. comm.)

Manoomin isn't just part of a ricer's life during harvest season; there are also ceremonies to be conducted, ricing tools to be crafted or repaired, and rice to be cleaned and bagged. In the winter months, the frozen ground allows access to normally waterlogged swamps to harvest long, straight tamarack and spruce trees for push poles. The dead trees are stripped of their branches and bark, sanded, and a hardwood fork attached to the widest end. These slender push poles are preferred over paddles to move the canoes through the rice beds because poles don't damage the Manoomin plants as much and they allow for easier navigation through the beds.

Historically, birch-bark canoes were used for ricing. Bark from the birch trees was peeled during winter through late spring to make both canoes and winnowing trays (plate 6). Lashing material was needed for both items, so forays were made into the peat bogs and swamps to harvest spruce roots, which had a thin outer skin that gave the roots a reddish color. Roots were pulled up from the muck hand-over-hand, as several hundred feet were needed to lash one canoe. The outer skin was stripped away and the roots were boiled and split in half before being used for lashing. Spruce roots or basswood were also used for tying the rimming of winnowing trays. Today, the birch-bark canoe has been replaced with modern canoes, but the winnowing trays are still made the same way.

To harvest the Manoomin, the plant needs to be shaken or tapped in order for the seeds to fall. The tool for that job is a smooth pair of ricing sticks, also known as "knockers." Because of the reverence in which Manoomin is held by the Anishinaabek, the sticks are carved out of cedar, one of the four sacred plants (plate 7). The sticks are about an inch or so in diameter and around 3 feet long, tapering to a dull point. Early ricing sticks were also shaped like narrow paddles, but over time they were replaced by round sticks that caused less damage to the plants.

When it is time to go picking, *Asema* is offered at the water's edge and a prayer is spoken before heading out to the wild rice bed. Then it is in the canoe and off you go. Ricing is done by two people, the knocker and the poler. The canoe is paddled out into the rice bed where the poler stands and swaps out the paddle for the pole. As the canoe is pushed through the Manoomin, the knocker reaches back and pulls over the rice plants with one of the cedar sticks, striking it with the other or stroking the plant to knock the grains into the bottom of the canoe. They will make several linear passes through the rice bed until they have filled their boat.

Once the rice is harvested, it is dried before being parched (plate 8). A variety of different materials were used under the rice while it was drying in the sun, basically chosen by what was most available. Roger LaBine of the Lac Vieux Desert Tribe teaches that deer hides and birch bark were used in the early days, and tar paper was employed later in the 1940s by his tribe (Robbins 1940). Present-day ricers favor plastic or canvas tarps for both drying and dancing on the rice (plate 9).

After the Manoomin is dry, it needs to be parched so that the hulls can be removed. Rice parching requires some form of large container that can be used over an open fire. In the 1940s, an evaporator pan normally used for boiling down maple sap was put to the task at Lac Vieux Desert, with the parchers using brooms to stir the Manoomin (figure 14). Basically, anything handy could be employed in the parching process. But the most common container used for the task is the old wash tub, with wooden paddles used to stir (plate 10). The tubs need to be treated prior to use because of the galvanized coating. New tubs are placed in a hot fire where the silver coating "slides" off the sides. Once all the coating is removed, the tub is taken off the fire and the inside is rubbed with liberal amounts of cooking oil, then placed back into the fire until it smokes. A second and third coating is often added until the tub is perfectly seasoned. Stainless steel tubs are available today; however the old washtubs are still preferred due to their low cost and availability.

Once the grains are sufficiently dried in the sun, it is time to parch. A fire is built and allowed to burn down a bit so as not to burn the Manoomin. It is fed with small logs throughout the parching process, with a focus

FIGURE 14. Parching in a maple-syrup evaporator pan, Getegitigaaning, circa 1940.

on keeping the temperature at just the right point. Some form of brace is constructed, often a metal pipe wedged between rocks or cinder blocks, and the tub is leaned against the brace over the fire. Both hands are used to grab as much Manoomin as you can and it is tossed into the tub. Two or three big handfuls is usually a proper amount to parch. A cedar paddle, boat oar, or anything handy is used to continuously stir the Manoomin in a circle until it is done. Some ricers judge the "doneness" by the color inside the grain when it is snapped in two. Others roll the grain between the finger and thumb to see if the "jacket" slips off easily. There is a warm, toasty smell to parched rice that is close to done.

Once parched, hulls are removed by the friction of grains rubbing against each other. This can be accomplished by dancing (jigging) (plate 11). Moccasins specially designed for treading or dancing on the wild rice are made from deer skin. These moccasins usually have attached leggings to keep the Manoomin from getting inside the foot cover and irritating the feet of the dancer, as rice hulls and awns have sharp barbs that can break off during the treading and work their way into the skin. Dancing was done in old wooden buckets and also depressions in the earth (figure 15). In a letter to anthropologist Albert Jenks in 1898, Chief Simon Pokagon described the Pottawatomie in the St. Joe River Valley sometimes putting dried Manoomin into bags and then pounding it to remove the hulls, and other times putting it in skin-lined holes. Most of the time that work was done by the women and children, according to the Chief.

Another way to remove the hulls is by pounding. Some people used pounders and a hollowed-out log called a *botaagan*, or in later years a wooden barrel, to pound the Manoomin to loosen the hulls. Several people would

FIGURE 15. Dancing or jigging Manoomin in a bucket.

stand in a circle around the Manoomin and lift the pounders into the air, bringing them down with just enough force to loosen the hulls, but not enough to crush the grains. But today, most folks that still practice the old ways use a tarp laid over a bowl-shaped depression in the earth and dance on it.

Once the hulls are removed, the chaff is the next to go. Winnowing trays are used to "fan" the chaff and separate the loose material from the grains (plate 12). The last step is the final cleaning, where the Manoomin is carefully examined for pieces of smut (rice fungus), stones, or grains that hold onto their jackets. The rice is put in a strainer and shaken to separate the broken pieces from the intact grains. It is during this process that many stories are shared, as often it is the elders and the children who participate in the final cleaning (plate 13). The Manoomin is then bagged and ready for storage or sale.

Today, some folks are building their own rice machines to assist with the dancing and winnowing part of the process, due to the high amount of labor involved in the traditional methods (plate 14). These are especially useful in communities where there are few people interested in traditional processing, or in situations where there are only one or two people involved in the finishing. Ricing, like other foodway traditions, requires many hands.

What is it like to be part of this beautiful, labor-intensive practice called ricing? The following is a fictional but historically accurate depiction of what ricing season might have been like a long time ago during the fur trade era at Getegetigaaning, based on my own personal experience and historical information:

It was the Ricing Moon, Manoominike-giiziz. Cedar paddles dipped in and pushed against the cool water as the canoes made their way under the gray blue autumn sky. Migizi, the bald eagle, circled high over the rice bed while sora rails sent out their greetings from deep within the marsh. As they approached the bed of waving grass, the woman in the bow of the canoe, who was facing backward toward the stern, picked up her ricing sticks and lightly brushed a little bug from her skirt. Her sister placed the paddle on the bottom of the canoe, grasped the sides for support, and slowly stood. She carefully plunged the push pole in the water until the hardwood prongs took perch on the bottom. With her feet balancing the canoe, she pushed the craft *forward* into the rice bed, the long tamarack pole sliding easily through her hand. A soft swishing sound could be heard as the birch bark canoe brushed against the stems of Manoomin.

The woman who was knocking the Manoomin reached back with her right arm as though doing the backstroke and used a ricing stick to pull the grass over the canoe. With her left hand, she took the other stick and tapped the first stick, knocking the ripe grains from the seed head at the top into the canoe. Then she quickly reached behind her with her left arm, pulled over another bunch of plants, and repeated the process. Soon a rhythm developed between them. Push, swish, knock, knock, knock, push, swish, knock, knock, knock. The Manoomin sounded like rain as it hit the bottom of the canoe. As the mound of rice grew, it started to look like it was growing fur as the long pointed awns pointed up into the air. Little spiders scurried out of the pile trying to make sense of the moment. Rice worms tickled the legs of the ricers as they crawled out of the growing pile and up a leg. The sisters riced for a good two hours and filled the canoe with nearly seventy pounds of fresh Manoomin. It was a good harvest. Along with several other ricers, they paddled to shore, canoes heavy. They bagged up the Manoomin and took their harvest back to camp on the lakeshore for processing the next day as the sun was getting low on the horizon.

Camp was bustling with activity the following morning. Hides and large pieces of bark were covered with fresh rice drying under the warm rays of the sun. Children squatted around the Manoomin and eagerly pulled out little rice worms that were trying to escape the heat and light. A rhythmic swishing sound rose up from the dried rice that was being stirred in one of the large black trade kettles. The fire warmed an old man as he stirred the rice grains with his cedar paddle. Around and around the rice moved like an eddy in the stream, until the awns were turned to black dust and the hulls turned a golden brown. Two young men lifted the heavy cast iron pot off the fire and the Elder ran his hands through the grains of rice, testing their "doneness." The warmth of the Manoomin felt so good on his hands, which were aching and sore from a day of hard work. He closed his eyes and inhaled the scent of freshly parched Manoomin. This was his favorite part of rice camp. But his bliss was cut short as the excited squeals of the children startled him. They had found another rice worm and were tossing it back and forth.

Once the hulls were dried, they needed to be removed from the grains. A bowl shaped hole slightly bigger than a person's feet was carefully carved out of the Earth. Every little stone and root was removed and the sides smoothed. The hole was covered with a clean deer hide. Next to the hole, a pole was erected and brace poles attached on either side so that the dancer could stiffen his arms and lift some of his body weight off the rice as he danced. Several handfuls of parched rice were tossed into the hole. The dancer put on special moccasins that went up his calf then stepped gently onto the rice. He grasped the support poles, straightened his arms, and began the dance. The balls of his feet pivoted on the Manoomin as his body twisted back and forth. Slowly the hulls started to pull free from the grains.

The youngest dancer stepped out of his hole, got down on his hands and knees, and ran his hands through the fluffy chaff. There were many grains with their hulls still attached, so he tossed the Manoomin back in, wiped the dust off his hands, and resumed dancing on the rice. Once the hulls had all let go, the young man scooped up the fluffy pile and placed it into a shallow birch bark basket. He handed it to one of the women, who began to winnow the Manoomin by dropping the basket out from under the grains, creating a draft that blew the chaff away. Up and down went the basket until all that was left were the beautiful black, brown, and olive colored grains. Some of the Manoomin was put in a pot to be cooked and eaten that day, some was stored in bags made from the skins of fawns killed that spring. These would be traded with the French at some future time. The rest was stored in woven cedar bark bags. The Band needed many pounds of rice to feed their families through the coming winter, so rice camp went on for several weeks until the last ripe grains had been harvested.

Harvesting techniques are different when gathering river rice in southern Michigan. Potawatomi ricers must work with Manoomin that towers high above them, growing on the shores and muddy banks of the rivers. Care must be taken not to break the fragile stems of these towering giants, which can snap at their joints, and skill is required to pull the seed heads into the canoes because they can grow up to 13 feet high.

In his 1898 letter to Albert Jenks, Chief Pokagon described how his people historically practiced the ricing tradition. Sometimes several families went ricing together and gathered Manoomin from the end of September until November. They used any boat that was available and would push them through the rice, bending the tops of the plants over the boat and "pounding" it out with a stick or flail. Men, women, and children all helped. The rice was divided equally among the family members, as was their way. Chief Pokagon said that generally women and children removed the hulls from the Manoomin, although sometimes men helped. They had a special sack that was made just for the purpose and would fill it with rice, then pound it. Or they would use a skin-covered hole in the ground, likely for dancing. They did not gather any particular amount of Manoomin each year. But, according to the Chief, his people stopped gathering and using Manoomin due to cultural interference.

Today, the Potawatomi tribes are back to ricing once again, and those harvesting Manoomin from the lakes use the same methods previously described. They also harvest river rice, according to Jennifer Kanine, director of Natural Resources for the Pokagon Band, and John Rodwan, environmental director for the Nottawaseppi Huron Band of Potawatomi. The grains of the river rice are much smaller than the northern lake rice, and because the plants can be up to 13 feet tall, old-style shepherd's hook ricing sticks are used, which allow a person to pull the tall plants over without breaking them (plate 16). The hooked ends are used to pull the rice over the boat, and then straight sticks are used to gently knock in the seeds. Stands of Manoomin growing on the rivers are very dense and linear, and it is difficult to pole a canoe into them. Ricers may harvest from the water side of the bed or from the river bank, depending on whichever is easier to access the Manoomin (Jennifer Kannine, pers. comm.; John Rodwan, pers. comm.).

There is a welcome resurgence of traditional camps since that first teaching camp held at Getegitigaaning, and Roger LaBine has continued to travel all over Indian Country sharing his knowledge with both tribal and nontribal people. Many of those who have attended Roger's camps have taken his teachings home and incorporated them into their communities. Others have become advocates for the conservation of Manoomin. Annual wild rice camps are now held by many of the tribes in Michigan, and every fall, stories of ricing abound. New stories of the old ways. The traditions are finally returning. Indeed, Manoomin is calling the people home.

CHAPTER 9

Manoomin, the Good Berry

In a pre-colonial context, manoomin was a staple among the tribes of the Great Lakes Region. It would not be unusual in those days to find people eating it on a daily basis. The ingredients used in manoomin recipes in those days would have all been Indigenous, whether occurring in the region naturally, or introduced by the people themselves.

The early colonial era ushered in new foods and opportunities to create Indigenous/non-Indigenous fusion recipes. It was not unusual to find manoomin still eaten on a daily basis, although it might have been mixed with foreign spices, vegetables, and meats.

In modern times, manoomin remains a staple for some families that live closer to the manoomin beds, and/or make a conscious effort to incorporate it into their diets. Unfortunately, for most folks, it does not appear on their tables with regular frequency. It is, however, often still a well anticipated component of feast meals at ceremonies and other traditional gatherings.

My early experience with manoomin was infrequent. Prior to my participation in the Decolonizing Diet Project (DDP) in 2012, I had only gone out wild-ricing a few times, and had only eaten manoomin at traditional gatherings and Indigenous food focused events like our annual food tasters. As such, I also had very little experience using it in my cooking. In 2012, that all changed with my 100 percent commitment to the DDP. I relied on manoomin so much that year that I really gained a deeper and more meaningful appreciation for its spirit. I have no doubt that it played a big part in my positive health outcomes which showed peak vitamin levels and decreases in weight and bad cholesterol levels.

The recipes that follow were shared by several tribal community members across the Great Lakes Region, and illustrate the diversity and evolution of manoomin recipes. Some focus on Indigenous ingredients only, while others are a mix of foods from different regions of Mother Earth. All of them show the versatility of manoomin as food, and the continuity of the special relationship people have with it.

—Dr. Martin Reinhart, Anishinaabe Ojibway, associate professor
of Native American Studies at Northern Michigan University
and the principal investigator for the Decolonizing Diet Project

Authentic (non-domesticated) wild rice grows in lakes and rivers across Michigan, Wisconsin, Minnesota, and Canada, yet it is hard to find hand-harvested Manoomin for sale in Michigan. It is common to see roadside signs advertising wild rice as you drive along US-2 in the Upper Peninsula, but these signs are somewhat misleading (figure 16). Those stores are likely selling paddy rice from California or Minnesota—or semi-domesticated rice from Canada—the same kinds of "wild rice" you are likely to find in the grocery stores. Domesticated wild rice grains are shiny and black, all the same length, and take an hour or more to cook. The rice is planted in a paddy; sprayed with fungicides, herbicides, and pesticides; and harvested and processed by machines. Wild, hand-harvested Manoomin is considered "true" wild rice by the Anishinaabek. It has not been altered through selective breeding, nor has it been sprayed with any chemicals. It cooks in about 15 to 20 minutes, and the grains pop open and curl after it

FIGURE 16. Sign
advertising wild rice,
which is actually paddy-
grown rice, not wild-
harvested.

COURTESY OF TERRY FOX.

soaks and cooks (plate 17). Due to the high amount of labor involved in its
harvesting and processing, hand-harvested Manoomin costs around $12
to $15 a pound, in contrast to the paddy wild rice, which often can be pur-
chased for less than $5 a pound. If you are lucky, you may find a bag labeled
"handharvested" or "tribally harvested" at one of the shops in the Upper
Peninsula or in a good natural-foods store. That label, along with a higher
price tag and the diversity of color and size of the grains, will tell you that
you are about to enjoy some truly "wild" rice.

Manoomin was a staple in the diet of the Anishinaabek in the Great
Lakes region and an important trade item with the trappers. Chief Pokagon
gave us a glimpse into the role Manoomin played in his tribe in the late
1800s in his correspondence with Albert Jenks (Pokagon 1898a, 1898b).
Wild rice was stored in boxes (he called them *mocoks*) or bags until needed,
and mostly eaten in the fall. But it was also consumed during the winter
months if they had it, which indicates that other foods played a larger role

in their diet the rest of the year. It is important to remember that they primarily harvested the southern river rice (*Z. aquatica*), which was difficult to gather in any quantity. The Pottawatomie never ground the Manoomin into flour or meal, but did boil it with meat for soups, or simply boiled it and ate it with maple syrup.

Today, Manoomin continues to be harvested and eaten as part of ceremonies, feasts, and daily meals. As the tradition of ricing continues to grow and spread within the tribes and new rice beds take hold, Michigan Manoomin will become more available to the eager consumer through the local ricers. But it is unlikely to ever be available commercially on a large scale as we have lost our large beds and there isn't enough to supply the greater market.

Once the Manoomin is harvested and processed, it can be stored for several years if packed in airtight containers. The protein-packed seed is a healthy food choice as it is high in dietary fiber, protein, magnesium, manganese, and phosphorus, and low in saturated fat, salt, and cholesterol (USDA 2017). Manoomin is one of the most versatile foods around and there are no shortages of recipes. It can be turned into a main dish, side dish, savory dish, or dessert. Manoomin can be ground into flour using a mill or grinder and made into pancakes, muffins, or bread (plate 18). Grains can be fried in oil to make "popped rice." But if you want to cook up a tasty dish of Manoomin, there are a few preparation steps you should do. The best way to prepare hand-harvested Manoomin is to first soak it overnight, then rinse it before cooking (plate 19). One cup of dried rice will give you four cups of cooked rice. Add two cups of water to your soaked wild rice, bring to a boil, then simmer until done, about 15-20 minutes. As one tribal elder told me, "Treat it like a sauna!" Several tribal folks have graciously shared their favorite Manoomin recipes. Enjoy!

WILD RICE

> —giiwegiizhigookway Martin, Getegitigaaning Ojibwe Nation ("Both of these are my mom's recipes, Rose Polar Martin, from her mother, Minnie White Polar.")

1½ cups wild rice (cleaned and soaked overnight)
salt pork

Cover the bottom of a 9 × 13 rectangular cake pan with wild rice. Add small pieces of salt pork. Fill the cake pan with enough water to cover the rice completely (about 4 cups of water). Cover tightly with tinfoil. Bake in oven at 350° until water is absorbed (about 25-30 minutes). Serves 6.

WILD RICE AND FRUIT

1½ cups wild rice
4 cups water
¼ cup maple syrup
fruit (of your choice)

Bring water and rice to a boil, then turn down the heat and simmer until rice is fluffy and tender (about 20 minutes). Drain. Add maple syrup and fruit (I always use blueberries). Mix well. Chill for two hours prior to serving.

WILD RICE WITH CINNAMON AND RAISINS

> —Terry Fox, Getegitigaaning Ojibwe Nation

1½ cups wild rice
4 cups water
¼ cup of raisins
¼ cup maple syrup
3 tbs. cinnamon
whipped cream

Soak rice overnight. Bring rice, water, and raisins to a boil, then turn down the heat and simmer until tender (about 20 minutes). Drain. Combine cinnamon with maple syrup. Stir mixture into the wild rice and raisins. Serve warm with whipped cream. Good as a breakfast dish.

WILD RICE CASSEROLE

1 lb. cooked wild rice (about 12 cups)

2 lbs. ground beef (or venison or chicken)

1 medium onion, chopped

2 beef bouillon cubes

2 cans Veg-all, undrained

1 can white or yellow hominy, undrained

2 cans cream of mushroom or cream of chicken soup

2 cans of water

Salt and pepper to taste

Brown ground beef with onions. Drain off excess grease. In large casserole dish or large roasting pan, mix above ingredients. Bake at 350° in the oven for 45-60 minutes. If preferred, mix all ingredients in large Crock-Pot or Nesco. Cook approximately 30 minutes on "high," then turn dial down to "serve."

WILD RICE FRUIT SALAD

—This recipe was borrowed from Terry's brother Wayne LaBine.

1 lb. wild rice

½ cup pure maple syrup

2 tbs. maple sugar or brown sugar

1 pint fresh strawberries, quartered

1 pint fresh blueberries

1 pint fresh raspberries

Prepare the night before: Rinse wild rice until water is clear. Soak wild rice in hot water, covered, overnight. Wild rice should be split and curled. Bring wild rice to a boil, shut off heat, cover. Let cool, drain off water. Mix maple syrup, maple sugar, and strawberries. Refrigerate until ready to serve. Before serving, gently fold in raspberries and blueberries into the rice.

MANOOMIN IN BIRCH BARK

—Renee "Wasson" Dillard, Little Traverse Bay Bands of Odawa Indians

Get a bed of hot coals with some steady rocks on the bottom. Rocks hold up the birch bowl.

Soak ½ cup of rice for about an hour. Place the rice in the bowl on the coals with 3 cups of water. Bring to a boil. Put in 1 cup diced cattail shoots. Add ¼ cup diced wild leeks. Add a handful of winter berries. Add 1½ cups diced filet fish. Simmer until fish is cooked. Take the birch bowl off the rocks. Some of the birch bowl edges may have burnt and fallen into the soup, which adds flavor. Eat hot and enjoy!

WARM WILD RICE AND BERRIES

—Shiloh Maples, Odawa and Ojibwe

4-5 cups cooked wild rice	1-2 cups blueberries
⅓ cup maple syrup	3-4 cups strawberries, halved

Toss cooked wild rice, blueberries, and maple syrup in small baking dish. Smooth out mixture. Place strawberries cut side down, covering the entire top of the mixture with a single layer of strawberries. Cover with foil and bake at 350° for 15-20 minutes.

All measurements are approximations. Adjust syrup to your desired sweetness; at minimum there should be a light coating throughout the rice.

AUTUMN WILD RICE SALAD

(6 meal-sized portions or 12 side-dish servings)

SALAD	BERRY DRESSING
2 cups cooked wild rice	½ cup oil
1 small sweet onion, minced	⅓ cup red wine vinegar
1 red bell pepper, chopped	1 tbs. maple syrup
1 small green apple, chopped	3 tbs. raspberry jam
1 cup walnuts, roughly chopped	½ tsp. dry tarragon
	Salt and pepper

WILD RICE MILK

—Martin Reinhardt, Sault Ste. Marie Tribe of Chippewa Indians.
This recipe also appears in the *Decolonizing Diet Project Cookbook*.

1 lb. manoomin (wild rice)   1 cup maple sugar, adjust to taste

Bring water to a boil in a large pot; add Manoomin and cook it down for about three hours by constantly stirring and adding water when it gets down to the top of the rice. After it reaches the consistency of rice pudding, use a blender to mix it with water in a one-to-one ratio. After blending, pour through a wire mesh strainer to remove solids from the liquid. Set the solids aside and then further strain the liquid through an old clean white T-shirt. What remains afterward is a slightly tan-colored liquid: the rice milk. Mix about ¼ cup of maple sugar with each quart of milk.

Cook's notes: The longer the rice is cooked, the thicker the milk will be. Use the solids that remain for breakfast mixed with blueberries and pecans, or use as a thickener in a pot of soup.

DDP DEER LIVER PÂTÉ

—This recipe also appears in the *Decolonizing Diet Project Cookbook*.

1 lb. deer liver   ½ tbs. sunchoke powder
2 cups wild rice milk   1 tsp. sweet fern
2 tbs. sunflower oil   1 tsp. sea salt
¼ cup leek bulbs   ¼ cup black cherry juice

Cut up liver into large, thin pieces. Soak liver in wild rice milk for an hour or more. Heat sunflower oil, leek bulbs, sweet fern, sea salt, and sunchoke powder in a large pan on medium heat for 3–5 minutes. Add liver slices and cook until brown on the outside but still pink inside. Add black cherry juice and cool until much of the liquid is evaporated and the liver is cooked thoroughly. Take pan off stove and let it cool. Add everything in the pan to the food processor and puree the mix until the liver is in a spreadable consistency. Add salt to taste.

Cook's notes: This tastes great on corn bread or with corn chips and green beans.

MANOOMIN (WILD RICE) SALAD

—Karen Schaumann-Beltran, Passamaquoddy Nation, European American

Start with Native-grown wild rice, 1 cup (it will increase in volume to between 3 and 4 cups when cooked). Boil 3 cups of water in a heavy pot (cast iron works the best)

RICE

Add 1 cup of wild rice, stir and bring to a boil. Reduce heat and simmer (gentle boil) for 30 minutes. Check to see if the water has been absorbed; when cooked (it may take 10-15 more minutes), there will be a little water at the bottom. Some people like it with some "tooth" or crunch to it. Cook it to your taste. Turn off heat, cover, and in 5 minutes, fluff rice.

Let rice cool to room temperature (though this recipe can use warm rice during the winter).

ADD

Use seasonal fruit (about 1 cup): blueberries, strawberries, cranberries, peaches, or your favorite fruit (dried if winter). If using canned fruit (peaches, tangerines, cherries, etc.), you can use the juice from the can for the sauce.

To make sauce, you can use 2 tbs. vinegar (balsamic or apple vinegar works well—don't use white vinegar because it is a petroleum-based product) and ¼ cup fruit juice (you can use apple juice, cider, or whatever you have on hand). To adjust to fit your taste, you can add 1 tbs. of maple syrup or agave syrup. The sauce should be a little sweet.

Top with toasted nuts (whatever is seasonal, your favorite, or what you have on hand). To toast nuts, spread in a baking sheet and cook in the oven at 350° for 7-8 minutes, shaking the baking sheet two or three times during the process. Keep separate until serving, then top each portion with a dusting of roasted nuts.

MANOOMIN ATIK AMEG RECIPE

—Aaron A. Payment (Biiwaagajiig), Bahweting Anishinabe

2 cups wild rice

1 lb. smoked whitefish

1 cup leeks

2 cups morel mushrooms

4 oz. of sun-dried tomatoes

2 cloves of garlic

3 tbs. olive oil

pinch of pepper

dash of hot sauce

1 Ramen Noodle spice pack
    (mushroom flavor)

Chop morels, leeks, and garlic and sauté in olive oil and ½ of flavor packet until just before they are softened. Flake the whitefish (watch for bones) and place in the sautéed mixture and let cool. Add pepper and dash of hot sauce. Thoroughly rinse wild rice and follow instructions for the water-to-rice ratio. Add all ingredients into a rice cooker and set to cook.

MANOOMIN DELIGHT

—Cathy Abramson, Wabanang Kwe, Ojibwe Sault Ste. Marie Tribe of Chippewa Indians

1 cup hand-harvested wild rice

2 cups water

½ tsp. cinnamon

3 tbs. Sugar Island maple syrup

½ cup dried cranberries

½ cup wild blueberries

¾ cup small chunked raw celery

½ cup pecans

Bring wild rice to a boil and simmer 20-30 minutes until it's cooked and fluffy. Set aside. Cool to room temperature. Mix in cinnamon, cranberries, and blueberries. Blend in maple syrup. Stir in celery and pecans. Serves four to six Nishnobs, depending on what tribe you're from. Delicious! Sometimes Cathy makes this without celery and adds it to her pancake mix.

WILD RICE CASSEROLE

—Adel Easterday, Seneca descendant, Sault Ste. Marie, Michigan

Purchase an authentic wild rice product and read everything before doing anything.

2 cups wild rice	pork chops
1 stick butter	1 can cream of chicken soup
2 onions	1 can cream of celery soup
1 bunch chopped celery	1 large can mushrooms

Boil 6 cups of water, add 2 cups of wild rice, return to boil, salt, and stir. Reduce heat and simmer covered 50-60 minutes or until kernels puff open. Uncover, fluff with a fork, simmer an additional 5 minutes, and drain off the liquid and pour into a Crock-Pot.

Melt one stick of butter in a large skillet; add 2 chopped onions, one bunch of chopped celery, a large can of mushrooms with the juice. Shake some basil over it and stir in the soups. Sauté the sauce for 20 minutes. In a separate skillet, sear pork chops.

With the wild rice on the bottom of the Crock-Pot, pour half of the sauce over it; then place the pork chops on top and pour the remainder of the sauce over the pork chops. Cook on low 3 hours. Yummy!

Afterword

I t is an amazing thing, the Internet. It allows one to search for information in a way that was never possible before. When I think about how many papers, books, newspaper articles, and figures I have discovered online that document Manoomin in Michigan, I feel very grateful I am alive in this period of time. While it is true that Michigan has been discounted by European writers as a place where Manoomin grew in any abundance, I can understand why on some level. If I had had to research this topic using traditional methods (pre-Internet era), it would have taken me a lifetime.

What is clear is that Michigan did indeed have a vast number of wild rice beds, some covering thousands of acres. Manoomin is present in archaeological sites and grew in abundance along the coastlines and river mouths of the Great Lakes. Our inland waters also had wild rice growing in the shallow zones of lakes and in the bayous and slow-moving waters of streams and rivers. And all these beds were intact until the arrival of the European colonizers and their destructive land practices.

The Anishinaabek gathered and traded the highly nutritious wild rice for hundreds of years, but eventually that tradition was interrupted when lands were ceded. Some of the people, such as the Saginaw Chippewas, were forcibly removed from their homelands and placed on reservations that were far away from their traditional ricing areas. The boarding-school era saw the removal of many Anishinaabek children from their homes. They were placed in residential schools and forbidden to speak their language or maintain their cultural identity, sometimes never seeing their families or communities again. This caused a devastating break in the continuity of traditional and cultural knowledge between generations.

Regrettably, Michigan has lost all of its large rice beds but one, due to activities by the European colonizers as they populated the state. The first impacts came during the logging era when much of Michigan was clear-cut, the bare soil left behind causing sedimentation and erosion. Log runs and storage areas along the shorelines of rivers directly destroyed aquatic vegetation. Mills dumped debris into the water, which can still be seen today. Water quality was harmed because of the sediment load coming off the cleared land.

The logging era also encouraged the damming of rivers in order to raise water levels to float logs down rivers in the springtime. When the dams were used for other purposes and water levels were raised during the growing season, Manoomin was often lost. The lowering of wetland water levels was also a problem as channels and ditches were cut through marshes to facilitate the construction of railroads, roadways, towns, and agricultural fields.

The drainage of our marshes was also related to the issue of public health. During the 1800s, malaria raged across Michigan and there was a major effort to eradicate as many swamps as possible to get rid of the disease. As we entered the twentieth century, people learned that the mosquito, not swamp gases, were the carriers of malaria, and an even more targeted effort was executed to eradicate the insects through more complete drainage and the application of oil on the surface of the waters. These activities further impacted the Manoomin beds and the decline continued.

In the early 1900s, the notion of muck farming was starting to catch on, as organic soils found in the marshlands provided the perfect growing medium for root crops such as onions, carrots, and rutabagas. So another reason to drain was born, and we lost even more large marshes, including the one surrounding Rice Lake in Newaygo County. Even the lake was not spared, as a ditch was dug right through the center, which drained all the water out of it.

Dredging for navigation also severely impacted our Manoomin beds. Beginning in the first half of the nineteenth century, the U.S. Army Corps of Engineers began channelizing rivers that outlet into the Great Lakes to facilitate the movement of goods via shipping. This was the beginning of the end for Monroe Marsh, one of our largest wild rice beds. Channelization led to further development at the mouth of the Raisin River, including the construction of industrial factories upstream. The original islands and channels have been completely altered, and today no rice can be found at the Monroe Marsh.

The industries that sprang up along the rivers used the water as a dumping ground for oil, waste, and chemicals. Water quality was poor, and massive die-offs of waterfowl occurred in the mid-twentieth century around the Detroit River and Lake Erie coastal marshes. Pollutants also impacted the wild rice beds. Most places that Manoomin gathered its life force from were compromised—the water and the bottom sediments. Sunlight could not penetrate the murky waters to allow germination of seeds embedded in the muck. Manoomin was being cut, dredged, poisoned, smothered, and drowned. It didn't stand a chance.

As duck populations began to decrease and wild rice beds declined, great effort was made by nontribal hunters, the Michigan Department of Conservation (MDC), federal agencies, and even the railroads to bring it back through planting seeds. For nearly forty years they tried and failed, leading the MDC to reverse their earlier proclamation that rice should be planted all over the state, instead recommending that planting efforts should stop. So for the next forty years Manoomin restoration stalled.

The tribes began working on bringing back Manoomin in the 1980s and 1990s and have intensified restoration efforts over the last two decades. Once again the winds have shifted and federal and state agencies are funding and promoting wild rice restoration all over the state. At last there is recognition by the nontribal agencies that Manoomin is important both culturally and ecologically. This is illustrated by the formation of a new interagency wild rice team within state and tribal governments, composed of representatives from most of the twelve federally recognized tribes, the State of Michigan's Departments of Environmental Quality, Natural Resources, Agriculture and Rural Development, Transportation, and the Economic Development Corporation. Because of the cultural significance of Manoomin to the Anishinaabek, the tribes are taking the lead role in this effort with state staff supporting efforts for the protection, restoration, and conservation of wild rice. How far we have come!

While great strides have been made and people are developing positive relationships with Manoomin, we still have a long way to go to protect and restore the rice beds. Lake and river shoreline property owners for the most part are not fond of Manoomin or any other aquatic plant that might impede their recreational use of the water. Sadly, it has become common practice to chemically treat our sacred waters to kill off these "weeds," or bring in giant harvesting machines to cut them down. Until we learn to live in *relationship* with other forms of life instead of assuming a dominant position over them, Manoomin will be threatened along with the other plants sharing its home. I hope that over time, education and cultural sharing will support growth and change, and through open hearts and minds, we will learn to honor and respect Manoomin so that it can abundantly hold its rightful place in this beautiful place we call home, Michigan.

Historic Locations of Manoomin

COUNTY	NAME	DATE
Alcona	Holcomb Creek	1988
Alcona	Hubbard Lake	1942
Allegan	Kalamazoo Lake	1916
Allegan	Kalamazoo River (near Saugatuck)	1903
Allegan	Old Kalamazoo Lighthouse and Pier	1881
Allegan	Pottawatomie Club Marsh	1881
Barry	Glass Creek	1965
Barry	Gun Lake	1945
Bay	Squaquanning Creek	1848
Bay	Tobico Marsh	1880
Bay	West of Old Saginaw Bay Light House	1856
Benzie	Pearl Lake	1919
Berrien	Benton Harbor Marsh	1837
Berrien	Benton Harbor St. Joe River/Paw Paw River	1860
Berrien	Galien River Estuary	1911
Berrien	Little Paw Paw Lake	1928

COUNTY	NAME	DATE
Berrien	Potawatomie Lake (extinct lake)	1887
Berrien	South Lake (Grand Mere)	1970
Calhoun	Athens	1988
Calhoun	Bedford	1960
Calhoun	C Avenue South	1960
Calhoun	H Drive North	1954
Cass	Beckwith Mill Pond (now called Lagrange Lake)	1928
Cass	Curtis Lake Marsh	1985
Cass	Mill Creek Wetlands	1979
Cheboygan	Black Lake Inn	1941
Cheboygan	Black River	1963
Cheboygan	Cheboygan East	1912
Cheboygan	Cheboygan West (mouth of the river)	1912
Cheboygan	Indian River	1925
Cheboygan	Indian River (near mouth of the river)	1919
Cheboygan	Mullet Lake	1885
Cheboygan	Pigeon River	1936

Cheboygan	Upper Black River	1951
Crawford	Simpson Lake	1881
Emmet	Carp Lake	1931
Emmet	Crooked River	1920
Emmet	Spirit Lake (Wycamp Lake)	1887
Genesee	Long Lake	1913
Genesee	Long Lake (now called Fenton Lake)	1916
Grand Traverse	Arbutus Lake	1919
Grand Traverse	Rennie Lake	1919
Huron	Heisterman Island (Stony Island)	1911
Huron	Maisou Island (Katechay Island)	1911
Huron	Rush Lake	1911
Huron	Sebewaing River Mouth	1874
Iosco	Lake Solitude	1902
Iosco	Tawas Lake	1874
Iosco	Tawas River	1918
Iosco	Van Etten Lake	1937
Iosco	Van Etten Lake	1916
Jackson	Baldwin Road Rice Bed	1975
Jackson	Eagle Lake (Haehnle Marsh)	1921
Jackson	Little Portage Lake	1976
Jackson	Trist Mill Pond	1937
Kalamazoo	Barton Lake	1938
Kalamazoo	Campbell Lake	1941
Kalamazoo	Gull Lake	1981
Kalamazoo	Portage Creek	1958
Kalamazoo	Sugarloaf Lake	1933
Kalamazoo	Sugarloaf Lake	1940
Kalamazoo	W Avenue	1985
Kent	Fallasburg Mill Pond	1880
Lapeer	Cramton Park	1977
Leelanau	Cedar River	1948
Lenawee	Cleveland Lake stream	1987
Lenawee	River Raisin (near Brooklyn)	1986
Livingston	Island Lake Rec. Area	1947
Macomb	Old Campbell Farm	1875
Manistee	Acadia Marsh	2016

Manistee	Arcadia Lake	1989
Mecosta	Bass Lake	1940
Mecosta	Big Evans Lake (Upper Evans)	1940
Mecosta	Chippewa Lake	1927
Mecosta	Grass Lake	1940
Mecosta	Little Evan Lake (Lower Evans)	1940
Monroe	La Plaisance Road	1962
Monroe	Monroe Piers	1924
Monroe	Raisin River Flats	1917
Monroe	Silver Creek (Pointe Mouillee)	1949
Montcalm	Duck Lake	1941
Muskegon	Markle Drain	1948
Muskegon	Muskegon	1916
Muskegon	Muskegon Lake	1930
Muskegon	Muskegon River	1902
Muskegon	Muskegon State Game Area 1951 parcel	1951
Muskegon	Snug Harbor	?
Newaygo	Rice Lake	1880
Oakland	Marl Lake	1916
Oakland	Milford Pond (now called Hubbell Pond)	1948
Oakland	Proud Lake	1954
Ogemaw	Spring Lake (now called Lodge Lake)	1958
Oscoda	Lake David	1940
Ottawa	Bruce Bayou	1987
Ottawa	Grand Haven	1928
Ottawa	La Plaisance Road	1962
Ottawa	Lake Macatawa	1910
Ottawa	Little Pigeon River Creek Marsh	1936
Ottawa	Millhouse Bayou	1988
Ottawa	N. Ottawa County Rod and Gun Club Seeding Site 1	1945
Ottawa	N. Ottawa Rod and Gun Club Seeded Sites 2	1945
Ottawa	Pigeon River	1940
Ottawa	Pottawattomie Bayou	1984
Presque Isle	Grand Lake	?

Presque Isle	Rainy River/Black Lake	1953		Wayne	Huron River Mouth	1951
Presque Isle	Swan Lake	1949		Wayne	Knaggs Creek	1827
Roscommon	Backus Lake	1956		Wayne	River Rouge Mouth	1887
Roscommon	Houghton Lake	1934		Alger	Au Train Lake	1925
Roscommon	Houghton Lake	1930		Alger	Bar Lake	?
Roscommon	Houghton Lake	1964		Alger	Crow Lake	1988
Saginaw	Crow Island	1880		Alger	Doe Lake	?
Saginaw	DuPraw (DuPrat) Marsh	1880		Alger	Echo Lake	?
Saginaw	Ferguson Bayou	1880		Alger	Grimes Lake	1930
Saginaw	Mistiguay Creek	1880		Alger	Hovey Lake	?
Saginaw	Mouth of the Tittabawassee River NE	1821		Chippewa	Munuscong Bay	1930
				Chippewa	Munuscong Preserve	1906
Saginaw	Saginaw River	1881		Chippewa	Pendills Lake	1928
Saginaw	Willow Island	1881		Chippewa	Potagannissing River	1930
Shiawassee	Owosso	1889		Chippewa	Spectacle Lake	?
St. Clair	San Souci Harsen's Island	1958		Delta	Foote Lake	?
				Delta	Jackpine Lake	?
St. Clair	Sarnia Bay	1914		Delta	Middle Eighteenmile Lake	?
St. Clair	Stocks Creek	1909				
St. Joseph	Mill Creek Wetlands	1950		Dickinson	O'Neil Lake	1914
St. Joseph	St. Joseph River Colon	1894		Gogebic	Conner Creek	1909
St. Joseph	Wulfenia Plant Preserve	1984		Houghton	Portage Lake (south part)	1923
Tuscola	Fish Point	1921		Houghton	Sturgeon Slough	1948
Tuscola	Murphy's Lake	1921		Iron	Marten Lake	1941
Tuscola	Shay Lake	1921		Iron	Otter Lake	1914
Van Buren	Magician Lake	1928		Keweenaw	Deer Lake	1909
Van Buren	Van Auken Lake	1928		Keweenaw	Lac Labelle	1909
Washtenaw	Barton Pond	1938		Luce	Dollarville Flooding	1935
Washtenaw	Dexter Mill Pond	1980		Luce	Hunters Landing Tahquamenon River	1935
Washtenaw	Geddes Dam	1909				
Washtenaw	Joslyn Lake Public Access	1976		Luce	Mud Lake	1956
				Luce	North Manistique Lake (Round Lake)	1883
Washtenaw	Mill Lake Waterloo Rec. Area	1959				
				Luce	Tahquamenon River (near Sage River)	?
Washtenaw	South Lake	1938				
Wayne	Belle Isle Park	1892		Mackinac	Brevort Lake	1942
Wayne	Detroit South	1915		Mackinac	Hay Lake	1884
Wayne	Ecorse River	1820		Mackinac	Le Cheneaux Islands	1934
Wayne	Grosse Isle, Detroit River	1885		Mackinac	Manistique Lake (Big Lake)	1883
Wayne	Henry Ford Pond near Fairlane Dam	1911				
				Mackinac	Millecoquins Lake	1930
Wayne	Hubbard Farm	1849		Mackinac	Mud Lake	?

Mackinac	South Manistique Lake	1922
Marquette	Lake Independence	1922
Menominee	Hayward Lake	1923
Menominee	Mud Lake (now called North Lake)	1923
Menominee	Spring Lake (Mud Lake)	1923
Schoolcraft	A-1 Pool Seney National Wildlife Refuge	1968
Schoolcraft	B-1 Pool Seney National Wildlife Refuge	1954
Schoolcraft	Bass Lake	?
Schoolcraft	Byers Lake	?
Schoolcraft	C-1 Pool Seney National Wildlife Refuge	1954
Schoolcraft	C-2 Pool Seney National Wildlife Refuge	1947
Schoolcraft	C-3 Pool Seney National Wildlife Refuge	1956
Schoolcraft	Cookson Lake	?
Schoolcraft	D-1 Pool Seney National Wildlife Refuge	1938
Schoolcraft	E-1 Pool Seney National Wildlife Refuge	1938
Schoolcraft	East Lake	?
Schoolcraft	F-Pool Seney National Wildlife Refuge	1938

Schoolcraft	G-1 Pool Seney National Wildlife Refuge	1938
Schoolcraft	H-1 Pool Seney National Wildlife Refuge	1938
Schoolcraft	Hub Lake	?
Schoolcraft	Indian Lake	1905
Schoolcraft	Indian Lake	1925
Schoolcraft	I-Pool Seney National Wildlife Refuge	1956
Schoolcraft	Ironjaw Lake	?
Schoolcraft	J-Pool Seney National Wildlife Refuge	1938
Schoolcraft	Little Bass Lake	?
Schoolcraft	McDonald Lake	1925
Schoolcraft	Murphy Lake	?
Schoolcraft	Old Goose Pen, Seney Wildlife Refuge	1938
Schoolcraft	Seney National Wildlife Refuge J Pool	1956
Schoolcraft	Show Pool Seney National Wildlife Refuge	1938
Schoolcraft	Thunder Lake	?
Schoolcraft	T-Pool Seney National Wildlife Refuge	1947

Manoomin Restoration Efforts as Reported in Historic Newspapers from Michigan, 1877–1939

DATE	NEWSPAPER	PUBLISHED LOCATION	TEXT FROM ARTICLE	WATER BODY
8/31/1877	*True Northerner*	Paw Paw	The Kalamazoo river margins are fast filling up with wild rice, and the channel is almost a third narrower in some places than five years ago.	Kalamazoo River
6/4/1880	*True Northerner*	Paw Paw	Wild rice is being planted in favorable places on the lakes and rivers forming the inland route from Petoskey to Cheboygan, and it is expected that it will grow and spread through that region, thus raising food to attract wild ducks to those waters.	Petoskey to Cheboygan
6/18/1880	*True Northerner*	Paw Paw	The wild rice sown around the lakelets and marshes in the vicinity of Houghton, to attract wild ducks, has failed to grow on account of imperfect planting and other causes.	Houghton
4/7/1881	*Crawford Avalanche*	Grayling	Our Prosecuting Attorney, Mr. J. O. Hadley, has lately received five bushel of wild rice from Janesville, Wis., which is to be distributed around in the various lakes and bayous in this vicinity, for the benefit of the wild duck and geese which frequent them, and when they become sufficiently numerous, our sportsmen propose to step in and have a "benefit."	Grayling
4/16/1881	*Northern Tribune*	Grayling	Five bushels of wild rice from Wisconsin will be sowed around the lakes near Grayling this spring, with the hopes of inducing wild ducks to visit these localities.	Grayling

5/19/1881	*Crawford Avalanche*	Grayling	Mr. Myron Dyer, under the direction of J. O. Hadley, Esq., has lately sown a quantity of wild rice in Simpson, Darker, and School Section lakes, the Goose pond and the Outlet, and if that don't draw ducks and geese there's no attraction in taffy.	Grayling
9/21/1881	*Detroit Free Press*	Detroit	COLDWATER REPUBLICAN—An effort is being made by the sportsmen of this vicinity to purchase a quantity of wild rice and sow in the lakes around our city. The experiment was made about five years ago, but the seed proved worthless, none of it ever coming up. Canada rice will be purchased this time. It is a move that should be made at once, as the ducks are becoming very scarce in this vicinity, having nothing to feed upon.	Coldwater
9/25/1884	*Lake County Star*	Baldwin	The sportsmen of Sault Ste. Marie will sow wild rice in Hay lake in the hope of making it a duck resort.	
11/17/1886	*Detroit Free Press*	Detroit	STATE ITEMS—About a year ago a quantity of wild rice was sown in the streams about Battle Creek, and the unusual large number of ducks this fall, in the creeks thereabout, is undoubtedly owing to this fact. A subscription paper is being circulated among those who enjoy duck hunting for the purpose of raising funds to purchase and plant more seed this fall, and is meeting with good success.	Battle Creek
2/11/1887	*Alma Record*	Alma	An effort is being made at Cross Village, Emmet County, to raise money enough by subscription with which to buy wild rice to sow on Weikamp lake, thus to encourage duck settlement, and by and by a paradise in northern Michigan for duck hunting.	Spirit Lake
10/12/1894	*Yale Expositor*	Yale	Allegan sporting men are creating a fund with which to buy wild rice seed to sow in the river bottom. It will grow, create a swamp, and attract ducks and there you are.	Kalamazoo River
8/20/1896	*Crawford Avalanche*	Grayling	While Lewis Shettler, aged 34 years, was in bathing at the iron bridge over the Huron river, four miles south of Pinckney, he became tangled In the weeds and wild rice growing in the river, and before help could reach him was drowned.	Huron River
9/4/1896	*Saginaw Evening News*	Saginaw	MICHIGAN BRIEFS—The hearts of Muskegon's sportsmen beat loud in sympathy for the poor wild ducks which used to inhabit the banks of the Muskegon river before grazing became so poor. They are now planting the river edges with wild rice so the ducks can return, get a nice, square meal and be shot.	Muskegon River
9/10/1896	*Crawford Avalanche*	Grayling	Muskegon sportsmen will sow wild rice seed along the Muskegon River in an effort to coax back the wild duck that of late have been giving the river the go by on account of the poor feeding facilities.	Muskegon River

12/27/1896	*Detroit Free Press*	Detroit	HELD A COCKING MAIN: THEY PROTEST AGAINST THE SOWING OF WILD RICE BY SPORTSMEN—The [Muskegon Horticultural Society] also protested against hunters and sportsmen sowing wild rice in lakes and rivers on the ground that it attracts enormous flocks of blackbirds who attack the growing crops.	
1/8/1897	*Alma Record*	Alma	Allegan county sportsmen are sowing wild rice in the lakes and streams of that county in the hope of attracting water fowl there.	Allegan County
4/15/1897	*Crawford Avalanche*	Grayling	The lovers of fishing and hunting in Grayling and the vicinity will organize a rod and gun club, and will sow wild rice in the streams in order to attract wild ducks.	Grayling
4/19/1901	*Detroit Free Press*	Detroit	ALL AROUND THE STATE—For several miles in the vicinity of Mendon the St. Joe river is densely covered with wild rice, and the stream is impassable for boats. The rice grows about two feet above the water's surface, and is fed upon by millions of black birds. A few years ago some wild rice was sown in the river near Colon Lake, to attract wild ducks. It proved a failure in that line, but the rice has increased year after year until the historic river, once so beautiful, has been changed to practically a marsh.	St. Joe River
4/27/1902	*Detroit Free Press*	Detroit	One of the attractions of Tawas Beach is Lake Solitude, a placid and beautiful sheet of water stretching east and west about three quarters of a mile and extending about a quarter of a mile across at its widest point. The unknown source of its supply is supposed to come through an underground stream. The lake is fringed with a forest, bedecked with wild rice and celery, which feed ducks driven in by the wind and waves of Lake Huron.	Lake Solitude
11/4/1903	*Jackson Daily Citizen*	Jackson	Munising sportsmen who are anxious for better duck hunting than they now have will sow wild rice in some of the numerous small lakes in that vicinity.	Munising
11/4/1905	*Flint Daily Journal*	Flint	MICHIGAN—MANISTIQUE—The Manistique Rod and Gun club is sowing wild rice in the marshes and swampy districts on the shores of Indian lake and along the banks of nearby streams. Better duck hunting is the object.	Indian Lake

10/12/1909	*Calumet News*	Calumet	MORE RICE PLANTED—More wild rice has been planted by Laurium residents in the Sibley river, Deer lake, and lac Labelle districts in Keweenaw county, so more wild ducks may be attracted to this northern clime. Johnson Vivian of Laurium inaugurated this step in Keweenaw county, and his example has been followed by other sportsmen. The rice planted in Lac LaBelle and other streams last year has ripened, and the grain has fallen into the water, thus helping to make a bigger harvest of next season. Ducks have already been seen and many more will be attracted as the fields become bigger and more heavily laden with grain, a delicacy that ducks will fly many miles to obtain.	Sibley River, Deer Lake, Lac Labelle
10/27/1909	*Calumet News*	Calumet	Wild ducks seem to be about as plentiful as ever, they are not hunted to any extent in this locality [Marquette]. Last year wild rice was sown in some of the marshes that were once favorite haunts of ducks, but the experiment seems to have been a failure, as the rice has failed to grow. It appears that what is supposed to be the rice plants in the summer, have proved to be a weed, the foliage which greatly resembles wild rice, which, however, has no attraction for ducks.	Calumet
11/13/1909	*Diamond Drill*	Crystal Falls	A number of sportsmen from this city banded together and ordered 100 pounds of wild rice. The seed arrived last week and was apportioned out among the several lakes in the vicinity. All of it has been planted and if there is any success at all with the sowing, next year ought to see a small crop in all of the surrounding bodies of water. The advocates of this move believe that in a few years the lakes and streams of this locality will be attractive grounds for wild ducks owing to the wild rice that will be growing therein.	Crystal Falls
8/11/1910	*Calumet News*	Calumet	PARTRIDGE ARE PLENTIFUL: SPORTSMEN LOOKING FORWARD TO EXCELLENT SPORT THIS FALL—Copper country sportsmen who keep in touch with conditions in the woods report that indications point to some exceptionally fine hunting this fall. Partridge are said to be especially plentiful this year, and while duck have not commenced to put in their appearance yet, the wild rice is growing nicely and it is thought that it will attract a large number of these birds. Not only will the bird hunting be excellent this year but deer are said to be more numerous than usual. The early spring was very helpful to the game birds and caused them to multiply rapidly.	Keweenaw County

8/19/1910	*Calumet News*	Calumet	WILD RICE IS GROWING: Reports from Bete Gris indicates that the wild rice planted in the chain of small lakes near that resort by Laurium sportsmen, several years ago, as food for the ducks, is growing nicely and that it should prove an attractive lure for the birds this fall. Several sacks of seed were planted and the growing rice now covers a large area. Those who are familiar with the surroundings, recognize the place as an ideal one for duck hunting and Lauriumites are anticipating some good sport there after October 1, when the season opens.	Bete Gris small chain of lakes
8/30/1910	*Calumet News*	Calumet	With the closing of the trout season comes the opening of the season for duck hunting and the indications point to some excellent sport. Although the birds are not as numerous now as they will be later in the fall, good sport is expected. Wild rice is growing nicely at various places where it has been planted and it is believed that it will prove the means of attracting a large number of these birds.	Calumet
9/8/1910	*Calumet News*	Calumet	Local hunters returning from Keweenaw county and other points report a scarcity of ducks. A few have been seen in the vicinity of the wild rice fields in the Bete de Gris district, but on the whole the birds are very scarce.	Keweenaw County
11/25/1910	*Muskegon News Chronicle*	Muskegon	MICHIGAN IN A NUTSHELL—KALAMAZOO—It is planned by the officials of the Chicago, Kalamazoo and Saginaw railroad to send out several men along the line of their road in the near future to plant quantities of wild rice in the various lakes, hoping to secure a permanent growth of the grain which is the principal food of the wild ducks. As soon as the water conditions are favorable the planting will begin.	Genesee County Lakes
2/6/1911	*Calumet News*	Calumet	Local hunters returning from Keweenaw county and other points report a scarcity of ducks. A few have been seen in the vicinity of the wild. A petition was circulated in the L'Anse last week for the purpose of arousing interest in the organization of a rod and gun club which will have headquarters here. The purpose of the movement will be to protection of game and fish in this vicinity, says the L'Anse Sentinel. Sixty signatures have been secured to the petition and the organization will be perfected sometime next week. The members of the club plan to procure large amounts of fry from the state hatcheries and stock the streams here. A large amount of wild rice will be planted in lakes and marshes which are numerous in this neighborhood.	L'Anse

11/5/1911	*Detroit Free Press*	Detroit	CREATING A BIRD PARADISE—RESTING PLACE FOR HERONS—At the upper end of the pond is a stretch of swamp that has attracted wild ducks, and it is hoped to increase their number another year. To assist in this work, as well as to provide for those who have already taken up their abode here, wild rice has been planted and this will give a feeding ground sufficient for all requirements.	Henry Ford Farm
11/17/1913	*Flint Journal*	Flint	MUCH WORK IS ACCOMPLISHED BY GAME ASSOC.—The association [Genesee County Fish and Game Assoc.] is not paying attention to protection only, however. It has already spent more than $50 to plant wild rice in the lakes of the county.	Genesee County Lakes
6/19/1914	*Flint Daily Journal*	Flint	WILD RICE GROWING WELL AT LONG LAKE—GOOD DUCK SHOOTING EXPECTED ON LAKE THIS FALL—The wild rice which was planted last fall by the Genesee County Fish and Game association in Long Lake is already showing up in quantities beyond the expectations of the association. Already the long ribbon-like leaves of the rice are floating on the top of the water although it was not expected that it would show until at least a month later. Sometimes the wild rice stays in the water as long as 18 months before it begins to grow. It is not unusual for the seed to stay on the lake bottom until the second season before it germinates. The wild rice was bought in Minneapolis, Minn., last September. The association planted 200 pounds, 150 pounds in Long Lake and the remainder in Forest township. Wild rice is one of the best duck foods known and was planted to attract ducks to the county. This spring as a result of the federal migratory bird law which stopped spring shooting ducks were numerous on all the lakes of the county and many of them have remained to nest. With the wild rice maturing it is expected that duck shooting this fall will be better than in several years.	Long Lake
9/29/1914	*Calumet News*	Calumet	PROPAGATING GAME: Continuing its campaign for the conservation of waterfowl, the Portage Lake Rod & Gun club has planted a quantity of wild rice, wild celery and wapato, the latter a species of waterlily on which ducks feed, at the Otter and O'Neil lakes. The planting was done by John A. Doelle, superintendent of schools, who with F. K. Helff, manager of the telephone company, was at Otter Lake on business over Saturday and Sunday.	Otter, O'Neil Lakes

3/6/1917	*Saginaw Daily News*	Saginaw	COMMONWEALTH CO. TO SPEND MILLIONS ON STATE PLANTS, *by Gurd M. Hayes*—We are also doing some constructive work in behalf of the fish and game interests of the state. We build fish ladders at all dam sites and this aids in the migration of fish during the spawning season. We also have a definite policy of stocking the different ponds throughout the state in the various rivers where we have a water power plant, and we plant wild rice and duck food in many ponds in order to develop better shooting.	Statewide
9/18/1920	*Flint Daily Journal*	Flint	MICHIGAN NEWS—MICHIGAN ROUTE FOR WILD DUCKS—*Lansing, Mich Sept. 18*—Efforts are being made to attract the ducks down across Michigan by supplying them with attractive feeding places, and this is increasing the flight this way. Wild rice and celery is being planted and with considerable success by the game department in lake beds and streams and it is claimed the ducks are learning the way to the dinner table as well as the hungry hunter learns his way to mess after a hard day of shooting.	Statewide
4/20/1921	*Alpena Argus*	Alpena	We learned from an exchange that a few bushels of wild rice from Wisconsin will be distributed around the various lakes and bayous in the vicinity of Grayling this spring. It is said that the sheets of water are destitute of all wild rice, and the wild ducks and geese give the place a wide berth in consequence.	Alpena
5/19/1939	*Cass City Chronicle*	Cass City	HERE AND THERE AROUND THE THUMB: ITEMS GATHERED FROM THE CHRONICLE EXCHANGES AND FROM OTHER SOURCES—A group of Sebewaing sportsmen consisting of John Eisengruber, Frank Clare, Carl Tredup and Ed Pitcher have recently devoted much time to an experimental planting of wild rice, duck potatoes, and pondweed along the shore from the south of Lone Tree Island and north of Defoe. About 40 pounds of wild rice was planted by the group, and a number of the other foods, all of which are enjoyed by ducks.	Sebewaing

Manoomin Plantings at Seney National Wildlife Refuge, 1938–1984

ANNUAL NARRATIVE REPORT— YEAR	TOTAL POUNDS WILD RICE	SURVIVAL	SEED SOURCE	NOTES
1938	870	"70% of wild rice is growing well but in danger of much damage from ducks and muskrats before seed matures."		Pools D, E, H, and I had ¼ acre each seeded with 10 lbs. Pools F and J each had 3 acres seeded with 200 lbs., Show had 205 lbs. over 3 acres, and Goose Pen 225 lbs. over 5 acres.
1939 Feb–Apr	800		Arrowwood Refuge, North Dakota	

1939 May–July		"State restriction on muskrat trapping is becoming a severe problem. For the past two years, initial growths of wild rice and American bulrush have been almost completely destroyed. Also, the plantings of hardstem bulrush and wild celery have been badly damaged. A series of field observations made on the growth of wild rice show that the proper environment exists on the refuge for this plant. If complete control of rats was allowed, we could have large beds of rice, better stands of bulrushes, and more luxuriant plots of some of the more valuable aquatics, such as wild celery. After the marsh and aquatic vegetation became established, muskrats within certain limits would be beneficial, because they would tend to open up extensive marsh beds, help in the control of weed species, and their houses might be of value as nesting sites for the diving ducks."		"Water fluctuations, especially sudden changes, are fatal to wild rice during June and July. Drops in water levels are conducive to the spread of vegetation of low value, primarily *Scirpus cyperinus* and some of the *Carex* spp."
1939 Aug–Oct	2,500			*Zizania aquatica* (nomenclature of that time)
1939 Nov–Jan 19				"Because of the prolonged mildness of the fall aquatic planting was continued into November. Wild rice was planted just before and during the freezeup. Planting of wild rice was done at this late date so that late remnants of the waterfowl flight would not eat the seed."
1941 May–July		"Gratifying indeed are some of the catches of wild rice, *Zizania aquatica*, in F pool, borne of the plants that are already over six feet tall and, from the appearance of the flowering stalks, should bear heavily this season. Three fine beds appear to have been established."		

1941 Feb–Apr		"One-fourth of all rice received was planted [in the fall of 1940] and the balance stored in Clear Creek, north of Seney, Michigan. This rice came through in fine shape and was planted on April 15 and 21 in select locations in the pools of Unit 1. The rice had begun to show slight signs of germination and was planted immediately thereafter. By April 30 most of the seed sown had germinated. It was noticed that refuge geese tore up many of the tender young sprouts. Blue-winged teal, black ducks, and mallards also showed signs of great interest in the young plants. On several occasions the planting sites were inspected and ducks and geese were observed not only feeding on seed, but also freely tearing up the young sprouts. The birds were chased away but invariably came back, for each visit was rewarded with the tell-tale marks of floating sprouts which had been uprooted. How to combat a situation of this kind is not known. Fencing and screening appears to be the only logical solution, but this seems like a very costly procedure."	Tamarac Refuge, Rice Lake Refuge	"22 man-days were expended by CCC during the last week in April in planting wild rice . . . The seed was stored over winter in a spring creek, and any apprehension that may be entertained by anyone does not seem to be justified. The germination was excellent. Seed received from Tamarac and Rice Lake International Wildlife Refuges in Minnesota."
1945 Jan–Dec	200			"Seedings made during this period were limited to the planting of 200 lbs of wild rice."
1947	200		Rice Lake Refuge	"The only aquatic planting made this period was 200 pounds of wild rice received from the Rice Lake Refuge. The shipment was received in good condition, well iced and apparently fertile. Due to the fact that the water level in T Pool had not reached the desired height at the time (the pool had been drained and fertilized during the summer) the rice was stored in the cooler of a local butcher shop. This was planted on October 27 as follows: T Pool 90 lbs, approximately 6 lbs, C-2 Pool 60 lbs., Approx. 4 acres, Show Pools and Goosepen 50 lbs., approximately 3 acres."

| 1949 | | | | "The aquatics are excellent. In many areas the geese ripped up the submerged plants; the wreckage of the celery beds was reminiscent of the black brant on the eel grass beds of Puget Sound. There is little room for improvement of this category. The emergents on the other hand, leave plenty to be wished for. Improvements should result from water manipulation, artificial planting, natural propagation, and in some instances, burning. Water manipulation gives greatest promise and is almost synonymous with natural propagation. Artificial propagation has promise for certain species as the roundstemmed bulrush and wild rice, but is pitifully slow and expensive. Burning should be a great value in dense stands of the so-called marsh hay types. Obviously, conditions must be exactly right, first to get the right degree of burn, and second, to minimize the danger of losing control of the fire, which is especially dreaded in this timbered country." |
| 1950 Sept–Dec | 100 | | Rice Lake Refuge | "… hundred pounds of wild rice was received from the Rice Lake Refuge in Minnesota and planted immediately in favorable locations throughout Units I & II." |

1951 Sept–Dec	438	"... uncovered promise of wild rice finally becoming established in small stands."	Rice Lake Refuge	"A total of 438 pounds of wild rice seed was received from the Rice Lake Refuge, This was immediately planted in the west bay of J pool and a canoe anchored in the middle for a scare-device. Because of excessive damage by rats and deer that often wiped out smaller stands it was considered advisable to concentrate the entire planting in one location. A total of 438 pounds of Wild Rice seed planted in west bay of J pool. 438 lbs. wild rice seed from the Rice Lake Refuge. Condition upon arrival appeared to be very good; it was planted immediately."
1952 Sept–Dec	200	"The wild rice planting in the west end of J pool suffered heavily this summer with deer, muskrats, ducks and geese all working it over. At one time geese mowed off the entire stand to a uniform height of about 4 inches above the water. Some seed was produced however but whether it will reproduce itself remains to be seen. The Wild Rice stand in C-I continued to flourish and expand."	Tamarac Refuge	"The only plantings for the period was that of 6 sacks of wild rice seed received from the Tamarac Refuge. This seed was planted September 23 in the inlet end of J pool, or about ¾ of a mile NE of last years plantings. Weight is estimated at 200 pounds as we are unable to find any record in our files. Some seed was produced however but whether it will reproduce itself remains to be seen. A second planting of wild rice was made in the northeast end of J pool. Perhaps if this can get a foothold it will take some of the pressure off the first planting.
1953 Sept–Dec	300		Rice Lake Refuge	
1954 Sept–Dec	2100		Rice Lake Refuge—A/B, Tamarac Refuge and local—C, Rice Lake Refuge—D, Tamarac—J, harvested 75 lbs from Mud Lake (marsh adjoining Tahquamenon River)	"Muskrats prefer wild rice, sedges, burreed. The only seed collected this period consisted of the 75 pounds of wild rice seed collected by refuge personnel. This was harvested in Mud Lake, a marshy body of water adjoining the Tahquamenon River northeast of McMillan. Collected by canoe 9/14—35 lbs, 9/15 40 lbs, received 625 lbs from Tamarac, 1400 lbs Rice Lake."

1956 Sept–Dec	11,131		9,991 pounds of wild rice seed from Rice Lake Refuge, 1,140 pounds of wild rice seed from Tamarac Refuge	"The unusually large amount of wild rice seed sowed this fall was a powerful attraction for ducks. The waterfowl food situation remained about the same this year with the exception of the wild rice planting. A total of 11,000 lbs. of wild rice was sowed in Unit I and C-3 pools between September 17 and October 3. In order to try to save some of the rice seed it was mixed with grain in hopes the ducks would take the grain first and bury the rice while feeding on the grain. The immediate result was that most of the ducks moved from one pool to the next with the rice sowing. We will not know how effective this was until next summer. A total of 11,131 pounds of wild rice seed was planted in the pools of Units I and III. A total of 11,131 pounds of wild rice seed was planted. Of this seed 1,140 pounds were received from the Tamarac Refuge, by Auto Freight; condition poor. The balance of 9,991 pounds was received from the Rice Lake Refuge by Railway Express and two loads on Service trucks; the condition was very good. 40 total acres planted."
1957	7,948	"The 11,131 pounds of wild rice seed, planted the previous fall, did quite well. However the seed production was very poor because of heavy grazing by the geese during the summer. The rice did provide a splendid source of browse."	Rice Lake Refuge	"Two truckloads of wild rice seed with a total of 7948 pounds were planted in A pool, beaver marsh below A pools, D pool, E pool, F pool and J pool of Unit I. All conditions were good. As usual the plantings were worked over by ducks and geese for a few days after the seed was scattered."
1958 Sept–Dec	6,600	"The 7948 lbs. of wild rice planted during the fall of 1957 did not mature to seed producing status. The plants and stems are clipped off repeatedly during the summer months by browsing activities of geese, deer and muskrat."	Rice Lake Refuge	"Approximately 5400 lbs. of wild rice received from Rice Lake Refuge was planted in I, J, Upper F, D, and C-3 Pools and in Sadie Willet Spur of the Riverside Dike on September 26. 1,200 lbs. were transferred to the Michigan Conservation Department."

1959 Jan–Apr	50			"Wild rice held over from last fall was seeded out in experimental plots in April— Approximately 50 lbs."
1968	800	"Last seedings were made in 1958. Only one (west end C-1) proved partially successful as deer and rats (perhaps geese too) clobbered the sprouts."	Tamarac Refuge	"Eight hundred pounds of rice picked up at Tamarac Refuge was planted to 15 acres in seven pool locations [A-1, A-1 Pool, E-1 Pool, F-1 Pool, J-1 Pool, North and South Show Pools] on September 14th. This trial was made in an effort to once again evaluate the ability of this plant to survive the deer, muskrats and water conditions of our pools."
1969		"Wild rice continued to grow in C-1. It appeared that geese grazed many of the plants before they had an opportunity to produce seed in the 1968 plantings on A-l, F-1, J-1 and the Show Pools. An unscheduled drawdown on J-1 (for spillway repairs) in August caused the loss of the plants that would have produced seed there. Production of seed was poor on all pools except C-1. The rice producing portions of this pool were heavily used by blacks, mallards, blue-winged teal and wooducks."		
1970		"The wild rice bed in the west end of C-1 produced well and appears to be expanding slowly into the pool. Only the A-l seepage area produced a scattered growth of the areas seeded to rice in the fall of 1968."		

1971		"The wild rice bed in west C-1 Pool appears to be expanding east along the shoreline and out into the pool. Heavy browsing by goslings on the staminate portions in June apparently did not harm the plants since seed was abundant on the plants in September, As many as 200 black ducks, mallards and wood ducks utilized the area in the fall. The water was clear and the average water depth where the rice plants grew was 10–12 inches. During September of 1968, seven areas in Unit I were planted with various amounts of wild rice. During September, 1971, each of these areas (A-1, C-1, E-1, F-1, J-1, North Show Pool and South Show Pool) were investigated to determine the success of the plantings and the location of any surviving rice was mapped. Wild rice was found in all but E-1 Pool. A drawdown in 1969 eliminated much of the rice in J-1 Pool. Most of the surviving plants on the east end were choked with submergent aquatics. The north planting in A-1 Pool contained scattered rice plants. Plants were thinly scattered on the south end and both areas received competition from *Brasenia schreberi* and other aquatics. Only a couple of plants survived in F-1 Pool. A few plants survived in the North and South Show Pools and appear to be choked as a result of siltation and encroaching emergent vegetation. Soil samples were taken at C-1 and J-1 Pools as well as C-2 and T-2 Pools to assist in determining if conditions are comparable for future plantings.		
1974		"Wild rice stands in west C-1 and A-1 seepage area produced well but have shown no evidence of farther expansion of the beds."		
1975		"Wild rice stands seem to be holding their own—but do not seem to be spreading."		
1984		"The wild rice bed in C-1 Pool still exists as a remnant artifact only."		
TOTAL	*33,437*			

Source: Compiled from Seney Annual Reports.

Bibliography

Adler, Richard. 2016. "The Impact of Cholera and Mosquito-Borne Disease in the 19th-Century Michigan Territory." Paper presented at the Michigan Mosquito Control Association 30th Annual Conference, Ann Arbor.

Aiken, S. G., P. F. Lee, D. Punter, and J. M. Steward. 1988. *Wild Rice in Canada*. Agriculture Canada.

Albert, Dennis A. 2003. *Between Land and Lake: Michigan's Great Lakes Coastal Wetlands*. Michigan State University Extension Bulletin, E-2902.

Albert, Dennis A., and Patrick J. Comer. 2008. *Atlas of Early Michigan's Forests, Grasslands, and Wetlands*. East Lansing: Michigan State University Press.

Alexander, Dave. 2012. "Natural Forces Create Uniqueness of Muskegon Lake." *NorthJersey.com*. June 4. http://www.northjersey.com.

Alexander, Jeff. 2006. *The Muskegon: The Majesty and Tragedy of Michigan's Rarest River*. East Lansing: Michigan State University Press.

Alma Record. 1887. "State News Condensed." February 11.

——. 1897. "State News." January 8.

Alpena Weekly. 1921, April 20.

Andreas, A. 1883. *History of the Upper Peninsula of Michigan*. Chicago: Western Historical Company.

Andrews, Israel DeWolfe. 1852. "Lake St. Clair." In *First Session of the 32nd Congress,* 11:192, 227. Washington, DC: U.S. Government Printing Office.

——— 1853. *Communication from the Secretary of the Treasury.* Washington, DC: Robert Armstrong, Printer.

———. 1976. *Report of Israel D. Andrews on the Trade and Commerce of the British North American Colonies, and upon the Trade of the Great Lakes and Rivers—1853.* Vol. 32. Ayer Co. Publishing. Manchester, NH.

Annual Report of the State Forester of Wisconsin. 1906. Vols. 1-4. Madison, WI: Democrat Printing Co., State Printer.

Appleton, D. 1881. *Appleton's General Guide to the United States and Canada: With Railway Maps, Plans of Cities, and Illustrations.* New York: D. Appleton and Company.

Arzigian, C. 2000. "Middle Woodland and Oneota Contexts for Wild Rice Exploitation in Southwestern Wisconsin." *Midcontinental Journal of Archaeology* 25: 245-68.

Associated Press. 2009. "Ford to Donate 242-Acre Monroe Marsh as Part of Detroit River International Wildlife Refuge." *MLive.* February 15. http://www.mlive.com/news/detroit/index.ssf/2010/02/ford_to_donate_242-acre_monroe.html.

Baird, John, and David R. Jones. 1919. *Michigan Game, Fish and Forests Biennial Report, 1917-1918.* Fort Wayne, IN: State Game, Fish and Forest Fire Department of the Public Domain Commission.

Barton, Gary J., and Norman G. Grannemann. 1998. *Water Resources of Lac Vieux Desert Indian Community and Vicinity, Western Upper Peninsula, Michigan.* Water-Resources Investigations Report 98-4051. U.S. Geological Survey.

Bates, John. 2001. *River Life: The Natural and Cultural History of a Northern River.* Mercer, WI: Manitowish River Press.

Biedes, Robert E. 1995. *Native American Communities in Wisconsin, 1600–1960: A Study of Tradition and Change.* Madison: University of Wisconsin Press.

Blair, Emma Helen. 1996. *The Indian Tribes of the Upper Mississippi Valley and Region of the Great Lakes: As Described by Nicolas Perrot, French Commandant in the Northwest; Bacqueville De La Potherie, French Royal Commissioner to Canada; Morrell Marston.* Lincoln: University of Nebraska Press.

Blois, John T. 1840. *Gazetteer of the State of Michigan.* New York: S. L. Rood and Company.

Blowe, Daniel. 1820. *A Geographical, Historical, Commercial, and Agricultural View of the United States of America.* London: Edwards and Knibb.

Bokern, James K. 1987. "History of the Primary Canoe Routes of the Six Bands of

Chippewa from the Lac Du Flambeau District." Master's thesis, University of Wisconsin-Stevens Point.

Bonnette, Donald J. 1998. "Ecosystem Management at Houghton Lake, Michigan with an Emphasis on Wild Rice (Zizania aquatica) Ecology." Master's thesis, Central Michigan University.

Bradford, Charles. 1917. *The American Angler.* New York: Angler's Publishing Company.

Bransky, James A. 1986. "Petition for Federal Recognition of the Lac Vieux Desert Band of Lake Superior Chippewa Indians." Petition presented to U.S. House of Representatives, Washington, DC.

Branstner, C. N. 1995. *Archaeological Investigations at the Cloudman Site (20CH6): A Multicomponent Native American Occupation on Drummond Island, Michigan 1992 and 1994 Excavations.* East Lansing: Department of Anthropology, Michigan State University.

Branstner, M. C., and M. J. Hambacher. 1995. *1991 Great Lakes Gas Transmission Limited Partnership Pipeline Expansion Projects: Phase III Investigations at the Casassa Site (20SA1021) Saginaw County, Michigan.* Williamston, MI: Great Lakes Research Associates, Inc.

Brinks, Herbert J. 1995. *Dutch American Voices: Letters from the United States, 1850–1930.* Ithaca, NY: Cornell University Press.

Brose, David S. 1974. *Preliminary Report of the 1974 Archaeological Survey of the Area around Burdickville, Leelanau Co., Michigan.* Lansing, MI: Department of State.

———. 2017. *The Dunn's Farm Site; 20LU22: A Late Middle Woodland Event in Northwest Michigan.* https://www.academia.edu/31549852/The_Dunns_Farm_Site_20LU22_A_Late_Middle_Woodland_Event_in_Northwest_Michigan.

Brown, Edgar, and Carl S. Scofield. 1903. *Wild Rice: Its Uses and Propagation.* Washington, DC: Government Printing Office.

Bulkley, John. 1913. *History of Monroe County Michigan: A Narrative Account of Its Historical Progress, Its People, and Its Principal Interests.* Vol. 1. Chicago and New York: Lewis Publishing Company.

Calumet News. 1909a. "Laurium: More Rice Is Planted." October 12.

———. 1909b, October 27.

———. 1909c. "Upper Peninsula: Planting Wild Rice." November 17.

———. 1910a. "Partridge Are Plentiful." August 11, sec. Sporting News of the World.

———. 1910b. "Laurium Department: Wild Rice Is Growing." August 19.

———. 1910c. "Laurium Department: Trout Season to Close; Sportsmen after Duck."

August 30.

———. 1910d. "Local Briefs." September 8.

———. 1911a. "Houghton Department: L'Anse Rod and Gun Club; Effort Will Be Made to Protect Game in Baraga County." February 6.

———. 1911b. "An Indian Harvest." September 11.

———. 1911c, September 9.

———. 1914. "Hancock Department: Propagating Game." September 29.

Campbell, Douglas H. 1886. "Plants of the Detroit River." *Bulletin of the Torrey Botanical Society* 13: 93-94.

Campbell, Henry Colin. 1898. "A Precursor of Marquette." *American Catholic Quarterly Review* 23: 248-59, 546.

Carlson, R. F. 1968. "Hydrology and Reservoir Control on the Wisconsin River Basin." Madison: University of Wisconsin Water Resources Center.

Carver, Jonathan. 1974. *Travels through the Interior Parts of North-America in the Years 1766, 1767, and 1768.* Toronto: Coles Publishing Company.

Cass City Chronicle. 1927. "State News in Brief: Monroe." October 14.

Cass City Chronicle. 1939. "Here and There around the Thumb." May 19.

Castle, Beatrice Hanscom. 1974. *The Grand Island Story.* Marquette, MI: John M. Longyear Research Library.

Catlin, George. 1866. *Illustrations of the Manners, Customs, and Condition of the North American Indians.* Vol. 1. London: Henry G. Bohn.

Cheruvelil, Jubin J., and Barbara Barton. 2014. "Wild Rice Adaptation to Climate Change." *ResearchGate.* https://www.researchgate.net/publication/260573079_Wild_Rice_Adaptation_to_Climate_Change.

Cole, Leon J. 1905. "German Carp in the United States." Washington, DC: Department of Commerce and Labor, Bureau of Fisheries. https://archive.org/details/germancarpinunit00cole.

Confer, Clarissa W. 2011. *Daily Life during the Sioux Indian Wars.* Santa Barbara, CA: Greenwood Press.

Cox, Isaac Joslin. 1905. *The Journeys of Rene Robert Cavelier, Sieur de La Salle.* Vol. 1. New York: Allerton Book Company.

Cram, Thomas Jefferson. 1841. "Report on the Survey of the Boundary between the State of Michigan and Territory of Wiskonsin." In *Message from the President of the United States,* 18. Washington, DC: Senate, 26th Congress, 2d Session.

Crawford Avalanche. 1881a. "Faber Fancies." April 7.

———. 1881b. "Faber Fancies." May 19.

———. 1896a. "Mirror of Michigan." August 20.

———. 1896b. "Mirror of Michigan." September 10.

———. 1897. "State of Michigan." April 15.

Crawford, Gary W., and David G. Smith. 2003. "Paleoethnobotany in the Northeast." In *People and Plants in Ancient Eastern North America*, ed. Paul E. Minnis, 172–257. Washington, DC: Smithsonian Books.

Danek, L. J., and J. H. Saylor. 1975. *Saginaw Bay Water Circulation*. Fluid dynamic measurements. NOAA Technical Report No. ERL359-GLERL 6. Ann Arbor, MI: U.S. Department of Commerce.

Davis, Charles Moler. 1964. *Readings in the Geography of Michigan*. Ann Arbor, MI: Ann Arbor Publishers.

Darby, William. 1827. *Darby's Universal Gazetteer*. Philadelphia: Bennett and Walton.

David, Peter. 2013a. *Manoomin (Wild Rice) Enhancement and Research in the Ceded Territories in 2011*. Report No. 13-5. Odanah, WI: Great Lakes Indian Fish and Wildlife Commission.

———. 2013b. *Manoomin (Wild Rice) Enhancement and Research in the Ceded Territories in 2012*. Report No. 13-9. Odanah, WI: Great Lakes Indian Fish and Wildlife Commission.

de Castro, Marcia Caldas, Roberto L. Monte-Mór, Diana O. Sawyer, and Burton H. Singer. 2006. "Malaria Risk on the Amazon Frontier." *Proceedings of the National Academy of Sciences of the United States of America* 103 (7): 2452–57.

Densmore, Frances. 1949. *A Study of Some Michigan Indians*. Anthropological Papers, Museum of Anthropology, University of Michigan. Ann Arbor, MI: University of Michigan Press.

———. 2014. *Chippewa Customs*. St. Paul: Minnesota Historical Society Press.

Detroit Free Press. 1868. "Long Point, Lake Erie: The Peninsula Abounding in Game." July 17.

———. 1871a. "Local Matters." August 18.

———. 1871b, August 24.

———. 1881. "General Items." September 21.

———. 1886, November 17.

———. 1889, November 3.

———. 1896a. "Belongs to the State: Submerged Lands under Lake Erie and Detroit." July 9.

———. 1896b, December 27.

———. 1896c. "Held a Cocking Main: They Protest against the Sowing of Wild Rice by Sportsmen." December 27.

———. 1901a. "All around the State." April 19.

———. 1901b. "America's Wild Rice: Furnished Wholesome Support for Traders and Hunters Years Ago." November 18.

———. 1902a. "Beautiful Tawas Beach to Be Opened as a Summer Resort July 1." April 27.

———. 1902b, April 27.

———. 1906a. "Duck Season Open: More Birds Than Ever Before on Monroe Marshes." September 2.

———. 1906b, September 2.

———. 1906c. "Hunters Paradise." September 30.

———. 1906d, September 30.

———. 1906e. "Morbid Mob at Funeral." October 17.

———. 1906f, October 17.

———. 1908. "As They Look from the Airship." August 18.

———. 1911. "Creating a Bird Paradise." November 5.

———. 1921. "Monroe Marsh Swept by Fire, Ducks Suffer." December 2.

———. 1930. "A Feast Awaits Ducks up around Wildfowl Bay." September 28.

Detroit News. 1915, November 1.

Detroit News/Tribune. 1902, October 19.

Diamond Drill. 1909. "Planting Wild Rice." November 13. Crystal Falls, MI.

"A Disappointing Duck Season." 1919. *Bulletin of the American Game Protective Association* (January).

Dobie, Richard, et al. 1888. "Numbers and Location of Indian Tribes." In *Historical Collections: Collections and Researches Made by the Michigan Pioneer and Historical Society Including Reports of Officers and Papers Read at the Annual Meeting of 1887,* 11:486. Lansing, MI: Thorp and Godfrey.

Dock, George. 1903. "Mosquitoes and Malaria, with Some Observations in Michigan." In *Proceedings and Addresses of the Sixth General Conference of the Health Officials in Michigan,* 40-48. Lansing, MI: Robert Smith Printing Company.

Dodge, C. K. 1914. "The Flowering Plants, Ferns, and Fern Allies Growing without Cultivation in Lambton, Ontario." In *Sixteenth Report of the Michigan Academy of Science*, 1:132-200. Lansing, MI: Wynkoop Hallenbeck Crawford Company.

———. 1921. *Miscellaneous Papers on the Botany of Michigan*. Vol. 31. Michigan Geological and Biological Survey 6. Lansing, MI: Wynkoop Hallenbeck Crawford Company.

Ducks Unlimited. 2007. *A Planning Tool for Sustaining and Improving the Health of Saginaw Bay's Coastal Habitat*. Conservation Report. Bay City, MI: Saginaw Bay Watershed Initiative Network.

Dunham, Sean. 2008. "Wild Rice in the Eastern Upper Peninsula: A Review of the Evidence." Paper presented at the Michigan Academy of Science, Arts & Letters, Botany and Plant Ecology, Western Michigan University, March 7. http://www.academia.edu/2027259/Wild_Rice_in_the_Eastern_Upper_Peninsula_A_Review_of_the_Evidence.

Durant, Samuel W. 1877. *History of Oakland County, Michigan*. Philadelphia: L. H. Everts and Company. http://name.umdl.umich.edu/BAD1021.0001.001.

Durbin, Richard D. 1997. *The Wisconsin River: An Odyssey through Time and Space*. Cross Plains, WI: Spring Freshet Press.

Durham, Charles. 1910. "The Reservoir Possibilities of the Sources of the Mississippi and Tributaries of the Upper Mississippi River with Reference to the Improvement of Navigation." *Engineering News* 63 (3): 63.

Dustin, Fred. 1915. "Saginaw County as a Center of Aboriginal Population." In *Michigan Historical Collections*, 39:299-308. Lansing, MI: Michigan Historical Society.

East Saginaw Courier. 1859, August 18.

Ellis, Franklin. 1880. "City of Howell." In *History of Livingston Co., Michigan: With Illustrations and Biographical Sketches of Its Prominent Men and Pioneers*, 181. Philadelphia: Everts and Abbott.

Evening News. 1897, February 19. Detroit.

Evening News, The. 1900, October 11. Mendon, MI.

Everett, Franklin, A.M. 1878. *Memorials of the Grand River Valley*. Chicago: Chicago Legal News Company.

Evers, David C. 1992. *A Guide to Michigan's Endangered Wildlife*. Ann Arbor: University of Michigan Press.

Falck, Miles. 1997. *Results of the 1997 Wild Rice (Manoomin) Survey in the 1842 Ceded Territory of Michigan*. Report No. 97-15. Odanah, WI: Great Lakes Indian Fish and

Wildlife Commission.

Farmer, Silas. 1878. "Map of Detroit River." Guide and Souvenir to Detroit. Detroit: Silas Farmer and Company.

———. 1890. *History of Detroit and Wayne County and Early Michigan: A Chronological Cyclopedia of the Past and Present.* Detroit: Silas Farmer and Company.

Farwell, Oliver Atkins. 1900. "A Catalogue of the Flora of Detroit." *Michigan Academy of Science*: 31-68.

Ferris, Jacob. 1856. *The States and Territories of the Great West.* New York: Miller, Orton, and Mulligan.

Fjetland, Conrad Alan. 1973. "History of Water Management at Seney National Wildlife Refuge." Master's thesis, Michigan State University.

Flint Daily Journal. 1905, November 4.

———. 1914, June 19.

———. 1920, September 18.

Flint Journal. 1913, November 17.

Foote, L. S. 1917. "Michigan Fish and Game." *American Angler.*

Ford, Henry. 1908. "Historical Detroit." In *Michigan Historical Collections*, 10:96. Lansing, MI: Wynkoop Hallenbeck Crawford Company.

Ford, Richard I., and David S. Brose. 1975. "Prehistoric Wild Rice from the Dunn Farm Site, Leelanau County, Michigan." *Wisconsin Archaeologist* 56 (1): 5-15.

Forest and Stream. 1888. "The Monroe Marshes." May 10.

Fornace, Kimberly M., Tommy Rowel Abidin, Neal Alexander, Paddy Brock, Matthew J. Grigg, Amanda Murphy, Timothy William, Jayaram Menon, Chris J. Drakely, and Jonathan Cox. 2016. "Association between Landscape Factors and Spatial Patterns of *Plasmodium Knowlesi* Infections in Sabah, Malaysia." *Emerging Infectious Diseases* 22 (2): 201-8.

Foster, Richard G. 1954. *Houghton Lake Level Control Special Engineering Investigation, Reedsburg Dam—Hydro (Drawdown) Test.* Lansing: Michigan Department of Conservation.

———. 1956. *Lac Vieux Desert Level Control.* Engineering Investigation. Gogebic County, Michigan, and Vilas County, Wisconsin: Michigan Department of Conservation Engineering and Architecture.

Fox, Truman B. 1868. *History of the Saginaw Valley: Its Resources, Progress and Business Interests.* East Saginaw, MI: Daily Courier Steam Job Print.

Francis, George. 1885. *The Sportsman's Guide to the Northern Lakes: With Hints on*

Fishing, Hunting, and Trapping. Chicago: G. F. Thomas.

Fuller, Kent, and Harvey Shear, eds. 1995. *The Great Lakes: An Environmental Atlas and Resource Book.* 3rd ed. Government of Canada and the U.S. Environmental Protection Agency. http://www.epa.gov/glnpo/atlas/glat-ch3.html.

Gansser, Augustus H. 1905. *History of Bay County, Michigan and Representative Citizens.* Chicago: Richmond and Arnold.

Garfield, Charles W. 1886. "The Forestry Problem." In *Annual Report of the Secretary of the State Horticultural Society of Michigan,* 69-128. Michigan State Horticultural Society.

Garg, Teevart. 2014. "Public Health Effects of Ecosystem Degradation." Job Market Paper. Ithaca, NY: Cornell University.

Geare, R. I. 1915. "Wild Rice of the Upper Great Lakes." *Merck's Report* 24 (9): 216-17.

Geiger, J. C., and W. C. Purdy. 1919. "Experimental Mosquito Control in Ricefields." *Journal of the American Medical Association* 72 (11): 774-79.

George A. Ogle and Company. 1900. *Standard Atlas of Newaygo County, Michigan: Including a Plat Book of the Villages, Cities and Townships of the County . . . patrons Directory, Reference Business Directory and Departments Devoted to General Information.* Chicago: George A. Ogle and Company. http://archive.org/details/3927906.0001.001.umich.edu.

————. 1915. "Standard Atlas of Clinton County, Michigan: Including a Plat Book of the Villages, Cities and Townships of the County . . . patrons Directory, Reference Business Directory . . ." Chicago: George A. Ogle and Company. http://catalog.hathitrust.org/Record/002911327.

Getsinger, Kurt D., Angela G. Poovey, R. Michael Steward, Michael J. Grodowitz, Michael J. Maceina, and Raymond M. Newman. 2002. *Management of Eurasian Milfoil in Houghton Lake, Michigan. Workshop Summary.* Report No. ERDC/EL TR-02-24. Washington, DC: U.S. Army Corps of Engineers.

Gibbes, Heneage. 1888. "The Pathology of Acute Miliary Tuberculosis." In *Transactions of the Michigan State Medical Society for the Year 1888,* 12:124-43. Detroit: O.S. Gulley, Bornman and Company.

Glyshaw, Paul, and Elizabeth Wason. 2016. "*Anopheles Quadrimaculatus.*" *Animal Diversity Web.* http://animaldiversity.org/accounts/Anopheles_quadrimaculatus/.

Goodrich, S. G. 1832. *A System of Universal Geography, Popular and Scientific, Comprising a Physical, Political and Statistical Account of the World . . . Illustrated by Engravings, Etc.* Boston: Carter, Hendee and Co.

Graham, James Duncan. 1859. *Lake Michigan—Harbors Of. Report for the Year 1857. Annual Report . . . on the Improvement of the Harbors of Lakes Michigan, St. Clair, Erie, Ontario, and Champlain.* Washington, DC: N.p.

Grant Area Yesterday-Today. 1979. Grant, MI: Grant Public Library.

Great Lakes Indian Fish and Wildlife Commission. 2010. *Circle of Flight.* Odanah, WI: Great Lakes Indian Fish and Wildlife Commission.

Greenberg, Joel. 2002. *A Natural History of the Chicago Region.* Chicago: University of Chicago Press.

Gulig, Anthony G. 2007. *An Historical Analysis of the Saginaw, Black River, and Swan Creek Chippewa Treaties of 1855 and 1864.* Whitewater: University of Wisconsin, Whitewater.

Hager, Daniel. 2001. "Michigan Settlers vs. Malaria, or How the Midwest Was Won." Mackinac Center for Public Policy. August 2. http://www.mackinac.org/3574.

Hahn, Micah B., Ronald E. Gangnon, Christovam Barcellos, Gregory P. Asner, and Jonathan A. Patz. 2014. "Influence of Deforestation, Logging, and Fire on Malaria in the Brazilian Amazon." *PLoS ONE* 9 (1): 1–8. https://doi.org/10.1371/journal.pone.0085725.

Hallock, Charles, and William A. Bruette. 1888. "The Monroe Marsh Case." *Forest and Stream* 30 (May): 350–51.

Hambacher, Michael J., James A. Robertson, and Donald J. Weir. 2009. *Phase III Archaeological Investigations along the Flint River, Saginaw County, Michigan.* FEMA Flint River Flood Control Project. R-0622. Jackson, MI: Commonwealth Cultural Resources Group, Inc.

Hambacher, Michael J, Kelly Hagenmaier, Kathryn E. Parker, Kathryn C. Egan-Bruhy, Terrance J. Martin, Randall Schaetzl, Jammi Ladwig, Linda Scott Cummings, Mary Malainey, Christopher T. Espenshade, and Timothy Figol. 2016. *Phase II and Phase III Archaeological Investigations at 20OT344, 20OT283, and 20OT3 for the US-31/M-231 Holland to Grand Haven Bypass Project, Ottawa County, Michigan.* Report #R-0960. Lansing: Michigan Department of Transportation.

Hamtramck. 1858. "Incidents of the War of 1812." *Detroit Daily Free Press,* August 8.

Hanley, Elizabeth Hines. 1926. *Pageant of Historic Monroe, June 23–24, 1926, Monroe, Michigan.* Lamour Printing Company.

Hansen, D. 2008. *Natural Wild Rice in Minnesota: A Wild Rice Study Document Submitted to the Minnesota Legislature by the Minnesota Department of Natural Resources, February 15, 2008.* Duluth: Minnesota Department of Natural Resources.

Hayden, Jim. 2009. "Five Decades Ago, Titanic Tornado Took Out

Century-Old Lighthouse." *Holland Sentinel*, April 2, sec. News Now. http://www. hollandsentinel.com/article/20090402/NEWS/304029862.

Heilman, Mark A., Kurt D. Getsinger, and Anthony F. Groves. 2003. "Management of Eurasian Watermilfoil in Houghton Lake, Michigan." *Michigan Riparian* 38 (4) (November): 17-21.

Helminiak, Jon. 2011. *Land O' Lakes*. Charleston, SC: Arcadia Publishing.

Herms, William Brodbeck. 1913. *Malaria: Cause and Control*. New York: Macmillan.

Herrick, Harold. 1910. "Ducks at Monroe, Michigan." *The Auk* 27 (1): 76-77.

Hickerson, Harold. 1974. *Ethnohistory of Chippewa in Central Minnesota*. New York: Garland Publishing.

Hill, E. J. 1891. "*Zizania* as Found by the Explorers of the Northwest." *Bulletin of the Torrey Botanical Society* 18 (2): 57-60.

Hinsdale, Wilbert B. 1931. *Archaeological Atlas of Michigan*. Ann Arbor: University of Michigan Press.

Historical Collections and Researches of the Michigan Pioneers and Historical Society. 1888. Vol. 11. Lansing, MI: Thorp and Godfrey.

Historical Society of Michigan. 1834. *Historical and Scientific Sketches of Michigan: Comprising a Series of Discourses Delivered before the Historical Society of Michigan, and Other Interesting Papers Relative to the Territory*. Detroit: Stephen Wells and George L. Whitney.

History of Bay County, Michigan, with Illustrations and Biographical Sketches of Some of Its Prominent Men and Pioneers. 1883. Chicago: H. R. Page and Co.

History of Calhoun County, Michigan with Illustrations Descriptive of Its Scenery, Palatial Residences, Public Buildings . . . 1877. Philadelphia: L. H. Everts and Company.

Hollister, C. E. 1884. "Drainage of Large Marshes." *Scientific American Supplement*, March 22.

Holmes, J. C. 1851. *Transactions of the State Agricultural Society, with Reports of County Agricultural Societies, for 1850*. Lansing, MI: R. W. Ingals.

Holmes, John C. 1907. "Narrative Concerning the Knaggs Farm, and the Knaggs Windmill, Located in Springwells, Near Detroit." In *Michigan Historical Collections of the Pioneer Society of the State of Michigan*, 4:500-502. Lansing, MI: Wynkoop Hallenbeck Crawford Company.

Hough, E. 1890a. "The Clubs of the St. Clair Flats, Part I." *Forest and Stream*, August 28.

———. 1890b. "The Clubs of St. Clair Flats, Part II." *Forest and Stream*, September 4.

———. 1890c. "The Clubs of St. Clair Flats, Part III." *Forest and Stream*, September 11.

———. 1900. "Chicago and the West: A New Sport in the West." *Forest and Stream*, October 6.

Houghton Lake Improvement Board. 2016. "Aquatic Plant Control." http://www. houghtonlakeboard.org/AquaticPlantControl.aspx.

Hubbard, Bela. 1887. "Birds of My Neighborhood—1850." In *Memorials of a Half-Century*, 286. New York: G. P. Putnam and Sons.

Hubbard, Leonidas, Jr. 1901. "Sportsmen's Clubs of the Middle West." *Outing: An Illustrated Magazine of Sport, Travel, Adventure and Country Life*. October.

Huggler, T. 1985. *Hunt Michigan! How To, Where To, When To*. Lansing: Michigan United Conservation Clubs.

Hulst, Cornelia Steketee. 1912. *Indian Sketches: Père Marquette and the Last of the Pottawatomie Chiefs*. New York: Longmans, Green and Company.

Hunding, C., and R. Lange. 1978. "Ecotoxicology of Aquatic Plant Communities." In *Principles of Ecotoxicology*, 239-55. New York: John Wiley and Sons.

Hungerford, Austin. 1880. "New Buffalo Township." In *History of Berrien County Michigan*, 270-78. Philadelphia: D. W. Ensign and Company.

Hunt, George S., and Howard E. Ewing. 1953. "Industrial Pollution and Michigan Waterfowl." In *Transactions of the Eighteenth North American Wildlife Conference*, 360-68. Washington, DC: Wildlife Management Institute.

Hunt, G. S. 1963. "Wild Celery in the Lower Detroit River." *Ecology* 44 (2): 361-70.

Hunter, James K. 1916. "Public Domain Commission Minutes, May 2, 1916." Lansing, MI: Office of the Public Domain Commission.

Houghton Lake Resorter. 2010. "Lake Association Plants Wild Rice in Houghton Lake, Flats and Muskegon." June 17, http://www.houghtonlakeresorter.com/news/2010-06-17/Outdoors/Lake_Association_plants_wild_rice_in_Houghton_Lake.html.

"Indians Harvesting Mah-No-Men (Wild Rice) at Lac Vieux Desert." 1940. *Michigan Education Journal* (November).

International Joint Commission. 1951. "Report of the International Joint Commission of the United States and Canada on the Pollution of Boundary Waters." Washington, DC, and Ottawa: International Joint Commission.

Ironwood Daily Globe. 1956a. "Committee Will Study a Report." November 19.

———. 1956b. "Proceedings for Control of Lake Level Reported." December 15.

Isham, Warren. 1849. "Notes by the Way: The Farm of Bela Hubbard, Esq." *Michigan Farmer*, January 1.

J. E. Tiffany and Sons. 2016. *2016 Dam Inspection Report for Houghton Lake Level Control Structure, Roscommon County*. Roscommon, MI: Roscommon County Board of Commissioners.

Jackson Citizen Patriot. 1922. "Poorest Land 20 Years Ago Now Is State's Best." December 7.

Jackson Daily Citizen. 1903, November 4.

Janette, Fred. 1928. "Pagan Indian Tribe in Michigan Wilds." *Detroit News*, October 28.

Jenks, Albert Ernest. 1901. *The Wild Rice Gatherers of the Upper Lakes: A Study in American Primitive Economics*. Washington, DC: U.S. Government Printing Office.

Johnson, J. A., and A. J. Havranek. 2013. *Effectiveness of Temporary Carp Barriers for Restoring Wild Rice Beds in Upper Clam Lake: 2010 to 2013*. Report to St. Croix Tribal Environmental Services. Webster, WI: St. Croix Tribal Environmental Services, Natural Resources Department.

Johnston, James Dale. 1855. *The Detroit City Directory and Advertising Gazetteer of Michigan for 1855–56*. Detroit: R. F. Johnstone and Company.

Kaeding, Danielle. 2015. "Wild Rice Beds Re-emerge Following Carp Elimination Efforts." *Wisconsin Outdoor Report*, Wisconsin Public Radio.

Karamanski, Theodore J. 1989. *Deep Woods Frontier: A History of Logging in Northern Michigan*. Detroit: Wayne State University Press.

Kedzie, R. C. 1874. "Report on the Resolutions, Referred to the Section on State Medicine and Public Hygiene, on the Use of Alcoholic Liquors, and the Establishment of a National Sanitary Bureau, and the Influence of Drainage on Public Health in Michigan." In *Transactions of the American Medical Association*, 25:401–24. Philadelphia: Collins.

———. 1880. "A Talk on Water Supply." In *Proceedings and Addresses at a Sanitary Convention*, 48–58. Lansing, MI: W. S. George and Company.

Kellogg, J. H. 1882. "The Climate of Michigan." In *Good Health*, 342–43. Battle Creek, MI: Good Health Publishing Company.

Kennedy, Stiles. 1872. "Malaria in Michigan." In *Magnetic and Mineral Springs of Michigan*, 23–25. Wilmington, DE: James and Webb, Publishers and Printers.

Kilar, Jeremy W. 1990. *Michigan's Lumbertowns: Lumbermen and Laborers in Saginaw, Bay City, and Muskegon, 1870–1905*. Detroit: Wayne State University Press.

Kincaid, R. E. 1975. "Draining of Rice Lake." In *The Beginnings of Grant*. Grant, MI: Grant Public Library.

Kinietz, William Vernon. 1947. *Chippewa Village: The Story of Katikitegon.* Bloomfield Hills, MI: Cranbrook Institute of Science.

Kroll, Roy W., Johan F. Gottgens, and Brian P. Swartz. 1997. "Wild Rice to Rip-Rap: 120 Years of Habitat Changes and Management of a Lake Erie Coastal Marsh." In *Transactions of the 62nd North American Wildlife and Natural Resources Conference,* 490–500. Washington, DC.

Lacy, Thomas F. 1976. "Stalking Wild Rice and Other Goodies." *Washtenaw Impressions,* Washtenaw County Historical Society. September.

Lake County (MI) Star. 1884. "The News around the State." September 25.

Lake, D. J., B. N. Griffing, F. (Frederick) Bourquin, and Worley and Bracher. 1873. "Atlas of Clinton County, Michigan." Map. Philadelphia: C. O. Titus. https://www.loc.gov/item/2010587156/.

Lee, P. F., and J. M. Stewart. 1982. "Ecological Relationships of Wild Rice, *Zizania Aquatica* 2. Sediment—Plant Tissue Nutrient Relationships." *Canadian Journal of Botany* 61 (6): 1775–84.

Leeson, Michael A. and Damon Clarke. 1881. *The History of Saginaw County, Michigan.* Chicago: Charles C. Chapman and Company.

Leeson, M. A. 1882. *History of Macomb County, Michigan: Containing an Account of Its Settlement, Growth, Development and Resources . . . churches, Schools and Societies; Portraits of Prominent Men and Early Settlers . . .* Chicago: M. A. Leeson and Company.

Leeson, Michael A. 1881. *The History of Saginaw County, Michigan.* Chicago: C.C. Chapman and Company.

Leonardi, Joseph M. 2008. *Status of the Fishery Resource Report: Murphy Lake.* Report No. 2008-44. Lansing: Michigan Department of Natural Resources.

Le Prince, J. A. A. 1915a. "Malaria Control: Drainage as an Antimalarial Measure." In *Public Health Reports (1896–1970)* 30 (8): 536–45. Washington, DC: Government Printing Office. http://www.jstor.org/stable/4571955.

———. 1915b. "Control of Malaria: Oiling as an Antimosquito Measure." *Public Health Reports* 30 (9): 599–608.

Leverett, Frank. 1909. "Open File Report XLV: Field Notes of Frank Leverett." General Land Office Surveyor Notes, Notebook No. 232-Leverett, U.S. General Land Office Surveys. Michigan and Wisconsin: U.S. Geological Survey. http://www.michigan.gov/documents/deq/OFR_45_Leverett_NB232_306628_7.pdf.

Lexden. 1898a. "Down the Wisconsin Part One." *Forest and Stream,* October 8.

———. 1898b. "Down the Wisconsin Part Two." *Forest and Stream,* October 15.

Longyear, J. M., and J. M. Case. 1884. *Forests, Streams, Lakes, and Resources of Northern Michigan*. Marquette, MI: L. P. Crary.

Lovis, W., K. Egan-Bruhy, B. Smith, and G. Monaghan. 2001a. "Wetlands and Emergent Horticultural Economies in the Upper Great Lakes: A New Perspective from the Schultz Site." *American Antiquity* 66 (4): 615–32.

Lovis, W. A., G. W. Monaghan, and J. A. Robertson. 2001b. "Landscape Change and the Late Archaic Occupation of the Lower Saginaw River in Bay City." Paper presented at the Midwest Archaeological Conference, La Crosse, Wisconsin.

Lyon, Lucius. 1825. "Notes from the Internal Lines Survey of Marengo Township in Calhoun County, Michigan in 1825." General Land Office Surveyor Notes. http://seekingmichigan.contentdm.oclc.org/cdm/compoundobject/collection/p16317coll7/id/50187/rec/1.

Lyster, Henry F. 1876. "Influence of Drainage in Removing Certain Forms of Disease, and in Promoting the Healthfulness of Cities." In *Third Annual Report of the Secretary of the State Board of Health of the Fiscal Year Ending September 30, 1875*, 149–60. Lansing, MI: W. S. George and Company.

———. 1880. "The Reclaiming of Drowned Lands." In *Seventh Annual Report of the Secretary of the State Board of Health of the State of Michigan for the Fiscal Year Ending September 30, 1879*, 233–60. Lansing, MI: W. S. George and Company.

———. 1883. "The State with Reference to Malarious Diseases." In *Michigan and Its Resources*, 70–72. Lansing, MI: W. S. George and Company.

Mackenthun, Kenneth Marsh, and William Marcus Ingram. 1967. *Biological Associated Problems in Freshwater Environments: Their Identification, Investigation and Control*. Washington, DC: U.S. Government Printing Office.

Malhiot, François Victor. 1910. "A Wisconsin Fur Trader's Journal—1804–05." In *Collections of the State Historical Society of Wisconsin*, 19:163–233, 489–528. Madison: Wisconsin Historical Society.

Manny, Bruce A., Thomas A. Edsall, and Eugene Jaworski. 1988. "The Detroit River, Michigan: An Ecological Profile." Biological Report 85 (7.17). Washington, DC: U.S. Fish and Wildlife Service.

Mansfield, John Brandt. 1899. *History of the Great Lakes*. Vol. 1. Chicago: J. H. Beers & Company.

McCrimmon, Hugh R. 1968. *Carp in Canada*. Ottawa: Fisheries Research Board of Canada.

McDonald, Malcolm E. 1951. "The Ecology of the Pointe Mouillee Marsh, Michigan, with Special Reference to the Biology of Cat-Tail (Typha)." Ann Arbor:

University of Michigan.

———. 1955. "Cause and Effects of a Die-off of Emergent Vegetation." *Journal of Wildlife Management* 19 (1): 24-35.

McGaffey, Ernest. 1892a. *Atlas of Newaygo County, Michigan.* Philadelphia: C. O. Titus. http://archive.org/details/3927793.0001.001.umich.edu.

———. 1892b. *Poems of Gun and Rod.* New York: C. Scribner's Sons. http://archive.org/details/poemsgunandrod00mcgagoog.

McLure, John. 1903. "Sebewaing Harbor (River), Saginaw Bay, Michigan." In *Report of the Chief Engineer of the U.S. Army,* 1140-41. Washington, DC: U.S. Government Printing Office.

McVicar, Brian. 2010. "Efforts to Reintroduce Wild Rice in Muskegon Lake Unsuccessful." *Mlive,* October 6. http://www.mlive.com/news/muskegon/index.ssf/2010/10/wild_rice_efforts_in_muskegon.html.

Mershon, W. B. 1923. *Recollections of My Fifty Years Hunting and Fishing.* Boston: Stratford Company.

Michigan Department of Agriculture. 2002. *Michigan Mosquito Manual.* Lansing: Michigan Department of Agriculture.

Michigan Department of Conservation. 1941. *Michigan Conservation.* Lansing: Michigan Department of Conservation.

Michigan Department of Conservation. n.d. *Survey of Wild Rice Plantings in Michigan.* Report No. 1022. Lansing: Michigan Department of Conservation.

———. 1959. *Proceedings of Conservation Commission.* Vol. 39. Lansing: Michigan Department of Conservation.

———. 1929. "Waterfowl." In *State of Michigan Department of Conservation Fifth Biennial Report,* 279-85. Lansing: Michigan Department of Conservation.

Michigan Department of Natural Resources. 1987. "Remedial Action Plan for Muskegon Lake AOC." Lansing: Michigan Department of Natural Resources.

———. 2016. "Tahquamenon River Basin Wetlands Management Area Summary." Lansing: Michigan Department of Natural Resources. http://www.midnr.com/publications/pdfs/forestslandwater/Ecosystem/EUP/final-MAsummaries/29_Tahquamenon_River_Basin_Wetlands_MA_summary_3_6.pdf.

Michigan Department of Natural Resources and Ontario Ministry of the Environment. 1991. "Stage 1 Remedial Action Plan for the Detroit River Area of Concern." Lansing: Michigan Department of Natural Resources.

Michigan Department of Transportation. 2014. *Michigan's Railroad History—1825-2014.*

Lansing: Michigan Department of Transportation. https://www.michigan.gov/documents/mdot/Michigan_Railroad_History_506899_7.pdf.

Michigan Education Portal for Interactive Content. 2016. "A Brief History of Lumbering in Michigan." *Michigan EPIC*. http://www.michigan-history.org/lumbering/LumberingBriefHistory.html.

Michigan Geological Survey. 1921. *Inland Lakes of Michigan*. Geological Series 25, Publication 30. Lansing, MI: Wynkoop Hallenbeck Crawford Company.

Michigan Natural Resources Commission. 1951. *Proceedings of Michigan Natural Resources Commission*. Lansing: Michigan Natural Resources Commission.

Michigan State Board of Health. 1894. "Alleged Nuisances in Michigan in 1891." In *20th Annual Report of the Michigan Department of Health*, 302-19. Lansing, MI: Robert Smith Printing Company.

Michigan's 50 Best Fishing Lakes: The State's Top Inland Waters. 1984. Lansing: Michigan United Conservation Clubs.

Miller, Albert. 1878. "Past and Probable Future of the Saginaw Bay Marshes from Personal Observation." Report of the Secretary, Michigan State Board of Agriculture. http://www.bay-journal.com.

———. 1890. "The Rivers of the Saginaw Valley Sixty Years Ago." In *Michigan Pioneer and Historical Society*, 14:495-510. Lansing, MI: Darius D. Thorp.

———. 1910. "Saginaw One Hundred Years Ago and the Origins of a Band of Indians, and a Name of a Locality in Genesee County." In *Collections and Researches Made by the Michigan Pioneer and Historical Society*, 17:446-49. Lansing, MI: Wynkoop Hallenbeck Crawford Company.

Miller, Herbert J. 1943. *Wild Rice in Michigan*. Conservation Report 2068. Lansing: Michigan Department of Conservation.

———. 1946a. *Report on the Grand River Marshes in Ottawa County*. Conservation Report 901. Lansing: Michigan Department of Conservation.

———. 1946b. *Report on Examination of Waterfowl Food Plantings on the Grand River Marshes near the City of Grand Haven*. Conservation Report 903. Lansing: Michigan Department of Conservation.

———. 1946c. *Sebewaing Bay Waterfowl Sanctuary*. Conservation Report 913. Lansing: Michigan Department of Conservation.

———. 1946d. *Report on Waterfowl Food Plantings at Middle Grounds on Saginaw Bay—Spring 1945*. DNR Report 914. Saginaw: Michigan Department of Natural Resources.

———. 1947. *Report on Duck Losses at Monroe and Erie Marshes*. DNR Report 647.

Monroe: Michigan Department of Natural Resources.

———. 1962a. "Development and Preservation of Wildlife Habitat on the Great Lakes Shoreline." Talk presented at the Semi-Annual Meeting of Great Lakes Commission, Mackinac Island, MI, July 23.

———. 1962b. *Pollution Problems in Relation to Wildlife Losses, Particularly Waterfowl, Detroit River and Lake Erie*. Report No. 2371. Lansing: Michigan Department of Conservation

Miller, Herbert J., and S. C. Whitlock. 1948. "Detroit River Waterfowl Mortality—Winter 1948." *Michigan Conservation Magazine*.

Monroe Commercial. 1871. "Wild Rice for Printing Paper." September 7.

Moore, Charles. 1915. *History of Michigan*. Vol. 1. Chicago: Lewis Publishing Company.

Moore, Lynn. 2015. "Lumber Mill Debris Being Dredged from Muskegon Lake as Part of $5 Million Cleanup." *Mlive*, October 1. http://www.mlive.com/news/muskegon/index.ssf/2015/10/lumber_mill_debris_being_dredg.html.

Morse, Grant M. 1903. *Eighth Biennial Report of the State Game and Fish Warden, 1901–1902*. Lansing, MI: Robert Smith Printing Company.

Morton, James Walter. 1977. "Ecological Effects of Dredging and Dredge Spoil Disposal: A Literature Review." *Technical Papers of the US Fish and Wildlife Service*, no. 94: 33.

"Muck Farmers Week 1968 50th Annual Meeting." 1968. East Lansing: Michigan State University.

Muskegon Chronicle. 1937. *Romance of Muskegon, Michigan: 1937 Centennial Year*, 23:41. Muskegon, MI: Muskegon Chronicle.

Muskegon Daily Chronicle. 1896, December 26.

Muskegon News Chronicle. 1910, November 25.

———. 1912. "Big Drain Will Reclaim Acres." January 10.

———. 1913, December 12.

Muskegon River Watershed Assembly. 2016a. "Houghton Lake Wild Rice Project." http://mrwa.org/mrwa_projects/houghton-lake-wild-rice-project/.

———. 2016b. "Muskegon Lake and Estuary Emergent Vegetation Restoration Demonstration Project (Wild Rice Project)." http://mrwa.org/mrwa_projects/muskegon-lake-estuary-emergent-vegetation-restoration-demonstration-project-wild-rice-project/.

NatureServe. 2015. *NatureServe Explorer: An Online Encyclopedia of Life.* Version 7.1. Arlington, VA: NatureServe. http://explorer.natureserve.org.

Nelson, Linda S., Chetta S. Owens, and Kurt D. Getsinger. 2003. *Response of Wild Rice to Selected Aquatic Herbicides*. Report No. ERDC/EL TR-03-14. Washington, DC: U.S. Army Corps of Engineers.

"New Buffalo Township, Berrien County Michigan, Southwest Michigan." 2016. http://www.newbuffalotownship.org/history.html.

"New Material for Paper, A." 1874. *Nature* 11 (November): 34–35.

Nicholas, Elmer. 1938. *Grant Herald-Independent*. In *Grant Area: Yesterday and Today*, 1979. Grant, MI: Grant Public Library.

Nicollet, Joseph N., and Martha Coleman Bray. 1970. *Journals of Joseph N. Nicollet*. St. Paul: Minnesota Historical Society Press.

"No Relaxation in Protective Laws—the Sportsman's Demand." 1918. *Bulletin of the American Game Protective Association* 7 (2): 1–2.

Northern Tribune. 1881. "State News." April 16. Grayling, MI.

Oates, William. 1917. *Michigan Game and Fish Biennial Report, 1915–1916*. Lansing, MI: Wynkoop Hallenbeck Crawford Co.

Palmer, Friend, Harry P. Hunt, and Charles Mills June. 1906. *Early Days in Detroit: Papers Written by General Friend Palmer of Detroit, Being His Personal Reminiscences of Important Events and Descriptions of the City for over Eighty Years*. Detroit: Hunt and June.

Paquin, Paul. 1892. "Michigan Climatology." *Bacteriological World and Modern Medicine, Bulletin of the Medical and Surgical Sanitarium, Battle Creek, Michigan* 1 (6): 220–22.

Partridge, B. F. 1881. "Bay County History—Its Pioneer Record and Wonderful Development." *Pioneer Society of the State of Michigan* 3: 337–38.

Patrick, Joyce. 1910. *One Room Country Schools of Newaygo County: History and Recollections*. Vol. 20. Charleston, SC: CreateSpace Independent Publishing Platform.

Payne, Fredrick C., Jane L. Schuette, Joel E. Schaeffer, Jerry B. Lisiecki, David P. Regalbuto, and Peter S. Rogers. 1985. *The Maisou Island Project*. Lansing: Michigan Department of Natural Resources.

Pedrose, Lawrence W. 1931. "Wanted: Wild Rice Harvester." *Scientific American*, May.

The Penny Cyclopaedia of the Society for the Diffusion of Useful Knowledge. 1839. Vol. 15. London: Charles Knight and Company.

Picotte, Alvin G. 1981a. "Wild Rice Damage and Loss." Fact Finding regarding BIA Claim 210.11. Bureau of Indian Affairs.

———. 1981b. *Michigan 2415 Progress Report for September, 1981*. Memorandum.

September 24.

Pictorial Keys to Arthropods, Reptiles, Birds, and Mammals of Public Health Significance. 1969. Public Health Publication 1955. Atlanta: Center for Disease Control of the U.S. Public Health Service.

Pirnie, Miles David. 1935. *Michigan Waterfowl Management.* Lansing, MI: Franklin DeKleine Company.

Pitezel, John H. 1857. *Lights and Shades of Missionary Life: Containing Travels, Sketches, Incidents, and Missionary Efforts, during Nine Years Spent in the Region of Lake Superior.* Cincinnati: R. P. Thompson.

Pokagon, Simon. 1898a. Letter to Albert E. Jenks, November 10. Albert Ernest Jenks Papers, Archives, Wisconsin Historical Society, Madison, WI.

——. 1898b. Letter to Albert E. Jenks, November 16. Albert Ernest Jenks Papers, Archives, Wisconsin Historical Society, Madison, WI.

Powell, J. W. 1899. *Eighteenth Annual Report of the Bureau of American Ethnology.* Washington, DC: Government Printing Office.

Powers, Perry. 1912. *A History of Northern Michigan and Its People.* Vol. 3. Chicago: Lewis Publishing Company.

Proceedings and Addresses at a Sanitary Convention Held at . . . Under the Direction of a Committee of the State Board of Health . . . 1880. Lansing, MI: W. S. George and Company.

Proceedings and Addresses of the . . . General Conference of the Health Officials in Michigan. 1903. Michigan State Board of Health.

Proceedings of the Sanitary Convention Held at East Saginaw. 1885. Lansing, MI: W. S. George and Company.

Progressive AE. 2006. *Houghton Lake: A Guidebook for Homeowners.* Houghton, MI: Houghton Lake Improvement Board.

Public Sector Consultants, Inc. 2000. "Measures of Success: Addressing Environmental Impairments in the Saginaw River and Saginaw Bay." Development Plan. Saginaw, MI: Partnership for the Saginaw Bay Watershed.

——. 2012. "Saginaw River/Bay Area of Concern: Restoration Plan for the Habitat and Populations BUIs." Development Plan. Lansing: United States Fish and Wildlife Service.

Radisson, Pierre Esprit, and Gideon Delaplaine Scull. 1885. *Voyages of Peter Esprit Radisson: Being an Account of His Travels and Experiences among the North American Indians, from 1652 to 1684; Transcribed from Original Manuscripts in the Bodleian Library and the British Museum; with Historical Illustrations and an Introduction.*

Boston: John Wilson and Son.

Ramsey, Alexander. 1850. "Conditions of the Indians—The Chippewas." In *Annual Report of the Commissioner of Indian Affairs, Transmitted with the Message of the President at the Opening of the Second Session of the Thirty-Second Congress, 1850*, 52-64. Washington, DC: Office of the Commissioner of Indian Affairs.

Raviele, Maria E. 2010 "Assessing Carbonized Archaeological Cooking Residues: Evaluation of Maize Phytolith Taphonomy and Density through Experimental Residue Analysis." PhD diss., Michigan State University, East Lansing.

Ravindran, Evelyn, Pamela Nankervis, and Kyle Seppanen. 2013. *Keweenaw Bay Indian Community Waterfowl Index Report and Wild Rice Report Results for 2013*. Conservation Report. L'Anse, MI: Keweenaw Bay Indian Community Natural Resources Department.

Read, Frederic. 1976a. *The First Two Hundred Years in Muskegon*. Frederic Read.

———. 1976b. *A Long Look at Muskegon*. Benton Harbor, MI: Patterson College Publication.

Rees, Thomas H. 1910. "Preliminary Examination of New Buffalo Harbor, Michigan." In *United States Congressional Serial Set Issue 5730*, 27:2. Washington, DC: U.S. Government Printing Office.

Reid, Edwy C. 1889. "Eighteenth Annual Report of the Secretary of the State Horticultural Society of Michigan, 1888." Horticultural Report. Lansing, MI: State Horticultural Society of Michigan.

Rice Lake Farms. 2016. "We Pick'm, Pack'm and Ship'm Fresh to Market." 2016. http://ricelakefarms.com/index.html.

La Salle, Robert Cavelier. 1901. *Relation of the Discoveries and Voyages of Cavelier de La Salle from 1679 to 1681, the Official Narrative*. Chicago: Caxton Club.

Robbins, E. B. 1940. "Indians Harvesting Mah-No-Men (Wild Rice) at Lac Vieux Desert." *Michigan Education Journal* (November).

Rockford Map Publishers. 1955. *Farm Plat Book, Newaygo County, Michigan*. Rockford, IL: Rockford Map Publishers.

"RRHX—Railroad History Time Line—1860." 2016. http://www.michiganrailroads.com.

Ruddiman, George. 1913. *Michigan Historical Collections*. Vol. 21. Lansing, MI: Wynkoop Hallenbeck Crawford Company.

Ruthven, Alexander G. 1911. *A Biological Survey of the Sand Dune Region on the South Shore of Saginaw Bay, Michigan*. Vol. 4. Biological Series 2. Lansing, MI: Wynkoop Hallenbeck Crawford Company.

Sabrosky, Curtis W. 1946. *Occurrence of Malaria Mosquitoes in Southern Michigan.* East Lansing: Michigan State College.

Saginaw County Mosquito Abatement Commission. 2012. "History of the Saginaw County Mosquito Abatement Commission." *Saginaw County Mosquito Abatement Commission.* http://www.scmac.org/history.htm.

Saginaw Daily News. 1917, March 6.

Saginaw Evening News. 1888, September 12.

———. 1896. "Michigan in Brief." September 4.

Saginaw News Courier. 1922, February 26.

Sands, Joseph P., Stephen J. DeMaso, Matthew J. Schnupp, and Leonard A. Brennan. 2012. *Wildlife Science: Connecting Research with Management.* New York: CRC Press.

Sawyer, Alvah. 1911. *A History of the Northern Peninsula of Michigan and Its People.* Vol. 1. Chicago: Lewis Publishing Company.

Scientific American. 1873. "Odd Materials for Paper Making." March 15.

———. 1881. "Wild Rice." May 21.

———. 1913. "How Indians Harvested Wild Rice." April 19.

Seney National Wildlife Refuge. 1938-84. "Annual Narrative Reports." U.S. Fish and Wildlife Service.

Sherzer, W. H. 1900. "Geological Report on Monroe County Michigan." Geological Survey vol. 7, part 1. Lansing: Michigan Board of Geological Survey.

Sherzer, W. H. 1913. *The Geology of Wayne County.* 1913. Michigan Geological and Biological Survey, Publ. 12. Geol. Series 9. Lansing, MI: Wynkoop Hallenbeck Crawford Company.

Shrady, George Frederick, Thomas Lathrop Stedman, and R. C. Kedzie. 1874. "Public Drainage." *Medical Record* 9 (January): 356.

Sievers, Rev. Ferdinand. 1848. "Second Letter to Rev. Loehe of Germany." Personal correspondence. August 11.

Smith, Harlan. 1894. "Ojibwas of Michigan." *Detroit Free Press,* July 1.

———. 1904. "The American Museum Journal." *American Museum of Natural History (1900–1901)* 1 (March): 3-24.

Smith, Loren M., Roger L. Pederson, and Richard M. Kaminski. 1989. *Habitat Management for Migrating and Wintering Waterfowl in North America.* Lubbock: Texas Tech University Press.

Spangle, Leon. 1910. "Hunting Coot on Big Mud Lake." *Hunter-Trader-Trapper,* June.

Stewart, C. B. 1911. "Preliminary Report on Storage Reservoirs at the Headwaters of the Wisconsin River and Their Relation to Stream Flow." Madison: Wisconsin State Board of Forestry.

Stout, William A. 2007. *Saginaw Bay Waterfowl Hunting and Decoy Carvers.* Bloomfield Hills, MI: Fanfair Enterprises.

Sunstrum, J., D. Lawrenchuk, K. Tait, W. Hall, D. Johnson, K. Wilcox, and E. Walker. 1998. "Mosquito-Transmitted Malaria—Michigan, 1995." Center for Disease Control. http://www.cdc.gov/mmwr/preview/mmwrhtml/00041534.htm.

T.C.A. 1876. "Ducking in the Monroe Marshes." *Forest and Stream* 7 (6): 81-83.

Terrell, Edward E., and Paul M. Peterson. 2009. "Annotated List of Maryland Grasses (Poaceae)." *Journal of the Botanical Research Institute of Texas* 3 (2): 905-19.

Terrell, Edward E., Paul M. Peterson, James L. Reveal, and Melvin R. Duvall. 1997. "Taxonomy of North American Species of *Zizania* (Poaceae)." *SIDA, Contributions to Botany* 17 (3): 533-49.

"To Place Rich Lands on Market." 1915. *Michigan Manufacturer and Financial Record*, November 13.

True Northerner. 1877. "Michigan Items." August 31. Paw Paw, MI.

———. 1880a. "Michigan News." June 4.

———. 1880b. "Michigan News." June 18.

Thompson, Richard I. 1977. "Township Rice Lake Marsh." Newaygo, MI. Grant Area District Library files.

Thwaites, Reuben G. 1887. "The Boundaries of Wisconsin." *Magazine of Western History*, May.

"Tribal Habitat Restoration—Caring for Our Land and Waters." 2015. Circle of Flight/ Great Lakes Restoration Initiative, Midwest Region.

"Tribal Habitat Restoration and Invasive Species Control." 2013. Midwest Region: Great Lakes Indian Fish and Wildlife Commission.

Tri-County Chronicle. 1903, October 16. Cass City, MI.

United States Army. 1880. *Annual Report of the Chief of Engineers, United States Army, Part II.* Engineering Report. Washington, DC: U.S. Army.

———. 1909. *Annual Report of the Chief Engineers of the US Army.* Washington, DC: U.S. Army.

———. 1911. *Annual Report of the Chief Engineers of the US Army.* Washington, DC: U.S. Army.

United States Army Corps of Engineers. 1872. *Report of the Chief of Engineers.*

Washington, DC: U.S. Army.

United States Bureau of Fisheries, and Leon Jacob Cole. 1903. *U.S. Fish Manual.* Washington, DC: U.S. Government Printing Office.

U.S. Department of Commerce, NOAA. 2014. "Great Lakes Water Level Dashboard." http://www.glerl.noaa.gov.

U.S. Department of Agriculture (USDA). 2004. *Lac Vieux Desert Wild Rice Plan.* Watersmeet MI: U.S. Department of Agriculture.

U.S. Department of Agriculture (USDA), Agricultural Research Service. 2017. USDA National Nutrient Database for Standard Reference, Release. Nutrient Data Laboratory. http://www.ars.usda.gov.

U.S. Geological Survey. 1996. *United States Geological Survey Water-Supply Paper.* Vol. 2425. Washington, DC: U.S. Government Printing Office.

Ustipak, R. D. 1995. *An Analysis of Wild Rice at Houghton Lake, Michigan.* Lansing: Michigan Department of Natural Resources.

Van Winkle, E. B. 1881. "Drainage of the Twenty-Third and Twenty-Fourth Wards, This City (Parts 1 and 2)." *Engineering News* 8 (August): 321–27, 337–41.

Vennum, Thomas. 1988. *Wild Rice and the Ojibway People.* St. Paul: Minnesota Historical Society Press.

Walters, Beverly. 2013. "Presently Accepted Nomenclature for *Zizania* Species in Michigan." Ann Arbor: University of Michigan Herbarium, November 19.

Warren, William Whipple. 1885. *History of the Ojibway People.* St. Paul: Minnesota Historical Society.

Waybrant, James R., and Troy G. Zorn. 2008. *Tahquamenon River Assessment.* Fisheries Division Special Report No. 45. Lansing: Michigan Department of Natural Resources.

Weaver, T. L., B. P. Neff, and J. M. Ellis. 2005. *Water Quality and Hydrology of the Lac Vieux Desert Watershed, Gogebic County, Michigan, and Vilas County, Wisconsin, 2002–2004.* Scientific Investigations Report 2005-5237. U.S. Geological Survey.

Weitzel, G. 1875. "Annual Report upon the Enlargement of Saint Mary's Fall Canal, and Improvements of Saint Mary's River, Harbors and Rivers on Lakes Huron and Saint Clair, Saint Clair Flats Canal, and Improvement of Detroit River." Annual Report of the Chief of Engineers. Michigan: U.S. Army.

Whitaker, John O., and William John Hamilton. 1998. *Mammals of the Eastern United States.* Ithaca, NY: Cornell University Press.

White, Stewart E. 1891. *Ornithologist and Oölogist.* Vol. 16. Hyde Park, MA: Frank B. Webster.

Wight, J. Ambrose. 1867. "Some Missionary Intelligence: Northern Michigan." In *Presbyterian Monthly*, 12th ed., 2:280-81. Philadelphia: Presbyterian Board of Publication.

Williams, William W. 1884. "Among the Otchipwees." *Magazine of Western History*, November.

Wilson, Thomas L. 1981. "Wild Rice Intake Forms." Fact Finding regarding BIA Claim 210.10. Bureau of Indian Affairs.

———. 1982. "R0001 Lac Vieux Desert Wild Rice—Claim 2415." Fact Finding regarding BIA Claim R0001. Bureau of Indian Affairs.

———. 1980. "Michigan 2415 Staff Briefing—Friday, February 29, 1980." Memorandum. February 26.

Wing, Talcott E., ed. 1890a. "Aquatic Sports and Oarsmen of the River Raisin." In *History of Monroe County*. New York: Munsell and Company.

———, ed. 1890b. "Business Interests of Monroe." In *History of Monroe County*, 415. New York: Munsell and Company.

———, ed. 1890c. "The United States Government Improvements of La Plaisance and Monroe Harbors." In *History of Monroe County*, 169-80. New York: Munsell and Company.

Wood, Edwin Orin. 1916. "Flint Township." In *History of Genesee County, Michigan, Her People, Industries and Institutions*, 293. Flint, MI: Federal Publishing Company.

Xu, Xin-Wei, Jin-Wei Wu, Mei-Xia Qi, Qi-Xiang Lu, Peter F. Lee, Sue Lutz, Song Ge, and Jun Wen. 2015. "Comparative Phylogeography of the Wild-Rice Genus *Zizania* (Poaceae) in Eastern Asia and North America." *American Journal of Botany* 102 (2): 239-47.

Yale Expositor. 1894. "Michigan Matters." October 12.

Ziibiwing Center. 2016. "History of the Tribe—Timeline." http://www.sagchip.org/ziibiwing/aboutus/history.htm.

Index

Page numbers in italics refer to figures.